Hoover Dam, Arizona & Nevada, USA → 72–73

Canales, Andalusia, Spain → 80–81

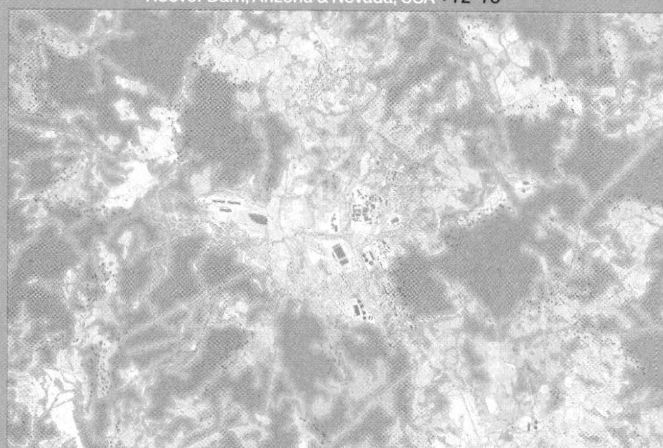
Larderello, Tuscany, Italy → 88–89

Imperial Valley, California, USA → 96–97

Las Gabias, Andalusia, Spain → 102–103

Sevilla, Andalusia, Spain → 110–111

Zahara de los Atunes, Andalusia, Spain → 118–119

Lelystad, Flevoland, the Netherlands → 124–125

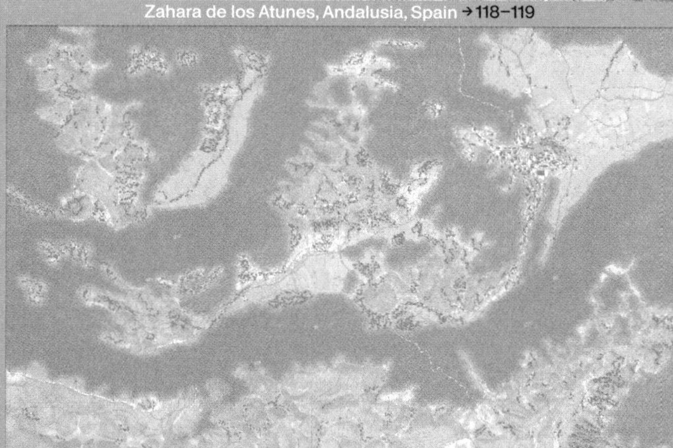
Viticuso, Latium, Italy → 132–133

Eggebek, Schleswig-Holstein, Germany → 138–139

The Power of Landscape

POWER OF LANDSCAPE

Sven Stremke, Dirk Oudes, Paolo Picchi

Novel Narratives to Engage with the Energy Transition

nai010 publishers

Learning from the Past

Questioning the Present

Imagining Alternative Futures

Preface

It was in the summer of 2016. A subject for research was sought for the Landscape Architecture Professorship and, in its wake, a new Professor for the Academy of Architecture. Perhaps there were several signs at the same time pointing in the direction of the energy transition. Was it a report in the Dutch national newspaper NRC Handelsblad that appealed to 'the creatives who, in this phase of climate policy, are the ones with the imagination to translate the scientific reports into visions for the future'? Or a report that China was going to invest 340 billion euros in sustainable energy generation, because otherwise its urban areas would become unliveable? Or a news item that the first Energy Commissioner of the Netherlands had been appointed to organize the National Energy Dialogue? Or an item that said Amsterdam wanted to be a gas-free city by 2050?

There was a growing awareness that energy transition would be one of the most far-reaching social and landscape challenges for the decades to come. Some telephone calls in autumn 2016 put us on the track of Sven Stremke, and Dirk Oudes and Paolo Picchi followed him to the Waterlooplein. The High-Density Energy Landscapes research group was a fact.

At the time of writing, the summer of 2022 has just begun so a few years have gone by since. Steps have been taken and many more will have to be taken before the use of fossil fuels is a thing of the past. In recent years, the High-Density Energy Landscapes group has made various contributions to the discourse on the energy transition, both inside and outside the Academy, in the Netherlands and abroad. The trio from HDEL has played an important role in training the future generation of designers in architecture, urbanism and landscape architecture. Research by design is increasingly becoming an indispensable link in the quest for answers to the major challenges, the energy transition certainly being one of them. It is a method to develop perspectives for an increasingly complex world and to learn to sketch scenarios for post-fossil futures. The power of imagination is essential here.

Parallel to the teaching, the group conducted research that resulted in the book that you, the reader, have in your hands: a journey through time, stories by experts, an inspirational book with photo essays, a book of wanderings to travel 'in' the maps, but above all, a wonderful reflection of several years of research at the Amsterdam Academy of Architecture. The power of imagination shines through every page.

Madeleine Maaskant, Director
Amsterdam Academy of Architecture

Introduction

SVEN STREMKE

What if we were focusing on the wrong things all this time and, if so, what should we be focusing on? This book questions a most common practice with respect to energy transition: the strong focus of politicians, policymakers, civil servants, engineers, designers and parts of the general public on energy *technologies* such as photovoltaic panels and wind turbines. The book illustrates that energy transition is *not* about technology, but about a changing environment. Energy transition changes the places where we live, work and recreate: rural and urban landscapes. In all these places, energy technology is the *enabler*—the means to realize some rational objective—but the technology is not what people are *concerned* about.

To illustrate this point, I like to refer to a thoroughly studied phenomenon: people, in general, do not oppose wind turbines. Quite the contrary, most people are in favour of renewable energy technologies. The picture changes dramatically once a technology—let's say a certain kind of wind turbine—is associated with a particular location; when the abstract turns into a prospective reality. The host of the until then abstract energy technology—a landscape—is not only 'pre-occupied' by other land uses but, much more importantly, possesses a multitude of characteristics and values ascribed by its inhabitants and other landscape users. Those qualities, not illustrated on official maps, are responsible for the success or failure of any kind of landscape change: and this is just a first encounter with the *Power of Landscape*.

What if energy transition is indeed not merely about energy technology, but about the transition of our living environment, the values we ascribe to it and the wishes we have for it? That would mean that energy transition is also about changes in the way we live, work and recreate. We can take some comfort in the knowledge that digitalization, another great challenge of the twenty-first century, is neither about servers nor internet cables, but about the possibilities and responsibilities that come with it. Digitalization too is about the way we live, work and recreate. Technology is the *enabler*—the means to realize some rational objective—but the technology is not what people are *concerned* about.

Just to be clear, this book is not going to argue at length why one thing is more important than another; it is about sharing our curiosity, wonder and fascination about the landscapes of energy. It draws attention to the qualitative and possibly emotional side of those landscapes that is *not* governed by statistics and economic optimization. This has been a long-cherished ambition of ours and we hope to contribute to a better understanding of energy landscapes that can inform decisions concerning energy transition. This book, in other words, is an expression of our passion and concern for landscapes that are formed by human development of energy sources together with natural processes. We have visited the great majority of landscapes featured in this book over the past decade or so. Other energy landscapes—long gone or 'rewritten' by continuous human development—were studied based on historical maps, writings, and paintings. A third group of energy landscapes—conceived through imagination, not yet actual physical landscapes—serves to research possible futures, nurture critical discussion and cultivate novel narratives about energy transition.

Our own writing is complemented by the work of key figures in the larger domain of energy landscape, from practice, government and academia. Their contributions to the book help to gain a renewed understanding of energy landscapes and, simultaneously, represent critical stimulus for the energy landscape discourse in those fields. The contributing authors, put differently, are ambassadors for a much-needed shift of focus from *enabler* to *concern*, from *technology* to *landscape*. Together, we visit both historic and present-day energy landscapes, and start to imagine future landscapes of energy.

What can we learn from past and present-day energy landscapes? What is it that people care about in their living environment and how can we acknowledge these values in the design of energy landscapes? Many relevant questions arise once we trade our preoccupation with energy technology for a more encompassing attention to a changing environment. This book, consisting of three parts—past, present and future energy landscape—offers some first, tentative answers. Tentative, because we are at the very beginning of decarbonization, often referred to as the take-off phase. If climate neutrality was a travel destination—conveniently placed in Paris because that is where the International Climate Agreement was signed in 2015—and we had departed from Amsterdam in the early 1990s, we would still be in the Netherlands. Globally, we still have 80 per cent of the work left, to realize energy transition. That is why any claim of all-encompassing and fully-validated answers deserves to be met with scepticism. While this situation admittedly presents challenges to many agents of energy transition and society at large, we draw energy from the exploration of uncharted territories and conversations with others about the future of our landscapes.

Our journeys to uncharted energy landscapes and conversations about the *Power of Landscape* are captured in this book. Mesmerized by the diversity, spatial expanse, and socio-economic implications of many energy landscapes, we asked experts to help us create solid foundations for the understanding of 'landscape' with respect to energy transition. What is the power of those landscapes, for its users and us as readers? Mike Pasqualetti, an early explorer of energy landscapes, accompanies us for our first encounter with the *Power of Landscape* in this book. For more than four decades, he has been helping others to learn to read the landscapes of energy, and to establish vocabulary and typologies that allow us to understand this particular kind of landscape. We then travel in time by means of landscape archaeology to witness how the Netherlands—known for its historical windmills—has been shaped by a series of very different energy systems, each one adding to the tapestry of today's cultural landscape. Jolanda de Jong helps to highlight the ties between human development and energy landscapes, which are part of the Dutch national identity. Andrea Cardoso and Emma Banks then take us on an anthropological journey to Columbia, to visit the *Landscape of Others*, confronting us with the socio-economic consequences of coal mining for the Global North. The coal ports, railroads and mines in Columbia are landscapes of energy colonialism. Above all, they illustrate human incapacity to develop true empathy for people living far away. While the efficiency of coal-fired power stations may have increased, we maintain that the sole focus on energy technology—fossil and renewable—is misleading. The inhabitants of the coal landscapes in Columbia, we are being told, are advocating to become agents in the transition to renewables and the shaping of their future energy landscape. Thinking about the future can be stimulated through design thinking, imagining the unknown. Architectural historian Lara Voerman introduces us to a selection of designers that have contributed to the creation of energy landscapes around the world. She illustrates how designers have employed the *Power of Landscape* over a period of 150 years to cultivate the discourse on the implementation of different energy sources ranging from coal to solar energy. She evidences how design attitudes, or paradigms, have evolved through time, how designers managed to emancipate the notion of energy landscape and, most importantly, moved 'energy' from the somewhat exclusive realm of engineering to the arts, humanities, and social sciences.

The second part of the book questions the status-quo of today's energy landscapes in Europe and North America. The British Geographer Dan van der Horst, well known for his sustained efforts regarding this subject, provides us with an introduction to a series of chapters on extensive fieldwork and ground-breaking research. The team of the High-Density Energy Landscape research group at the Amsterdam Academy of Architecture reports from their immersive fieldwork in the United States, Italy, Spain, the United Kingdom, Germany, and the Netherlands. They illustrate another *Power of Landscape*: energy landscapes and their users can teach us many things. In some places, energy development creates a sense of place and local identity. Elsewhere, energy technologies undermine stewardship of landscapes and erode local quality of life. That is why Dirk Oudes, in the next chapter, focuses on what is currently considered best practice in the development of solar energy landscapes. He reminds us of the need to quickly mainstream the knowledge from frontrunner projects while continuing to innovate and pursue new solutions for solar energy and other renewable energy sources. In the last chapter of the second part of the book, Canadian scholar Kate Sherren draws our attention to the societal opposition to landscape change, be it for energy development or other purposes. She evidences how so-called climax thinking, rooted in twentieth-century theories of ecology, continues to affect the way many of us perceive landscapes as permanent and static. While climax thinking has long been replaced by the dynamic equilibrium theory in ecology, many still want to preserve landscape as it is now or even return to earlier states. Sherren's work underlines the importance of *Learning to Change*. She illustrates another *Power of Landscape*: a source of knowledge and almost infinite body of reference for many important questions of the twenty-first century.

In the third part of the book, we leave the domain of descriptive inquiry. The remaining chapters are devoted to imagining alternative futures instigated by the eminent need to decarbonize and continue improving the quality of our living environment. What if the transition to renewable energy no longer poses a threat to our landscapes, providing an impulse to the quality of life instead, like the precious public park on the dam of the Canales hydropower plant in Spain? The first chapter presents the findings of our research on the work of the next generation designers of energy landscapes. We illustrate how energy transition is a given for young designers, no longer concerned with whether or not to engage in climate action. Instead, creativity is focused on what they are best at: designing desirable futures. To these young designers, the objective is no less than shaping the cultural landscape of the twenty-first century. Many established design professionals are also starting to embrace energy transition as a key challenge and a means to a better quality of life. The second chapter comprises a series of projects curated by Elizabeth Monoian and Robert Ferry from the Land Art Generator Initiative (LAGI). They reveal how renewable energy—which requires more space than fossil fuels and is situated closer to where we live—should no longer be pursued as a mere engineering exercise. It deserves the attention of many other disciplines and, above all, the landscape users. Developing *Energy Landscapes as Public Art* represents a renaissance of design thinking in the world of infrastructure. Above all, the ground-breaking designs presented in their chapter continue to succeed in engaging parts of the society in energy transition that have, so far, remained silent. And, not unimportantly, raised the interest of the larger design community to contribute to this transition. Dutch state advisor for the living environment Jannemarie de Jonge concludes the third part of the book with an essay on the *Design Dialogue* as a bridge between landscape and technology. She thus adds another important means for the creation of novel narratives: dialogue. Knowledge of the past (first part of this book), critical reflection on the present (second part of this book), and imagination of the future (third part of this book) are three key constituents of any such dialogue.

The epilogue of this book, finally, is dedicated to pressing questions that many of us face in our daily life. Should energy development be managed at the national scale or locally? Should renewable energy landscapes comprise multiple functions, and should they be large or small in size? Do we continue to hide energy infrastructure, or can we start to embrace new elements in our landscapes? And, not unimportantly for any kind of policymaking, who should have a say about the prospective changes in our living environment? The final chapter of this book illustrates the *Power of Landscape* in resolving all of those and many other questions. Enjoy the read.

Learning from the Past

The Foundations of Energy Landscapes

1.1

MARTIN J. PASQUALETTI

1

For most people, most of the time, energy landscapes are the visual equivalent of the noises that make up the background hum of everyday life. While we commonly ignore them, annoyance grows once we start to notice them. Breaching this threshold of awareness, any illusion of tranquillity vanishes, and we start yearning for places with characteristics at the calmer end of the landscape spectrum: solitude and unspoiled beauty. Sadly, humanity's avaricious rush to develop and market energy resources at any expense can only be slowed by securing high-level official protection.

Such protection of the land and the people who cherish it is sometimes elusive. However, we should remember that the unintended costs of energy borne by all of us are not new. Before humans entered the scene, many energy landscapes existed in their natural state. The oozing bitumen at Tar Pits Park on the beach in Carpinteria, California [→fig. 1] and a little to the south La Brea Tar Pits in downtown Los Angeles; Pitch Lake on Trinidad, the largest natural deposit of asphalt in the world; the fumaroles of Larderello in Tuscany; and landscapes leaking fossil fuels in 'The Land of Fire' in Azerbaijan. With a few exceptions, such energy landscapes were relatively small and most people did not take particular notice of them. Nowadays, they are more pronounced, more varied, and more expansive.

The human role in creating energy landscapes started as soon as we acquired enough knowledge and the means to change the land cover and remould the terrain. The earliest of such landscapes resulted from activities such as stream diversions and fire drives. But human landscape changes were, for several reasons, relatively minor and impermanent. The global population was small and migratory, tools were primitive, and Nature's regenerative powers mighty. However, in time, such benign patterns were overwhelmed by the multiple influences of rising numbers of people, technical innovations, and the repeated damage to ecological cycles.

Our abilities to create energy landscapes accelerated once we developed the skill to convert forested land into fuel for heating. History records the notable disappearance of large areas of European forests more than ten centuries ago. By the 1700s,

1 Oil has been oozing to the surface for thousands of years along the Pacific Ocean at Tar Pits Park, Carpinteria, California (Photo by the author).

great swaths of virgin North American forests had also been felled for fuel. In both places, some areas regenerated, but many forests were permanently erased. In some ways, history is repeating itself today in the Global South.

The pattern of forest removal was repeated in many areas of the world until coal became the favoured substitute. In this sense, one could claim that coal saved the forests, even though the transition heralded an entirely new form and more damaging scale of energy landscapes. Although the source of this new landscape was not renewable, its higher energy density made it more suitable for ironworking. The price for such an advantage was the creation of landscapes that were appalling, often even alarming, and inherently resistant to resurrection. They often evoked despair among visitors who lamented the natural landscape features being sacrificed. Today still, many countries, for example in Latin America, are suffering the spoliation of their landscapes to provide fuels to northern countries: the forest fires in Paraguay to make room for intensive cultivation of energy crops are not so different from the violent coal mining practices in Colombia Cerrejon described in the subsequent chapter.

Occasionally, these emotions led to public resistance and calls for reform. But it was slow in coming; despite the public misery that attached itself to coal like glue, the other benefits that the fuel engendered muffled concerns about the social turmoil and the egregious energy landscapes that resulted. Instead, for those living in those landscapes, jobs carried the day. Economic development was paramount. What the coal mines and pits, slag heaps, poisoned soils, dead trees, and befouled streams created were landscapes of necessity, the bargained price of progress.

Whether living near Dudley, in the Black Country of England, the gritty industrial cities along Germany's Ruhr River, or the working-class towns of north-eastern Pennsylvania in the United States, local residents rarely mixed with 'polite' society. Affluent people typically lived at a substantial remove from such landscapes, while those whose labour had created them were left to accept that the past's bucolic landscapes had been lost to the pure pragmatism of the present. The 'high-rent' people benefitted from the dirty and backbreaking efforts at the coal mines, iron foundries, glass factories, brickworks and steel mills, but they deigned to visit the resulting energy landscapes unless insulated from the experience by dreams of power and prestige.

In the early days of the coal economy, energy landscapes developed around the shallow underground mines then dominating recovery activities. As time passed, technological advances increased productivity and everything that went with it. Such improvements included more powerful water pumps, safer underground supports, more reliable ventilation, larger earth-moving equipment, and eventually devices to carry the mined coal, machinery, and workers vertically. These changes allowed mines to plunge deeper into the earth and access the coal that rested there. Meanwhile, the resulting energy landscapes expanded in scale, impact, and irreversibility.

Eventually, traditional coal mining was augmented by a new approach designed for flatter terrain where coal measures lay near the surface. Surface mining—specifically strip mining (often called open-cast mining)—vastly increased coal energy landscapes. While underground mining commonly has a surface expression of fewer than 100 acres, strip mining can create energy landscapes many times that size. Striking examples are the landscapes south of Gillette, Wyoming; or those south of Leipzig, Germany →fig. 2.

2

3 → 18–19

4

In the Appalachian Mountains of the United States, coal mining techniques evolved to accommodate its convoluted and dissected topography. Such mining techniques included extensive contour mining and, more recently, mountain-top removal. Both mining techniques produce graphic energy landscapes that are, compared to strip mines, particularly difficult to reclaim or repurpose when the mining activities come to an end. These energy landscapes are likely to remain discernible for hundreds of years. Their presence, in other words, is permanent in nature → fig. 3.

Throughout the world, the coal economy has created an assortment of energy landscapes ancillary to the mines themselves. Close to mines, we find emblematic apparatus such as ventilation equipment, headframes, access roads, storage silos, conveyor belts, and heaps of discarded non-combustibles. Together, these compose the energy landscape. Away from the mines, we find a complex network of ancillary energy landscapes that include railroads, tunnels, viaducts, bridges, canals, and port facilities for bulk carriers.

Most mined coal is destined for power plants. The larger ones consume 1,000 tonnes of coal per hour and produce a substantial footprint on the land with their power block, emission control equipment, switchyards, cooling towers, chimneys, water treatment facilities, coal storage, and ash disposal. Taken together, a coal plant can easily stretch across 1,500 acres (6 km^2) or more. Many of those are found in our large seaports, for example in Rotterdam and Amsterdam.

It would also be short-sighted to believe that coal's energy landscapes are limited to mining operations, supporting neighbourhoods, transportation infrastructure, and powerplants. Sometimes they result from the toxic brew of emissions that transform nearby and distant landscapes in ways no one predicted, let alone imagined. Such landscapes include forests poisoned by acid precipitation, for instance in the Adirondack Mountains of New York State, Great Smoky Mountains National Park in North Carolina, and the Black Forest in Germany.

A new form of energy landscape started taking shape once the first oil well was drilled in Titusville, Pennsylvania in 1859. The resulting landscapes took on a much different appearance than those resulting from coal mining. Exoskeletal drilling rigs starting marching across the land like an invading army as frenzied speculators scrambled to extract the black liquid from the land.

As enthusiasm spread over the next two dozen years, energy landscapes started appearing all over the world, including in remote Baku, Azerbaijan; the then Dutch East Indies; Beaumont, Texas; Signal Hill, California; Lake Maracaibo, Venezuela; the permafrost expanse of Siberia, the blistering deserts of the Persian Gulf, and hundreds of other places → fig. 4. Especially with the appearance of gulping inventions such as the automobile and the airplane, oil promised an attractive alternative to every other employment option that existed at the time.

As oil speculators rushed in, oil gushed out. Like magic, forests of trees were reshaped into forests of drilling rigs. Everyone was in a hurry, driven by the 'rule of capture': claim your part now, or someone else will beat you to it. No one worried about the energy landscapes they were creating.

Historically, energy landscapes have proved to have a long half-life. Travel today through areas of former energy development and you will see concrete foundations

2 Lignite mine near the now demolished village of Heuersdorf to the south of Leipzig in Germany represents the extensive surface landscape transformation of mines around the world (Photo by D. Stremke, 115559).

3 Permanent landscape transformation caused by coal mining in the Appalachian mountains, Wise County, Virginia, USA (Alan Gignoux / Alamy).

4 Oil blowouts were common in the early days of oil development, as here in the Signal Hill region of present-day Long Beach, California, circa 1925 (Huntington Library. Public Domain).

and crumbling buildings, ponds of toxic water, broken piping in all shapes and sizes, sterile soils, and rusted debris littered about. Many residual energy landscapes are destined to become permanent reminders of past get-rich dreamers who felt no responsibility for the damage they were leaving behind.

The energy landscapes of oil took on an appearance vastly different from the landscapes of coal. These novel landscapes included not only drilling rigs, but miles of pipes, bundles of drilling bits, webs of access roads, rickety shantytowns, tank farms, labyrinthine processing equipment, railroads, water transport docks, and many other landscape features that quickly became impossible to overlook and showed no signs of fading → fig. 5.

5

6

Today, the human rush of individual fortune-seekers has morphed into the merciless competition of giant oil companies and state-run monopolies. But for the energy landscapes of oil, not much has changed; we find them in one form or another in every country that produces oil. As long as prices stay above $55–60 per barrel, people will continue to start drilling and fracking in new places. Once this happens, it will be immediately followed by the creation of new energy landscapes, with all the resulting impacts in terms of land alterations and the social and emotional reactions that go along with them. They will expand in areas such as western China, eastern Siberia, and the coastal regions of Brazil, Guyana, and Suriname. As the landscape changes, so too will the lives of those who depend on it.

As numerous and long-lasting as present oil landscapes are, future developments are likely to be more disruptive and long-lasting. And we are not just talking here about the push of traditional oil recovery into fragile Arctic environments, but also about energy landscapes of a whole new scale, created through oil sands development, for instance in north-eastern Alberta, Canada → fig. 6. Using giant land-sculpting machinery, several companies have joined to create an energy landscape larger than the USA State of Rhode Island. As astronauts on the International Space Station pass 220 miles above northern Canada, they have no trouble picking out the scars from these activities far below.

Just the magnitude of landscape change alone would be sufficient to attract public attention, but public opposition to the oil sands development has transcended that single issue. It has grown to include how and where it is marketed. After squeezing oil from the host sands, the end product is fed into a distribution network for use in all three North American countries and a small but growing number of overseas customers. Because the oil sand reserves are enormous, Canada wishes to enlarge the USA market if it can get the necessary permission. Crossing the border into the USA requires a presidential permit. Because the landscape damage of oil sands developments is well known, and because there are many other serious environmental drawbacks associated with its development and use, oil sands have attracted widespread and protracted public attention → fig. 7. There has been strong and sustained public opposition to continued operation, both in the USA and in Canada.

In response to the public outcry, including chains of protesters risking arrest by linking arms around the White House, the Biden Administration, in January 2021, withdrew the presidential permit necessary to complete the required pipeline that would bring additional product into the United States. In this instance in particular,

7 → 22–23

the scale of the energy landscapes has promoted a complete public rethink as to the wisdom of tapping into these costly and dirty oil reserves.

As we slowly transition away from fossil fuels and the energy landscapes they produce, we increasingly entertain other options. One possibility is to leave some reserves in the ground, untouched. This option has been an argument against approving further oil development in wilderness areas and offshore. Similarly, the steep decline in coal use in many countries will likely lead to the preservation of natural landscapes.

The turn away from coal and oil is sharpening the focus on the renewable alternatives and the energy landscapes they create. One of these renewables is hydropower, as witnessed most notably in China, India, Brazil, Canada, and Ethiopia. However renewable the source, the resulting energy landscapes can be large and devastating to ecological and social stability. Hydro installations aside, other renewable options include geothermal, biomass, wind and solar, all of which produce their own unique landscape signatures. Of these, wind and solar are attracting most of the attention from investors and governments, especially in North America, Europe, and China.

8

9

Both wind and solar energy have unique characteristics. Wind power is site-specific. For this reason, 'wind farms' have to be developed where the resource is concentrated, or it won't pay back. Wind energy landscapes are therefore created at those specific sites. This can lead to conflicts between pre-development land use and, on occasion, post-development land use. For those living or working nearby, convenient disinterest is not possible. The spinning blades inevitably attract the eye. Raising the challenge further, the relatively low energy density of wind means that wind developments commonly stretch over large areas to provide adequate economies of scale for access, construction and distribution.

Considering current applications of wind power may trigger memories of a bygone era. As in Europe, settlers in the Netherlands used wind power to grind grain and dewater the polders. Today these structures are considered 'quaint', important tourist attractions. Everyone seems to cherish them → fig. 8. We see a similar reaction to the squat and scattered wood-lattice wind machines of ninteenth-century farms that were scattered about the Great Plains of the US. So essential to farming and survival at the time, their visage never attracted a disparaging look.

This earlier sanguine experience has not, as a rule, transferred to the era of modern wind turbines. On the contrary, they commonly bring people together in strong group resistance to their installation. Reaching the height of a 40-storey building and the wingspan of a Boeing 747, hardly anyone would describe them as quaint. Modern wind turbines transform landscapes so thoroughly that public complaints about them have become common, if not universal.

These reactions began attracting sustained notice in the 1980s. For example, in 1985, articles appeared in opposition to the wind farms altering the landscapes in places like Palm Springs, California. Between 1984 and 1985, hundreds of such turbines rose out of the hot desert sand like a vast mirage. For locals familiar with apparitions, these were not an illusion → fig. 9.

The Palm Springs experience holds a solid place in the history of public reactions to renewable energy landscapes. The first reaction to their appearance north of town was a chorus of protest, starting with some loud voices from celebrities who lived

5 The Schwechat refinery, Vienna, Austria, illustrates the industrial landscape necessary to refine crude oil before commercialization is possible (Photo by the author).
6 A small part of the extensive landscape disruption (essentially permanent) that has resulted from the mining of the Athabascan Oil Sands, north-eastern Alberta, Canada (Photo by author).
7 Wildfires in oil sands region near Fort McMurray, Canada. Highway 63 south of town on 5th of May 2016 (MCpl van Putten / Alamy).
8 Historical windmills in the salt flats in Mazara del Vallo (Sicily, Italy). The windmills were pumping the sea water into the flats. This energy landscape is currently under the process of recognition by UNESCO as world heritage (Photo credit Filippo Innocenti, 2011).
9 Wind energy landscape near Palm Springs, California, United States. View is to the southeast (Photo by the author).

nearby. They and other locals realized that this new energy landscape differed from any other that had ever existed. It was, for one thing, an energy landscape that was impossible to hide.

Making the energy landscape even more noticeable, the 2,700 turbines were installed on both sides of Interstate10, one of the busiest highways in the country. They would spin, sometimes glint and flicker, getting noticed by millions of people traveling in and out of the Los Angeles Basin. Prodded by citizen complaints, City officials expressed worry that the fields of wind turbines would degrade visitors' entryway to their elegant resort town. All these circumstances meant that Palm Springs would become a forerunner of public reactions to wind energy landscapes in other parts of the country and most other places in the world where they appeared.

Population growth, greater public mobility, and—at least in the United States—an expanding preference for exurban living have converged to increase encounters between the public and the energy landscapes created to serve their needs. In these places, wind energy landscapes have attracted a level of public disdain akin to finding trash along a wilderness trail. It is not what people expect, and negative reactions can reach the point of outrage.

The growing intolerance for these new energy landscapes reflects changes in public awareness, rising empowerment, and a greater sophistication about how to oppose unwanted landscape changes, even when those who complain admit to the broader benefits that hastened them.

In response, these people have been taking two courses of action. The first one is to oppose new energy landscapes at their initial proposal. This approach is frequently attempted and sometimes successful, such as with the Cape Wind project near Boston. This approach cannot be successful everywhere, though, as energy demands will not abate. Also, it is not always easy for people to acquire sufficient knowledge about proposals in time to effectively oppose them.

A second approach is to propose, insist on, and even mandate the 'recycling of energy landscapes' beyond the minimum limits of standard reclamation regulations. The following are examples of this approach.

- A mountain-top removal site in Pennsylvania has been re-contoured into a golf course, United States.
- Mined-out lignite pits near Leipzig have become coveted and popular recreational lakes, Germany.
- Near Essen, art installations have been placed on top of heaps of mining waste, Germany.
- Subsidence depressions from underground coal mining have become a wildlife refuge near Leeds, United Kingdom → fig. 10.
- The site of a former coal-fired power plant has been repurposed with solar panels in Nijmegen, the Netherlands.

10

Such repurposed energy landscapes can provide a welcome tempering of the public criticisms about the deterioration of such landscapes caused by the long-term abandonment of equipment, buildings, and brownfields.

Despite such adjustments, a fundamental question persists: will the coming energy transition improve the appearance of energy landscapes or make matters worse? It is difficult to tell which possibility will dominate. Still, there is growing acknowledgment—especially in the Global North—that we cannot keep relying so strongly on conventional energy resources. In this instance, it may be that our concern about global warming and the more regional concerns over landscape destruction will meld into more sensitive, respectful forms of energy that align with landscapes rather than ignore their innate forms and sensitivities.

While our dependence on conventional energy resources is not likely to decline quickly, renewables are beginning to establish themselves more rapidly than previously expected. Compared to fossil and nuclear energy, the environmental impact of renewables is less serious. For example, solar power landscapes are stationary, quiet, need none of the copious amounts of water used in thermal power plants, produce no emissions, require little maintenance, and have the significant added advantage that they can be placed over existing surfaces such as roads and buildings.

Wind power, however, is another matter, but it too is a significant improvement on conventional energy development. Although turbines are inescapable attention-grabbers, they are almost as benign as solar power, despite what detractors like to charge about bird mortality, low-frequency noise, and shadow flicker. With appropriate consultation and care, none of those issues need bring wind developments to a halt. In some of the windiest areas of the US, for example, they are welcomed additions on previously disturbed lands such as ranches[1].

1
Apostol, D., Palmer, J., Pasqualetti, M.J., Smardon, R. & Sullivan, R. (2017). The renewable energy landscape: preserving scenic values in our sustainable future. Abingdon, Oxon: Routledge.

You might note that there seems to be a pattern to the historical sequence of energy resources: we are heading back to where we began, a near-total reliance on the sun and many of its gentle derivatives. The concept is simple. Just as thousands of generations of humans depended on renewable energy resources before the industrial age, we are now beginning to return to them, not because they are the only option, but because of their many advantages. We recognize that the era of fossil fuels has come with a price we can no longer afford, despite the fact that these have underpinned our present ways of life. In short: we started with a reliance on renewable energy, and we are looping back as we have come full circle in a sense, now that we turn our attention and hope toward a greater reliance on the sun once again.

As we increase our use of these resources to provide our energy, we will also gain environmental and geopolitical advantages. Although these renewable energy sources can transform landscapes, their potential interference with landscape values will vary with topography, land cover, occupancy, financial circumstances, and public attitudes. As the costs of traditional energy resources mount—both financially and environmentally speaking—we will increasingly see the wisdom of replacing our reliance on conventional energy as we look to the future. Significantly, the visible changes of these less harmful alternatives will help remind all humanity that the energy we use must come from somewhere. As we transition to alternative energy, some of the landscapes created by traditional energy resources will have a chance to heal. Others have an important role to play in the ongoing transition to renewables: they need to be recycled, even upcycled, and thus gain new relevance in the exploration of post-carbon futures.

11 → 26–27

10 Subsidence Fairburn LNGs, east of Leeds, United Kingdom, February 1985.
11 Wind energy landscape near Palm Springs, California, United States (Photo by Sven Stremke).

1

Power from the Landscape: One Thousand Years of Landscape Transformation

1.2

SVEN STREMKE and JOLANDA DE JONG

STUDYING THE PAST TO LEARN LESSONS FOR THE FUTURE

Most of us will fall silent when standing in front of one of the impressive landscape paintings from the Dutch masters. Few can think of the Netherlands without picturing their historical windmills, first recorded by the artist Jacob van Ruisdael and his contemporaries in the seventeenth century. Times have changed considerably. Present-day wind turbines are met with scepticism in the Netherlands and many other countries. Yet, we are starting to comprehend that our landscapes are transformed by the transition to renewable energy (see Martin Pasqualetti's chapter in this book).

Landscape transformations for the sake of energy are not a new phenomenon. Large-scale deforestation, for example, was common in societies that relied on firewood[1, 2]. For the largest part of human history, the main energy sources were muscle power, wood, wind and peat. Those were followed by fossil fuels: coal, natural gas and oil. The period of change from one main energy source to another is commonly referred to as energy transition, often entailing technological innovation, socio-economic changes, and environmental transformations. Sustainable energy transition refers to decarbonisation—the most recent shift from fossil fuels to renewable energy motivated, among others, by climate change[3].

While past energy transitions are well understood with regards to technological innovation and socio-economic developments, little is known about the large-scale landscape transformations that took place. At the brink of yet another transition, there is a need to study the history of landscape transformation for energy development. Studying landscape transformations in the past offers valuable knowledge for a more sustainable planning and designing of future landscapes.

The research presented in this chapter has been supported by The Dutch Cultural Heritage Agency (RCE). The region of the western Netherlands serves to exemplify historical developments. It was selected because there are records of landscapes transformations over a period of more than 1,000 years. Please note that another part of the project with RCE has been published previously in an open-access journal[4].

1
Smil, V. (1994). Energy in World History. Boulder, CO, USA: Westview Press.

2
Sieferle, R.P. (2001). The Subterranean Forest—Energy Systems and the Industrial Revolution. Cambridgeshire, UK: The White Horse Press.

3
International Panel on Climate Change (2011). Special Report on Renewable Energy Sources and Climate Change Mitigation [O. Edenhofer, R. Pichs-Madruga, Y. Sokona, K. Seyboth, P. Matschoss, S. Kadner, T. Zwickel, P. Eickemeier, G. Hansen, S. Schlömer, C. von Stechow (eds)], Cambridge University Press, Cambridge, United Kingdom and New York, NY, USA.

4
De Jong, J. & Stremke, S. (2020). Evolution of energy landscapes: A regional case study in the Western Netherlands, Sustainability, 2020, 12, 4554.

1 A Mill on a Polder Canal, Known as 'In the Month of July', Paul Joseph Constantin Gabriël, c. 1889, oil on canvas, h 102 cm × w 66 cm × d 14 cm (Source: Rijks Museum, The Netherlands).

FAMILIARIZING WITH THE TERM 'ENERGY LANDSCAPE'

When we started to familiarize ourselves with the term 'energy landscape', we learned that the great majority of publications is primarily concerned with the *sources* of energy rather than with the *landscapes* that come into existence due to the human development of energy. We discovered that eight main energy sources are distinguished: muscle power, biomass energy, wind energy, water energy, solar energy, thermal energy from the underground, fossil fuels and nuclear energy. It soon became clear that the term 'energy landscape' can have different meanings. Blaschke et al. stress that 'the concept of an energy landscape—like the landscape concept in general—may appear vague and difficult to grasp, being viewed from different perspectives by different disciplines. It is a concept in which object and subject overlap and interact'[5]. Yet, the term is used by many and deserves attention. Let us look at several authors who have worked on and written about energy landscapes over the past years.

Goshn[6] refers to 'energy landscape' as a landscape of energy extraction. Lambussiere and Nadai[7], Nadai and Van der Horst[8], and Maxwell[9] take a broader perspective and describe their object of study as 'landscape of energy / energies'. Others follow a different path and focus on particular kinds of energy landscapes such 'sustainable energy landscapes'[10], 'landscapes of carbon neutrality'[11], 'third generation energy landscapes'[12] and 'energy landscapes of the sustainable economy'[13]. More recently, Pasqualetti and Stremke have put forward the first typology of energy landscapes and provided a more encompassing definition of energy landscapes as 'observable landscapes that originate directly from the human development of energy resources'[14].

When researching the 'crossroads' of landscape and energy, 'two basic questions come to mind... what could we gain by looking at landscapes through energy? And what would we gain by looking at energy through landscapes?'[15]. This book chapter embraces both perspectives because 'the more capable we become at reading the energy landscape, the more we appreciate how we can use this ability to recall the past, explain the present, and foretell the future'[16].

LANDSCAPE AND CULTURAL HERITAGE

As indicated above, landscapes have been, are and will continue to be shaped by human energy development. Landscapes that originate directly (first order effects, as opposed to indirect) from the human development of energy resources are referred to as 'energy landscapes'[17]. But what do we actually mean by 'landscape' and how does energy transition relate to cultural heritage?

The European Landscape Convention refers to 'landscape' as 'an area, as perceived by people, whose character is the result of the action and interaction of natural and / or human factors' (Council of Europe, n.d). In this book, we embrace this definition and consider energy development as one of the key human factors for the origin and reshaping of landscapes. Cultural processes are a significant part of landscape development, giving rise to so-called cultural landscapes.

The Cultural Heritage Agency (RCE) of the Netherlands defines 'cultural landscape' as 'the part of the Netherlands defined and shaped by human ideas and actions: all of our landscape, comprising land and water, urban and rural areas'[18]. RCE recognizes sustainable energy transition as a cultural process and acknowledges that

5
Blaschke, T., Biberacher, M., Gadocha, S. & Schardinger, I. (2013). Energy landscapes—Meeting energy demands and human aspirations. Biomass and Bioenergy, 55, p. 3–16.

6
Goshn, R. (Ed.). (2009). Landscapes of Energy. New geographies 02. Cambridge: Harvard University Press.

7
Lambussiere, O. & Nadai, A. (2014). Unexpected wind power 'potentials'—The art of planning with inherited socio-geographical configurations (France). Scottish Geographical Journal, 130(3), p. 152–167.

8
Nadai, A. & Van der Horst, D. (2010). Introduction—Landscape of energies. Landscape Research, 35(2), p. 143–155.

9
Maxwell, K. (2011). Beyond verticality—Fuelscape politics and practices in the Andes. Human Ecology, 39, p. 465–478.

10
Stremke, S. (2010). Designing sustainable energy landscapes—Concepts, principles and procedures. PhD thesis. Wageningen: Wageningen University.

11
Selman, P. (2010). Learning to love the landscapes of carbon-neutrality. Landscape Research, 35(2), p. 157–171.

12
Noorman, K., & De Roo, G. (Eds.). (2011). Energielandschappen—de 3de generatie [Energy Landscapes, the 3rd generation]. Assen: Provincie Drenthe.

13
Pasqualetti, M.J. (2013). Reading the changing energy landscape. In: S. Stremke & A. Van den Dobbelsteen (Eds.). Sustainable energy landscapes—Designing, planning and development (pp. 11–44). Boca Raton: CRC Press.

14
Pasqualetti, M.J. & Stremke, S. (2018). Energy landscapes in a crowded world: A first typology of origins and expressions. Energy Research and Social Science, 36, p. 94–105.

15
Nadai, A. & Van der Horst, D. (2010). Introduction—Landscape of energies. Landscape Research, 35(2), p. 143–155.

16
Pasqualetti, M.J. (2013). Reading the changing energy landscape. In: S. Stremke & A. Van den Dobbelsteen (Eds.). Sustainable energy landscapes—Designing, planning and development (pp. 11). Boca Raton: CRC Press.

17
Pasqualetti, M.J. & Stremke, S. (2018). Energy landscapes in a crowded world: A first typology of origins and expressions. Energy Research and Social Science, 36, p. 94–105.

18
RCE (Rijksdienst voor Cultureel Erfgoed) (n.d.). Landscape and historic setting, Retrieved 31 January 2017 from https://culturalheritageagency.nl/en/landscape.

19
Van 't Ven, C. (2017). Preamble. In: H+N+S Landschapsarchitecten, Erfgoed in transitie—Energielinie, Retrieved from https://erfgoedenruimte.nl/publicaties/energielinie-erfgoed-in-transitie.

renewable energy will affect cultural heritage[19]. These are fundamental premises for the research presented in this chapter and potentially for other studies on historical energy landscapes elsewhere in the world.

GENERAL HISTORY AND ENERGY PERIODS

20
Bridge, G., Bouzarovski, S., Bradshaw, M. & Eyre, N., (2013). Geographies of Energy Transition: Space, Place and the Low-Carbon Economy. Energy Policy, 53, 331–340.

21
Rotmans, J., Kemp, R. & Van Asselt, M. (2001). More evolution than revolution: Transition management in public policy. Foresight, 03 (01), 1–17.

Energy transition refers to the change between energy sources and / or technologies that often involves socio-economic as well as spatial change[20]. This chapter focuses on energy transitions that resulted in observable changes in the landscape, for example through peat extraction. We call the times between transitions, dominated by certain energy sources, 'energy periods'. These energy periods will allow us to study the development of Dutch energy landscapes through time. However, the boundaries between periods are somewhat fuzzy because most energy transitions are gradual transformations of existing systems: transitions are 'more evolution than revolution'[21]. To understand the evolution of energy landscapes in the Netherlands, we consider the developments of energy in relation to the general Dutch history. The most important moments and (social) developments in the history of the Netherlands can be summarized in five general periods.

- Period 1: Agrarian society / Early Middle Ages until circa 1000 (population 200,000)
- Period 2: The Great Exploitation / Middle Ages from circa 1000 to 1500 (population 1,000,000)
- Period 3: Early Modern Time / pre-industrial from circa 1500 to 1800 (population 2,100,000
- Period 4: Modern time / industrialization from circa 1800 to 2000 (population 15,800,000)
- Period 5: Post-industrial time, present (population 2021 circa 17,000,000)

22
Pasqualetti, M.J. (2013). Reading the changing energy landscape. In: S. Stremke & A. Van den Dobbelsteen (Eds.). Sustainable energy landscapes—Designing, planning and development (pp. 11–44). Boca Raton: CRC Press.

23
Noorman, K., & De Roo, G. (Eds.). (2011). Energielandschappen—de 3de generatie [Energy Landscapes, the 3rd generation]. Assen: Provincie Drenthe.

24
Smil, V. (2015). Power density—A key to understanding energy sources and uses. Cambridge: MIT Press.

Overlaying these five historical periods with the different sets of energy systems[22, 23, 24], we can start to distinguish five energy periods for the western Netherlands:

- Period 1: The period of muscle power—human and draft animals, mainly visible through the presence of fields for feedstock;
- Period 2: The period of peat fuel—characterized by large-scale peat extraction starting in the Early Middle Ages;
- Period 3: The period of wind energy—observable through the presence of windmills in the landscape;
- Period 4: The period of fossil fuels—conspicuous increase in use since the Industrial Revolution;
- Period 5: The period of renewable energy—renaissance of renewable energy sources in the post-industrial time (present)

25
Smil, V. (2008). Energy in Nature and Society: General Energetics of Complex Systems. Cambridge: MIT Press.

The above energy periods help to understand the development of different energy landscapes through time. Not surprisingly, energy landscapes themselves are constituents of larger energy systems. How can these systems and in particular their spatial components be described? In line with energy science[25], we conceptualize

Energy sources and subcategory (where applicable)			Examples in the Netherlands	Functioning when?	Visual component(s) of the energy chain
Muscle power	Draft animals		Grasslands near settlements agrarian society period	Past	Source (feedstock)
	Human labour		Arable fields near settlements agrarian society period	Past	Source (food)
Biomass energy	Wood	Firewood	Wassergeest, Zuid-Holland	Past	Source
		Charcoal	Beekman te Uddel, Gelderland	Past	Source and conversion
	Peat	Hoogveen (raised bog)	Fochteloerveen, Drenthe	Past, remnant	Source and transport
		Laagveen (peat bog)	De Ronde Venen, Utrecht	Past, remnant	Source and transport
	Peat gas		Midden-Beemster, North Holland	Past	Conversion
	Energy crops		Schiphol Trade Park, North Holland	Present	Source
	Waste	Solid	Waste to energy plant Hengelo, Overijssel	Present	Conversion
		Liquid	Waste to energy plant Dordrecht, South Holland	Present	Conversion
		Gaseous	PlantPower Stadskanaal, Groningen	Present	Conversion
Wind energy	Windmills		UNESCO Kinderdijk, South Holland	Past, present	Conversion
	Wind turbines		Windpark Noordoostpolder, Flevoland	Present	Conversion
Water energy	Water mills		Water mill Singraven, Overijssel	Past	Source and conversion
	Hydropower		Weir Maurik, Gelderland	Present	Conversion
	Blue energy		Test case Breezanddijk, Friesland	Present	Conversion
Solar energy			Zoneiland Almere, Flevoland	Present	Conversion
Fossil fuels	Coal		Wilhelminaberg, Landgraaf, Limburg	Past, remnant	Source and conversion
	Natural gas		Gas field Slochteren, Groningen	Present	Conversion
	Crude oil		Oil field Schoonebeek, Drenthe	Present	Conversion
Nuclear energy			Borselle Nuclear Power Station, Zeeland	Present	Conversion
Various sources	Electricity generation		Eemshavencentrale, Groningen	Present	Conversion
	Energy transport / transmission		Betuweroute, South Holland / Gelderland	Past, present	Transport / transmission

2

energy systems as consisting of four spatial components: the three main stages along the energy chain—source, conversion / storage and end use—plus transport / transmission between the main stages. Each of those four main components of energy systems may affect the physical environment, which is why they are functional in the subsequent analysis and representation of historical and contemporary energy landscapes in the Netherlands.

LOOKING AT LANDSCAPE THROUGH ENERGY

Energy landscapes may take various forms. One could think of the old windmills at Kinderdijk in the Netherlands (UNESCO World Heritage Site), the open pit coal mines in Lusatia in Germany (International Building Exhibition site) or Lake Mead with the iconic Hoover Dam near Las Vegas in the United States (another major tourist attraction). While the energy periods and energy system components introduced above allow us to 'locate' an energy landscape both in time and along the energy chain, research on (historical) energy landscapes requires additional descriptors to characterize the object of study. Pasqualetti and Stremke[14] have recently put forward a framework for the systemic study of energy landscapes. Below, we summarize their three qualifications that were applied for the study and characterization of energy landscapes in the Netherlands.

Firstly, energy landscapes are shaped by the energy source that is developed for human usage. Pasqualetti and Stremke[14] refer to this descriptor of energy landscapes as substantive qualification and suggest that the density of the energy source(s) can help to compare energy landscapes with each other. A biomass energy landscape, for example, belongs to the sub-category of *low-density* energy landscape as opposed to *high-density* energy landscapes such as hydro-power plants.

Secondly, the appearance of energy landscapes is determined by the spatial expanse and visual dominance of the means to utilize the source: energy technology / infrastructure or biological converter. While discussing this spatial qualification, Pasqualetti and Stremke[14] distinguish between *component energy landscapes*—energy infrastructure constitutes one of many landscape components (windmills at Kinderdijk, the Netherlands)—and *entity energy landscapes*—energy development constitutes the sole land use (coal mines in Lusatia, Germany).

Thirdly, Pasqualetti and Stremke[14] introduce the temporal qualification. Energy landscapes may exist only for a relatively short period of time, for example due to the short lifetime of energy technologies such as photovoltaic panels. Other energy landscapes, for example those that came into existence due to peat extraction, will remain or leave marks almost indefinitely. The respective descriptor—degree of permanence—may range from relatively *dynamic* to *permanent*.

We like to add another consideration that is particularly helpful for the study of *historical* energy landscapes. While Pasqualetti and Stremke (2018) distinguish between energy landscapes that existed in the *past* but have disappeared and those that *exist* in the present, they briefly refer to the 'traces' of past energy landscapes. These traces or remnants of past energy periods are of key importance to the study and appreciation of historical energy landscapes. While remnants may no longer be functional in the present-day energy system, they still present visual cues of historical landscape

2 Types of energy landscapes in the Netherlands, organized according to energy source.

transformation and they are important anchors of cultural heritage. The few remaining coals heaps in Limburg, a former mining region in the south of the Netherlands, are one prominent example of such local cultural heritage.

TYPES OF ENERGY LANDSCAPES IN THE NETHERLANDS

As stated before, we discovered eight main energy sources in the literature: muscle power, biomass energy, wind energy, water energy, solar energy, thermal energy from the underground, fossil fuels and nuclear energy. All eight sources have been developed in the Netherlands but not all of them gave rise to energy landscapes. Thermal energy from the underground is among the exceptions.

One specific and often overlooked type of energy landscape is illustrated in figure 3. The painting depicts how the chopping of trees and collection of firewood reshaped large parts of Europe that were originally covered with large forests. Few traces of this *past energy landscape* can be found today but many of today's open landscapes used to look very different only a few centuries ago.

Figure 2 presents an overview of the types of energy landscapes that resulted from our extensive literature review, organized according to energy source. The table indicates whether an energy landscape exists at present or existed in the past and, if so, whether or not remnants of past times are still visible. The table also indicates for each energy source which components of the energy system dominate the landscape (last column). For some types of energy, it is the actual energy source that gives shape to an energy landscape (e.g., peat energy landscape). For other types, the technology used to convert energy (e.g., wind turbines) or the infrastructure used the transport / transmit energy (e.g., power lines) determines the spatial appearance of energy landscapes.

When looking at the evolution of energy landscapes through time, it becomes clear that each type can be linked to the discovery of new energy sources and / or technological innovation. Environmental concerns also played a role in some of the earlier transitions. Coal, for example, was preferred over whale oil and helped whale populations to recuperate. Coal, in turn, was later replaced by natural gas, which reduced local air pollution[26].

Figure 4 presents an overview of how the different energy sources have been developed through time in the Netherlands. The figure illustrates which components of the energy system have been or are still visible in the landscape. The figure shows that some energy sources experience a revival. Water mills, for example, were first replaced with coal-fired steam engines and later substituted by electrical machines powered, among others, by hydropower generated elsewhere. The figure also shows that some energy sources have been found below the ground, and others are harvested on or above the surface. Not surprisingly, there is a clear link between this property of the energy source, the choice of energy technologies and the experience in the landscape. It appears that for the largest part of history, above-surface energy sources have been utilized. Except for a relatively short period of time—no more than a few hundred years—the Dutch (and many others) used energy sources from above the surface.

26
Smil, V. (2008). Energy in Nature and Society: General Energetics of Complex Systems. Cambridge: MIT Press.

3 Large-scale deforestation for energy development transformed many landscapes: Winter landscape, Paul Bril (copy after), 1615–1650, oil on panel, h 58.1 cm × w 79.1 cm × d 1.3 cm (Source: Rijks Museum, The Netherlands).

4 Energy sources and components of the energy system that have been or are visible in the Netherlands, from pre-medieval time to the twenty-first century.

3

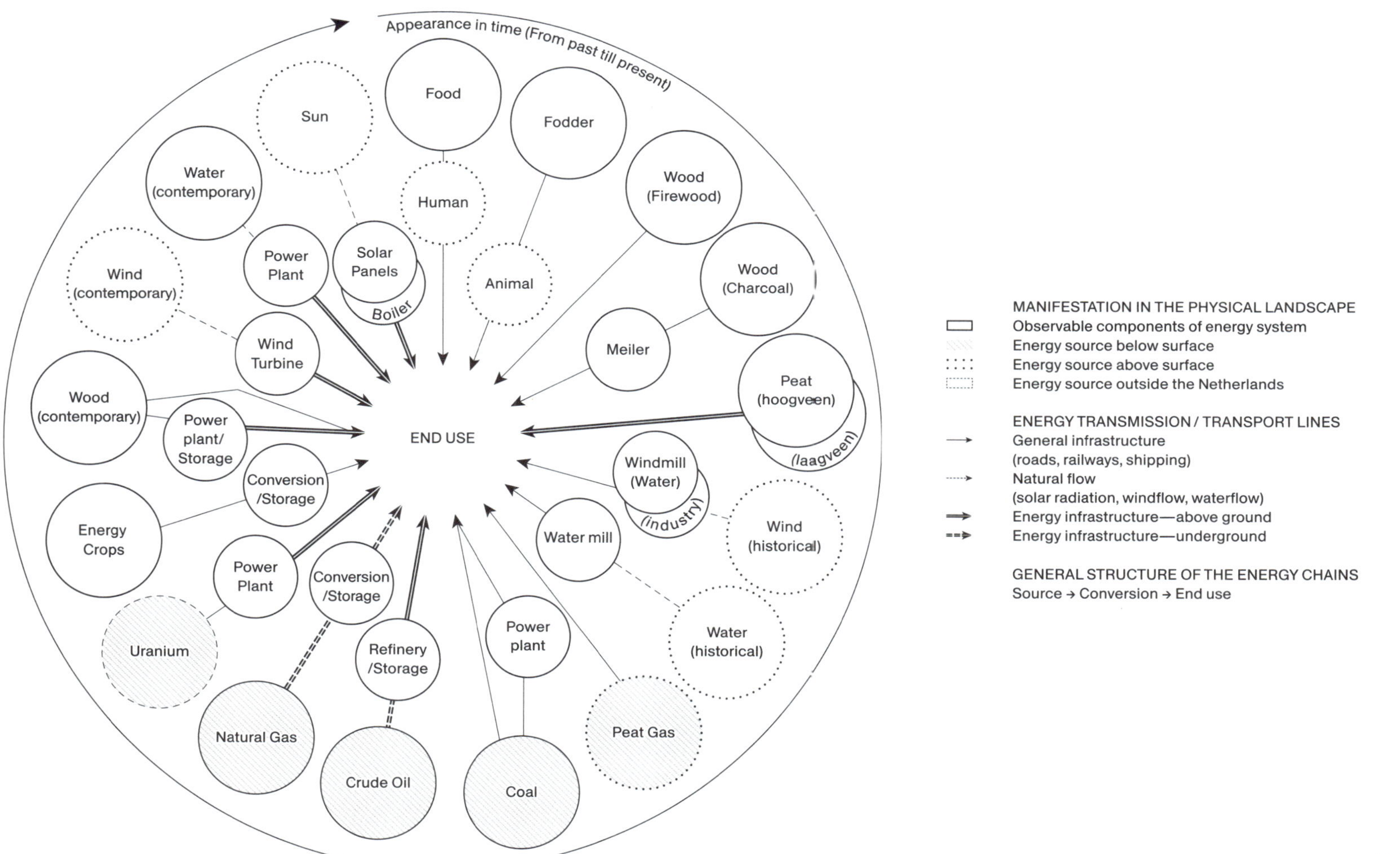

Appearance in time (From past till present)
Sun
Food
Fodder
Water (contemporary)
Human
Wood (Firewood)
Wind (contemporary)
Power Plant
Solar Panels
Boiler
Animal
Wood (Charcoal)
Wind Turbine
Meiler
Wood (contemporary)
Power plant/ Storage
END USE
Peat (hoogveen)
(laagveen)
Conversion /Storage
Windmill (Water)
(industry)
Energy Crops
Water mill
Wind (historical)
Power Plant
Conversion /Storage
Uranium
Refinery /Storage
Power plant
Water (historical)
Natural Gas
Crude Oil
Coal
Peat Gas
MANIFESTATION IN THE PHYSICAL LANDSCAPE
Observable components of energy system
Energy source below surface
Energy source above surface
Energy source outside the Netherlands
ENERGY TRANSMISSION / TRANSPORT LINES
General infrastructure
(roads, railways, shipping)
Natural flow
(solar radiation, windflow, waterflow)
Energy infrastructure—above ground
Energy infrastructure—underground
GENERAL STRUCTURE OF THE ENERGY CHAINS
Source → Conversion → End use

4

Afbeelding van de Hollandsche Veenen na 't Dorp AMSTERVEEN te zien, met de wyze van het Turf maken.

5

6

7

EVOLUTION OF ENERGY LANDSCAPES IN THE WESTERN NETHERLANDS

After we have shown how the different energy sources have been developed through time, each one of them leaving traces in the Dutch landscape, we will now exemplify this development for the western Netherlands. The region of the western Netherlands was chosen because distinct energy landscapes have come into existence during each of the five energy periods. Many of which (or their remnants) are still visible in this part of the country[→fig. 5, 6, 7].

During each energy period, the landscape changed due to the development of energy sources, namely muscle power, peat, wind energy, fossil fuels and renewable energy. This does not necessarily mean that people stopped using other sources. While the energy source responsible for major landscape transformations changed, for example from muscle to peat, some functions such as transport were still powered by muscles.

THE FIRST ENERGY PERIOD: THE LANDSCAPE OF MUSCLE POWER

Since prehistoric times, people burned wood to cook and keep themselves warm. Large-scale deforestation had already been taken place prior to the period described here. During the last centuries of the first millennium (before 1000 CE), the western Netherlands was the home to an agrarian society that reclaimed land to live on and for agricultural purposes. Muscle power was the main resource shaping the western Netherlands during the first millennium. Human labour and draft animals were used for mechanical work. 'One horse can accomplish the same amount of work as ten people in one hour. Horse and ox power were some of the first substitutes for human power and contributed to improving the quality of human life'[27]. This period was characterized by very low energy densities; energy was used directly or in proximity of the source[→fig. 8].

THE SECOND ENERGY PERIOD: THE LANDSCAPE OF PEAT EXTRACTION

The second energy period lasted from around 1000 until 1500 CE. The peat area in the western Netherlands was cultivated on a large scale[28]. State formations and centralization allowed the extraction of peat in the *laagveengebieden* within less than 300 years. The main purpose of this cultivation was to create space for settlements and agricultural use. On the local scale, however, peat was extracted for energy purposes. Although peat did not become the main national energy source until the seventeenth century[29, 30, 31], it was already used as fuel in the western Netherlands during the Middle Ages. Peat extraction irreversibly changes the landscape; many remnants can still be found. The peat landscape can therefore be characterized as permanent[→fig. 9].

THE THIRD ENERGY PERIOD: WIND ENERGY LANDSCAPE

Around 1500, while ever more peat was extracted for energy purposes, a new type of technology was introduced to the western Netherlands: the windmill. The first large polders (in Dutch *droogmakerijen)* were created making use of this advanced technology. The third energy period was dominated by wind energy development and lasted until approximately 1800 CE. The majority of windmills in the western Netherlands were used to drain water from the land; land that otherwise was no longer suitable for agricultural use due to excessive peat extraction and / or land subsidence. When windmills were demolished (many were), the energy landscape changed and other landscape

27
Pimentel, D. & Pimentel, M.H. (2008). Food, energy and society, 12. Boca Raton: CRC Press.

28
Cultureelerfgoed.nl. (n.d.). Landchap 6—Laagveengebied, Retrieved July 18, 2017 from https://cultureelerfgoed.nl/sites/default/public_ftp/CultGIS/laagveen.pdf.

29
Cornelisse, C.H. (2006). The economy of peat and its environmental consequences in Holland during the late middle Ages. Jaarboek voor Ecologische Geschiedenis, 2005–2006, 95–121.

30
Unger, R.W. (1984). Energy sources for the Dutch Golden Age—peat, wind and coal. Research in Economic History, 9, 221–253.

31
Jongepier, I., Soens, T., Thoen, E., Eetvelde, V., Crombé, P. & Bats, M. (2011). The brown gold—a reappraisal of medieval peat marshes in Northern Flanders (Belgium). Water history, 3(2011), 73–93.

5 Peat extraction near Amstelveen in the western Netherlands: View of the peatlands near Amstelveen, Jan Caspar Philips, 1741–1742, etching and engraving, h 171 mm × w 293 mm (Source: Rijksmuseum, The Netherlands).

6 Wind energy landscape in lower peat areas: Polder landscape, River landscape with barge, J.H. Weisenbruch, 1824–1903, oil on panel, h 245 mm × w 365 mm (Source: Groninger Museum, The Netherlands).

7 Location case study area (dashed line) of the Western Netherlands, encompassing parts of the provinces North Holland, South Holland and Utrecht.

features gained visual prominence. Therefore, the temporal qualification for the wind energy landscape is 'dynamic' even though some of the windmills lasted for hundreds of years. While many windmills have vanished, the remaining ones have become highly valued and well-preserved elements of the cultural landscape →fig. 10.

THE FOURTH ENERGY PERIOD: FOSSIL FUEL LANDSCAPES

The introduction of coal powered steam engines to the western Netherlands in the early ninteenth century marks the start of the fourth energy period: the period of *fossil fuel landscapes*. The introduction of machines powered by fossil fuels (coal, petroleum and natural gas) allowed for land reclamation at an unprecedented pace and spatial extent. Large lakes and abandoned polders could be reclaimed throughout and beyond the western Netherlands. Initially, coal and oil were brought to the region to manage water levels. Later, after the invention of power plants and high-voltage power lines, electricity was generated and transmitted to the user. The power plants and electricity infrastructure are components of the complex energy landscape of this period. On a small scale, natural gas and oil were extracted in the western Netherlands; extraction sites are included in figure 11. These landscapes have an intermediate degree of permanence. After energy facilities are closed, the landscape may evolve. The energy landscapes associated with the generation and transmission of electricity (power plants and high-voltage power lines) are considered dynamic because the energy infrastructure can be completely removed.

THE FIFTH ENERGY PERIOD: RENEWABLE ENERGY LANDSCAPE

Around the brink of the new millennium, the Netherlands started to transit towards a post-carbon economy causing the revival of renewable energy sources such as wind energy. This energy transition is starting to transform the landscape in the western Netherlands too. New landscape components—wind turbines, solar panels and energy crops—are emerging along with an improved electricity network, to transmit renewable electricity →fig. 12. Together they give rise to a number of distinct energy landscapes (e.g., Slufter wind energy landscape on the Maasvlakte, Rotterdam). Elsewhere, renewable energy technologies and electricity infrastructure present components of the larger, multifunctional landscape. The energy landscapes of the renewable energy period in the Netherlands are considered dynamic. Solar panels and wind turbines can be removed at the end of their life cycle—the energy landscape is reversible.

LEARNING FROM THE PAST

What types of energy landscapes have existed or still exist in the Netherlands and how have they evolved chronologically? That is the question that drove the research presented in this chapter of the book. First, we found that the large majority of publications is primarily concerned with the energy sources and technologies rather than with the energy landscapes that came into existence due to the development of energy. Will this change now that renewable energy is experiencing a renaissance and society is actively involved in the shaping of the sustainable energy transition? A question that will be taken along to the following two parts of this book.

Eight types of energy landscapes (according to energy sources) could be distinguished. Seven of them existed or still exist in the Netherlands, only thermal energy from the underground has not (yet) resulted in a distinct energy landscape. Figure 4 lists 23 different types of energy landscapes and shows which components of the energy system were / are visible. This brings us to the second important finding: energy development can manifest itself in the landscape in fundamentally different ways. The type of energy system component—source, conversion technologies or transmission / transportation infrastructure—that gave rise to an energy landscape, ultimately, affects the appearance and perception of that energy landscape.

Our research was aimed at gaining insights on the manifestation of energy development in the landscape in general, but we also examined the evolution of Dutch energy landscapes. The research shows that, apart from a relatively short period of time, people have used energy sources from above the surface. Moreover, we learned that the use of specific energy sources—wind and water—has revived with time. Some of the energy landscapes that emerged hundreds of years ago can still be seen today. A second group of energy landscapes can be experienced through its remnants, such as windmills and the extensive networks of canals.

The case study carried out for the western Netherlands shows that five energy transitions have taken place in the region. Each transition not only defined the start of a new energy period in the western Netherlands but also gave rise to distinct energy landscapes with different substantive, spatial and temporal characteristics. Peat extraction was one of the main drivers of landscape transformation in this part of the Netherlands. After the peat had been exploited, technologies such as windmills and coal-powered water pumps were deployed to continue cultivation of the land.

From this historical perspective, the ongoing sustainable energy transition can be understood as yet another stage in the (more or less) continuous landscape evolution mirroring human needs and societal values. The maps of energy periods in the western Netherlands show the spatial expanse of all energy landscapes in the case study area. It is important to realize that the observable landscapes that originate directly from the human development of energy over the centuries cover a large part of the total surface area.

The energy landscapes that developed in the western Netherlands never substituted their predecessors completely, let alone at once. During each energy period, one can find past energy landscapes or remnants of previous periods. Some energy landscapes have, through time, turned into much-appreciated cultural landscapes, for example the UNESCO World Heritage Site Kinderdijk. This finding offers some perspective for the currently eroding support for solar panels and wind turbines.

To conclude, energy development has given rise to new energy landscapes, and continues to do so today. While energy sources and technologies may change rapidly, some of the resulting landscape transformations are permanent and affect future developments. The spatial expression of energy in the physical landscape becomes richer time and again; the complexity of these cultural landscapes increases through time. The notion of cultural landscape will receive more attention in the remainder of this book, because we have learned that historical energy developments shaped the landscapes we live in today and that these are responsible for some of the qualities we cherish so much.

8 The Western Netherlands During The First Energy Period: Wood Energy

LAND USE
- Indication of habitation area
- Open water (1219 km²)
- Peat landscape (2838 km²)
- Other terrestrial area (1475 km²)

ENERGY IN THE LANDSCAPE
- Indication of areas used for
  - Food for muscle power
  - Fodder for draft animals
  - Chopping wood (deforestation areas)

9 The Western Netherlands During The Second Energy Period: Peat Energy

LAND USE
- Urban settlements (7 km2)
- Indication of habitation area
- Open water (1219 km2)
- Natural peat landscape (2422 km2)
- Other terrestrial area (1466 km2)

ENERGY IN THE LANDSCAPE
- Indication of areas used for
  - Food for muscle power
  - Fodder for draft animals
  - Chopping wood (deforestation areas)
- Indication of peat extraction areas

10 The Western Netherlands During The Third Energy Period: Wind Energy

LAND USE
- Urban settlements (17 km²)
- Indication of habitation area
- Open water (1484 km²)
- Natural peat landscape (1457 km²)
- Other terrestrial area (2154 km²)

ENERGY IN THE LANDSCAPE
- Windmill related to *Droogmakerijen*
- Industrial wind energy area 'Zaanstreek'
- Oldest windmill in the case study area
- *Droogmakerijen* (420 km²)

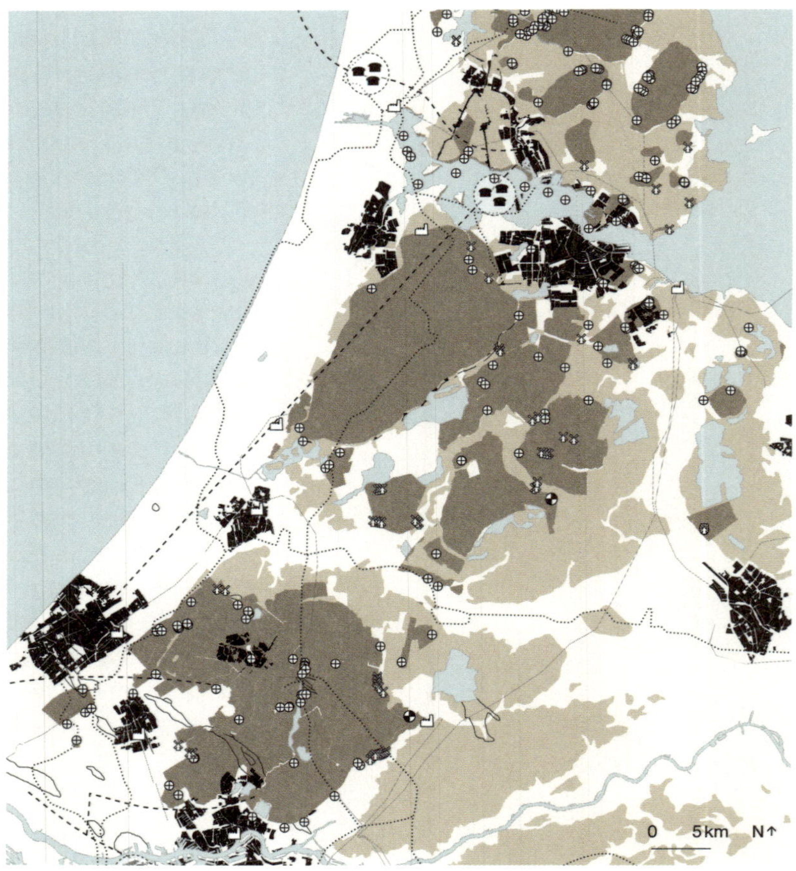

11 The Western Netherlands During The Fourth Energy Period: Fossil Fuels

LAND USE
- Urban settlements (254 km²)
- Open water (1421 km²)
- Remnants natural peat landscape (1034 km²)
- Other terrestrial area (2314 km²)

ENERGY IN THE LANDSCAPE
- Coal driven water pumping station
- Oil driven water pumping station
- Electric water pumping station
- Oil fields
- Fossil fuel storage
- Powerplant
- Overhead power line (50, 150 and 380 kV)
- High pressure gas network
- Large oil pipeline
- Historical windmill related to Droogmakerijen
- *Droogmakerijen* (929 km²)

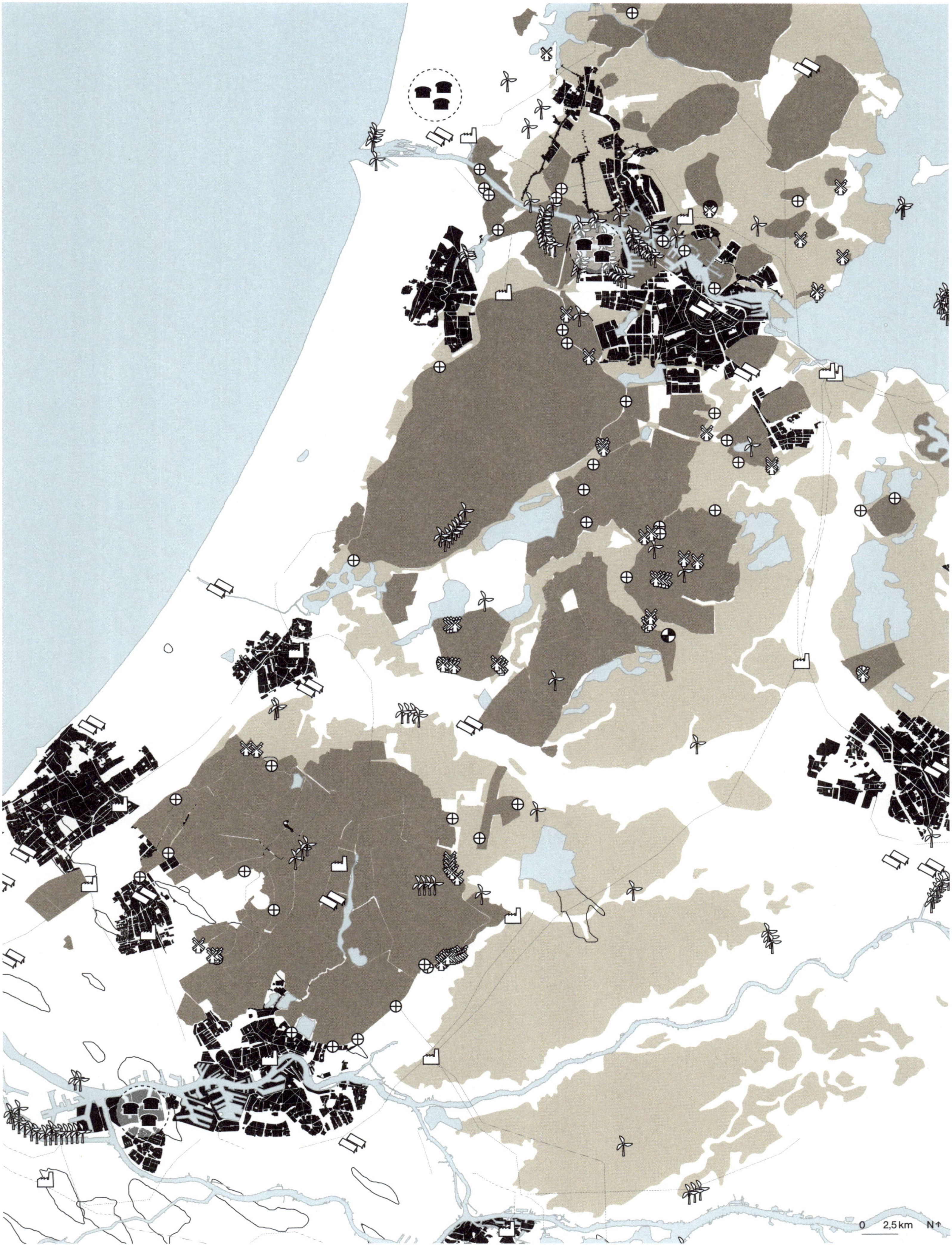

12 The Western Netherlands During The Second Energy Period: Peat Energy

LAND USE
- Urban settlements (339 km²)
- Open water (1387 km²)
- Remnants natural peat landscape (1013 km²)
- Other terrestrial area (1918 km²)

ENERGY IN THE LANDSCAPE
- Windturbine
- Solar park
- Coal driven water pumping station (partly non-functional remnants)
- Electric water pumping station
- Oil driven water pumping station (partly non-functional remnants)
- Oil fields
- Fossil fuel storage
- Powerplant
- Overhead power line (50, 150 and 380 kV)
- Historical windmill related to *Droogmakerijen*
- *Droogmakerijen* (929 km²)

1

The Landscape of Others 1.3

ANDREA CAROLINA CARDOSO and EMMA BANKS

In the Global North, you can wake up each morning and switch on your high-tech coffee machine. But where does the electricity that powers that machine come from? If just one coal-fired power plant is part of the network, even if your home has solar panels or your municipality hosts a wind farm, you will be consuming fossil fuels. We know that coal is one of the leading causes of climate change, and yet coal power plants are still operating today. Technologies inside the power plant have advanced over the past 100 years, but coal still produces the types of landscapes Charles Dickens depicted in his nineteenth-century novels. Today, those bleak and contaminated landscapes have moved from the Global North to the Global South. For example, the United Kingdom and Germany are closing most of their coal mines, while across the Atlantic Ocean in Colombia, open-pit coal mines are expanding day by day, eroding the traditional landscapes of the peasant, Afro-descendant, and indigenous communities there[1].

Despite the commitments made by 190 countries at COP26 to eliminate coal from their energy mix by 2030 for developed countries and 2040 for developing countries, the international coal market is ambiguous[2]. It does not respond to the need for decarbonization but to external factors such as the Covid-19 crisis, the increase in gas prices, and the recent sanctions on the Russian energy sector. The countries of the Global South that depend on coal continue to expand their operations, thinking that a growing demand in other countries in the South will compensate for the coal market fluctuations in the Global North[3].

In Colombia, 92.5 per cent of the coal extracted is exported[4]. All the exported coal comes from the Guajira and Cesar regions. The main Colombian coal destinations in 2019 and 2020 were Turkey (25 per cent), Chile (10 per cent), Brazil (7 per cent) and Israel (7 per cent)[5]. Until 5 years ago, the Netherlands and Germany were the main importers of Colombian coal. Most consumers never consider the real energy costs of their lifestyle. They see their energy bills, but not the costs to the landscape of Colombian communities. We invite you on a journey along the coal chain, in reverse order, from your coffee machine to a Colombian coal mine.

1
Cardoso, A. (2015). Behind the life cycle of coal: Socio-environmental liabilities of coal mining in Cesar, Colombia. Ecological Economics, 120, p. 71–82.

2
Vargas-Guevara, Ó., Corral-Montoya, F., Cardoso, A., Ruiz-Arroyave, J., Bonilla-Camargo, Ó., Gómez-Camargo, M., López-Orellano, L., Brito-Bouriyu, L., Guzmán-Angulo, N., Padilla-Guzmán, N., Soto-Sierra, M., Ortiz-Bouriyu, Y., & Malz, N. (2022). Impulsos desde abajo para las transiciones energéticas justas: género, territorio y soberanía. Editorial Unimagdalena, Fescol.

3
Yanguas-Parra, P., Arond, E., Strambo, C., & Vega-Araújo, J. (2021). El ocaso del carbón y la necesidad de una transición justa en Colombia. www.sei.org

4
UPME. (2020). BECO. Consulta. In BECO. Balance Energético Colombiano. http://www1.upme.gov.co/InformacionCifras/Paginas/BECOCONSULTA.aspx

5
UPME. (2021). Carbón. Producción, regalías y comercio exterior. https://www1.upme.gov.co/simco/Cifras-Sectoriales/Paginas/carbon.aspx

1 The vastness of Cerrejón coal mine (Photo credit Alejandro Valbuena H.).

Our journey could start in Rotterdam, the largest coal port in Europe, or in Amsterdam →fig. 2. In the port, we can board an empty coal barge departing to Colombia's Puerto Bolivar, located in the Guajira region, or to Puerto Nuevo and Puerto Drummond in the Magdalena region.

Over the past 40 years, several multinational companies have been granted open coal mining concessions to extract and export coal in La Guajira and Cesar regions. The Cerrejón open-pit coal mine extends over 69,000 hectares—three times the area of Amsterdam—and is one of the ten largest in the world. Cerrejón is the biggest exporter of thermal coal in the world[6]. Cerrejón ships its coal in Puerto Bolivar. These multinational companies also own the barges that travel between ports.

To reach the Cerrejón coal mine, we board a barge in Amsterdam where we will start our journey passing the wind turbines along the North Sea canal. This first part of our journey will take 17 days, with an average speed of 15 knots per hour to traverse 6162 nautical miles. We will move along the coasts of France, Spain, Portugal, Morocco, and the Western Sahara to then cross the Atlantic Ocean to the Caribbean Sea between the British Virgin Islands and Puerto Rico. When coal exports increase, so do the number of shipping accidents, resulting in coal spills in the ocean. Coal spills kill coral and important reef species in coastal zones[7].

Once we reach Cerrejón's port, Puerto Bolivar, we witness that the coal loading technique does not safeguard against critical dust dispersion affecting the coasts and the spilling of coal into the sea. This spillage impacts indigenous people's fishing industry and cuts coastal communities off from their traditional territory. The port looks like empty desert-like land—in Spanish, this zone is now called *Media Luna* (literally in the middle of the moon); coal companies displaced the community originally living here in the 1980s to make room for infrastructure. Today, communities living near the port continue to fight with the company over fishing rights, access to potable water, and territorial rights.

Coal reaches Puerto Bolivar via a dedicated train track that stretches 150 kilometres through indigenous lands. The trains run ten times a day, cutting through indigenous Wayúu settlements. On our ride south toward to the mine, we travel past the arid landscape of the Guajira peninsula rich in biodiversity and an awesome natural environment, which is a famous ecotourism destination, to the town of Albania. Before reaching Albania, the railway track circumscribes with a large curve the lands of the local community of Wayúu people. In these settlements, we will see families living in simple earthen homes and sleeping in brightly coloured hammocks woven by the women. Most families still herd goats for subsistence and income; the more goats you have, the higher your social prestige. All of these communities struggle to access drinking water; their traditional reservoirs have dried up and become contaminated over the years as the coal on the train leaves particulate matter and mining itself drains aquifers[8]. In these quiet settlements, plain-clothed security guards on horseback constantly monitor the population. A Wayúu elder described how the train 'has taken over our territory; now it is not ours'[9]. The train regularly kills their goats and livestock. Worse still, these railways do not have clear regulations regarding safety and the prevention of harm, resulting in frequent accidents. In Cesar, for example, 25 people died and 280 were injured between 2008 and 2011 along the lines in the Magdalena region operated by Fenoco →fig. 3[10].

6
Oei, P.-Y. & Mendelevitch, R. (2019). Climate Policy Prospects for steam coal exporters in the era of climate policies: a case study of Colombia Prospects for steam coal exporters in the era of climate policies: a case study of Colombia. Climate Policy, 19(1), p. 73–91.

7
Berry, K.L.E., Hoogenboom, M.O., Flores, F. & Negri, A.P. (2016). Simulated Coal Spill Causes Mortality and Growth Inhibition in Tropical Marine Organisms. Scientific Reports 6 (1): 25894.

8
Fierro, J., & Llorente, A. (2016). Consideraciones ambientales acerca del proyecto carbonífero de El Cerrejón, operado por las empresas BHP Billiton, Angloamerican y Xstrata en La Guajira. http://media.wix.com/

9
Jakobsen, Line Jespersgaard. 2020. "Corporate Security Technologies: Managing Life and Death along a Colombian Coal Railway." Political Geography 83: 102273, p. 5.

10
Cardoso, A. (2015). Behind the life cycle of coal: Socio-environmental liabilities of coal mining in Cesar, Colombia. Ecological Economics, 120, p. 71–82.

2

3

We then arrive at the Cerrejón mine located in the valley of the Ranchería River. For centuries, this has been the region's breadbasket, as the fertile soils in the valley and hills provide the right conditions to grow tropical fruits, coffee, tubers, and beans. In the eighteenth and nineteenth century, escaped slaves found refuge here, forming small settlements around tributary streams that provided water and fish[11]. Their descendants still occupy this region today alongside Wayúu communities and *mestizo* populations. The intercultural mixing in the region has produced Colombia's popular *vallenato* music, rich food traditions, and unique handicrafts.

Visiting today, it is hard to imagine people, plants or animals thriving in this region. Since 1985, coal companies have forcibly evicted Wayúu indigenous and Afro-Colombian communities to make room for the coal mine's expansion. The loss of traditional lands for agriculture has contributed to malnutrition especially among children[12].

After facing legal and social pressure over displacement, the Cerrejón company began to build resettlements for these communities, moving families from their rural homesteads to plaster homes located near the regional motorway. Here, community leaders have fought for better conditions including jobs to replace their rural livelihoods, potable water, and education for their children. They have lost their territories, which gave them subsistence, and which were an important part of their culture and identity. In a statement released in March 2022, three Afro-descendant and Wayúu communities relocated by Cerrejón described how they could no longer sustain themselves when they were removed from their territory, making them dependent on the company. They wrote: 'At this time, the communities do not have job opportunities because ancestrally we dedicated ourselves to the field—agriculture, ranching, small livestock, subsistence farming, and fishing. Today, because of our relocation, we do not have the territory or space to carry out these activities that would allow us to produce what is necessary to satisfy the needs of an entire population.' The communities demanded job opportunities and development funding to sustain themselves once again, calling on both the company and state institutions to pay attention to their plight.

Coal mining has degraded the surrounding soils and contaminated or dried up water sources, with devastating impacts on farming and livestock. The main concern in the whole Guajira region is air pollution, resulting from the coal dust that spreads not only during extraction but also during transportation to the port, resulting in respiratory diseases. Children suffer from malnutrition and illness due to coal mining. To illustrate this point, we turn to the story of Luz Angela Uriana, a mother and activist in the indigenous reserve Provincial. Luz Angela did not think of herself as an activist until her young son Moises fell sick and almost died as an infant. Moises has a rare lung disease caused by the coal dust. Luz Angela began working with lawyers to petition the company to cover her son's treatment and to halt mining near Provincial. Although she won her case, little has changed. Like many activists, Luz Angela keeps fighting nonetheless. 'I need to fight for all the children so that they don't die. I am scared that my Moises will die. Which is why I ask people to help and tell people our story and to say that there are many other communities suffering. We come to ask for doctors from this county to go to La Guajira to show that the coal mining here causes countless problems' → fig. 4[13].

11
Arregocés Pérez, S., Granados Castellanos, M., Múnera Montes, L., Naranjo Vásquez, J.E., Ramírez Díaz, R., Rodríguez Gaitán, L.F., Teherán Sánchez, S. & Ustate Arregocés, R. (2015). Bárbaros Hoscos: Historia de La (Des) Territorialización de Los Negros de La Comunidad de Roche.

12
Vega, M., & Rodriguez, L. (2018). CARBÓN TÓXICO: daños y riesgos a la salud de los trabajadores mineros y población expuesta al carbón-Evidencias científicas para Colombia. In Fundación Rosa Luxemburgo (Vol. 2). https://rosalux.org.ec/pdfs/FRL_Carbon_toxico_WEB_compressed.pdf.

13
AIDC. 2017. "Mum's Colombian Mine Protest Comes to London." AIDC | Alternative Information & Development Centre (blog). March 6, 2017. https://aidc.org.za/mums-colombian-mine-protest-comes-london/.

2 The coal terminal of Amsterdam Port (Photo credit aerostockphoto.com).
3 The coal railway cutting through the rural landscape (Photo credit Mauricio Lozano on flickr).

4

5

6

In 2015, the Cerrejón company began diverting 3.6 kilometres of the Arroyo Bruno (Bruno Stream) for the mine expansion. The stream is one of the main tributaries to the río Ranchería and a source of water for local Wayuu communities as well as for the town of Albania. The relocation threatened one of the main dry tropical forest reserves in the region, the Montes de Oca[14]. The Guajira is a water-scarce region; none of the municipalities has sufficient access to water[15]. Wayúu communities who live in the hills that surround the stream have long managed water and forest resources. For the Wayúu, water is part of their connection to *Wounmainkat* (Mother Earth). One community described how diverting and privatizing water went against Wayúu beliefs: 'God makes the water and land, and they are not for humans to take. So, we oppose the diversion. Human beings should not destroy what God has created'[16]. Despite sustained protests against the diversion plan and court orders to consult with indigenous communities, the company continued with the diversion plan → fig. 5, 6.

Social movements in the Guajira region have been fighting for more inclusion in the process with the support of NGOs and academics, and to reduce the strong support of the regional and national government to large-scale mining[17]. Carmen Yaneth Sierra, a local activist and teacher at the primary school in the community of El Rocío (impacted by the diversion of the Arroyo Bruno), contemplated the ethics of diverting water sources that are essential to life for a coal mine while the United Nations calls for decarbonization of the world's energy sources[18]. These environmental costs will be never paid back by the company whose concession rights expire in 2034.

Energy consumption in the Global North afflicts the landscapes of others along the coal chain far away from home. At the very beginning of that chain in Colombia, we found communities fighting for rights to landscape, health, food, and water. Dutch NGOs such as PAX have been active in the past in the Dutch Coal Dialogue involving governments, coal buyers, coal suppliers, and industry associations to better understand how mining could become more responsible and transparent[19]. However, this dialogue did not end in any tangible results. It hasn't brought any changes in for instance the application of standard mitigation measures to the real conditions of communities such as those impacted by the Arroyo Bruno diversion.

In the context of the global energy transition, fossil fuels such as coal run the risk of being replaced in the medium and long term. Those who suffer the most from the impacts of coal mining also stand to lose the most from mine closures, due to the lack of productive alternatives, both for mining workers and for those who sell them goods and services. The closure of the mines would imply profound socioeconomic trauma[20].

The extraction and use of coal is not only a local problem, it is a chain of social, cultural, and economic impacts that transcends borders and generates a collective feeling of mobilization for just transition; this must be designed and structured according to the conditions of each territory, community, and society. Just transition implies guaranteeing communities access to electricity and respect for all their rights, including the right to breathe healthy air, access to drinking water, and soils clean of carbon traces, their constitutional right to land, decent work, collective rights, human rights, and the rights of nature[21].

For the future a path should be to stop importing coal while safeguarding a timely and just transition to renewables for this region, avoiding the diversion of other

14
Llorente-Valbuena, A., Fierro-Morales, J., & Cuida-López, E. (2019). Arroyo Bruno, La Guajira, Colombia. Informe Técnico. Evaluación Preliminar de calidad de agua superficial en zonas afectadas por el proyecto carbonífero el Cerrejón.

15, 16
Banks, E. (2017). We Are Bruno: Citizens Caught Between An Absentee State And A State-Like Corporation During Water Conflicts In La Guajira, Colombia. Urban Anthropology and Studies of Cultural System and World Economies 46: p. 61–94.

17
Cardoso, A. & Turhan, E. (2018). Examining new geographies of coal: Dissenting energyscapes in Colombia and Turkey. Applied Energy, p. 224.

18
Contagioradio. (2020). Carbones del Cerrejón incumple sentencia que protege a comunidades y al Arroyo Bruno. https://archivo.contagioradio.com/carbones-del-cerrejon-incumple-sentencia-que-protege-a-comunidades-y-al-arroyo-bruno.html (accessed 1 February 2020).

19
Cardoso, A. (2018). Valuation Languages Along the Coal Chain From Colombia to the Netherlands and to Turkey. Ecological Economics, 146, p. 44–59.

20
Corral-Montoya, F., Santamaria- Guerrero, R., Mejia-Brito, A., Sánchez-Pérez, Y., Cardoso, A., & Malz, N. (2021). Hechos, realidades y perspectivas de la minería de carbón en el Cesar y La Guajira.

21
Santamaría-Guerrero, R., Cardoso, A. & Caselles-Martínez, C. (2022). Co-creation of the energy transition agenda in the colombian caribbean. In: Co-creation of the energy transition agenda in the Colombian caribbean. Universidad del Magdalena.

4 Coal mining has dried up water sources and the member of the Wayuu community need to collect water far from their dwellings. Their home landscape id dominated by the presence of the mine (Photo credit Anadolu Agency, 2021).
5 The Arroyo Bruno's diverted course (Photo credit PAX).
6 And the original one (Photo by Emma Banks).

rivers and destruction of the landscape of others. And, simultaneously, learn from and assist the local Guajira community who are now advocating for participation in the development of wind energy projects[22]. Next time you make coffee, remember those coal landscapes and opt for renewable energy, like you already choose to buy organic coffee produced by small Colombian farmers in Antioquia. Then you can help preserve the cultural landscapes recognized by UNESCO as world heritage.

22
González-Posso; Camilo, & Barney, J. (2019). El viento del Este Lega con Revoluciones. Multinacionales y transición con energía eólica en territorio Wayúu.

Note: We would like to take the opportunity and thank Paolo Picchi for his enthusiasm about our work in Colombia and assisting with the conception of this chapter.

The Poetics of Power 1.4

LARA VOERMAN

1

The title of the book you are reading now is made up of the same four words as a publication written some 65 years ago, and not without reason. *The Landscape of Power,* by British landscape architect Sylvia Crowe, was published in 1958. Just as this book, it opens with a statement. At an alarming rate, economic prosperity and growth, powered by energy, was destroying the landscape that had kept us rooted and sane for thousands of years. Oil refineries, nuclear reactors, power stations, and the electricity network had brought unprecedented material wealth, but at the same time resulted in impoverished landscapes, according to Crowe → fig. 1.

Crowe was one of the first designers to make inspiring efforts to reconcile the growing need for energy with the need for a liveable landscape. She brought the power of design and poetics to a sector dominated by technology. The historical quest to unite these seeming opposites and the role that designers had in it is the subject of this chapter[1]. The unique characteristics of energy structures—often polluting, rather large and immensely high, or even kilometres long, sometimes with almost cosmic instead of terrestrial forms—makes shaping something that literally powers all our actions a unique task.

In 1958, Crowe lamented that one of the reasons for the chaotic energy landscapes she saw developing around her was that there was little design tradition to fall back on. Today, we have a legacy of 150 years of designing energy landscapes to learn from. This chapter is not organized chronologically, but instead discusses three design attitudes from those 150 years, complemented with a variety of examples that can inspire or deter. At the basis of each attitude is a certain understanding of landscape and the role us humans are allowed to play in shaping it.

The first attitude is to *camouflage*, a defensive approach building on the notion that landscape is a fixed and pristine backdrop to our daily lives. The second attitude is to *reconcile*: trying to unite the seeming opposites of landscape and energy infrastructure by placing them in well-designed living environments. Here, designers have a less dogmatic idea with regard to what is considered landscape and what is not.

1
With many thanks to Sven Stremke, Paolo Picchi, Dirk Sijmons and Joost Emmerik.

1 Portrait of Sylvia Crowe at the photographic library of the Council of Industrial Design (Source: Design Council Archive, University of Brighton Design Archives).

The third attitude is to *integrate*, based on the understanding that landscape has always been a co-production of people and nature. It is driven by the notion that designing energy landscapes is a complex task, which is only viable when it is treated as a combined technological, spatial and cultural enterprise.

CAMOUFLAGE

Masking the true function of energy technology is a design attitude that is as old as the invention of electricity itself. In 1882, Thomas Edison opened the first two power stations in the world that generated electricity for public use. Not that this was celebrated in a grand design: Pearl Street Station in New York and Holborn Viaduct power station in London were disguised as terraced houses. The tall chimneys on the roof, the humming noises and the stinking clouds of smoke were the only evidence of the hypermodern electricity-generating machines inside →fig. 2.

Later on, and for a short period only, architects like Giles Gilbert Scott in England, Piero Portaluppi in Italy, and Hans Heinrich Müller in Germany designed 'cathedrals of energy', roaring and exciting installations that powered the urban fabric with cables as tentacles. But as concerns for the hygienic conditions within cities grew and the effects of energy production's filth-spewing processes became intolerable, the energy technology was soon removed from its architectural skin and exiled to the urban periphery[2]. Gas pipes and electricity cables went discreetly underground, creating an illusionary landscape, as Dutch landscape architect Dirk Sijmons calls it, in which energy lost its place as a visual productive cultural and urban endeavour[3].

Camouflaging originated as a defensive attitude, arising from the view that energy infrastructure is a polluting and ugly intruder in the city and the countryside. Words referring to disease, monstrosity and decay were used very early on to describe their impact. In the 1930s, people in the Netherlands spoke of the 'pole plague', the historical variant of the word 'horizon pollution', which appeared for the first time when wind turbines were introduced in the 1980s. It is significant that simultaneously with the 1911 decision to build provincial power plants in the Netherlands—which would mean great lengths of wires on wooden poles stretching out into the open countryside—the Bond Heemschut was established, an activist association for the preservation of heritage[4]. The members of this association embraced the notion that landscapes are organically grown, innocent and in dire need of protection. And while camouflaging is certainly not the strategy with which one can tackle today's energy transition entirely, in some places it may still be a valid way to go. Sylvia Crowe used camouflaging sometimes because she was convinced that the value of some landscapes—at least visually—lies in the minimal presence of modern society. And more recently, in the outskirts of Valentano, a historical town in the Latium region of central Italy, a solar farm was meticulously hidden behind poplars to protect the landscape views from the provincial road, with exactly the same conviction behind it.

One of the most fascinating historical examples of this attitude are four islands right off the coast of popular Long Beach, just South of Los Angeles in the United States. Since their creation in 1965, four offshore oil drilling plants have been behind a décor of cascading waterfalls, palms, banana trees and luxurious, brightly coloured apartment buildings. It is a full-on Thunderbirds landscape. The plans for the islands sprung out

2
Blostein, B. (2008). Toward a productive excess. In: Tilder, L. & Blotsein B., Design Ecologies: Essays on the Nature of Design. Princeton: Princeton Architectural Press, p. 245.

3
Sijmons, D., Hugtenburg, J., van Hoorn, A. & Feddes, F. (2014). Landschap en Energie. Ontwerpen voor transitie. Rotterdam: nai010 publishers, p. 17.

4
Vredenberg J. (2003). Trotse Kastelen & Lichtende Hallen'. Architectuur van elektriciteitsbedrijven in Nederland tot 1960. Utrecht: Matrijs, p. 105.

2

3

5
Meares, H. (2018). Long Beach's deceptive islands. Curbed.com, visited December 2021.

of the growing pains of environmentalism that were a major factor in industrial design during the 1960s[5]. Landscape architect Joseph Linesch was hired not only to minimize the visual pollution, but also to add to the existing natural beauty of the coastland. He collaborated with artists and architects who had designed much of the original Disneyland, including the park's famed fictional landscapes. This resulted in convincing fantasy environments that successfully masked the mechanical equipment of the oil production. The large oil derricks are disguised as typical sixties beach apartments and large waterfalls muffle the industrial sounds. Some trees and shrubs are placed on tracks for quick mobility, a trick borrowed from Disney → fig. 3.

On the other side of the Atlantic Ocean, we find one of the most poetic historical examples of camouflaging. In 1960, Geoffrey Jellicoe designed the landscape atop the Rutherford High Energy Laboratories in Harwell, United Kingdom. There was a particle accelerator in this laboratory with a massive amount of contained energy. What does humanity do when it gets its hands on such powerful energy, Jellicoe wondered. Will we use it for good, or will it ultimately lead to the destruction of humanity? The design history of the Harwell Hills is, in Jellicoe's words, a light-hearted exploration of that sinister idea[6]. As guardians of the particle accelerator, the landscape architect placed three hills on it. The two largest he named Zeus, after the capricious supreme god, and Themis, after his second wife and the symbol of justice. The smallest hill was called Klotho, after their daughter and one of the Fates who determine the fate of humankind. It turned out that Klotho would impede certain rays emanating from the particle accelerator. It was not constructed, so that, according to Jellicoe, 'the fate of mankind still hangs in the balance'[6].

6
Spens, M. (1994). The complete landscape designs and gardens of Geoffrey Jellicoe. London: Thames and Hudson, p. 86–87.

RECONCILE

Sylvia Crowe was also one of the first designers to realize that designing energy plants and energy infrastructure was a spatial and social challenge, one that had a huge, and often negative, impact on people's living environments. With her books and her many attractive energy landscape designs Crowe is perhaps the most prominent spokesperson of a category of designers that tried to *reconcile* the alien forms of energy installations with its surroundings—at least visually.

In *The Landscape of Power*, published in 1958, Crowe meticulously dissects the character of each energy source, and the sources in relation to the landscape as well as to human proportions. In a sense, steam and coal could still be seen as a natural force of the earth, she writes, while electricity belongs in the air, traveling through thin wires, carried on thin grey structures and there is no reason to relate it to a human scale. The dam, on the contrary, was the most magnificent of all organic engineering structures. When properly designed they seemed to emerge from the landscape, with the impersonal grandeur of a rocky mountain range. Nuclear power has no natural boundary

2 Scale model of Thomas Edison's Pearl Street power station, made in 1927 (Source: National Museum of American History).

3 Design concept of Island A, Joseph H. Linesch, around 1965 (Source: Architecture and Design Collection. Art, Design & Architecture Museum; University of California, Santa Barbara).

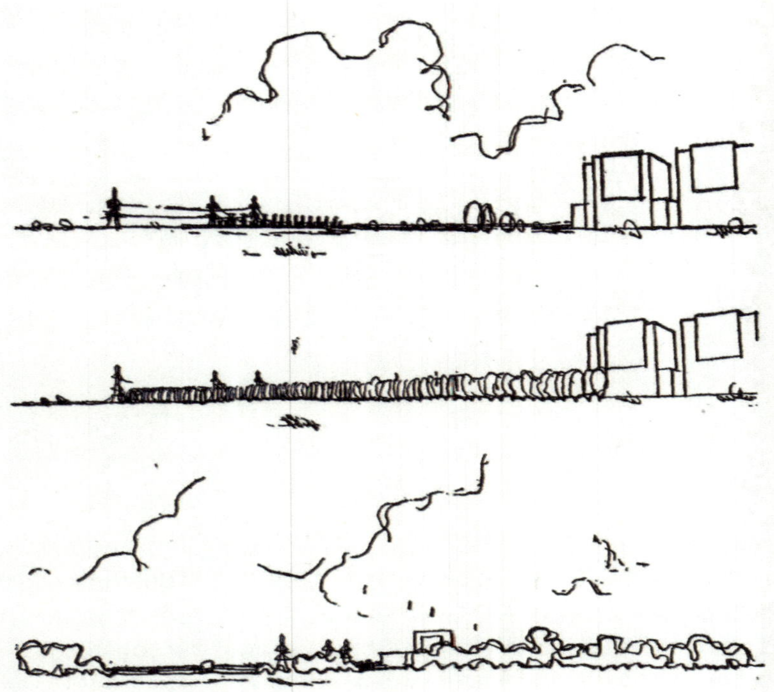

4

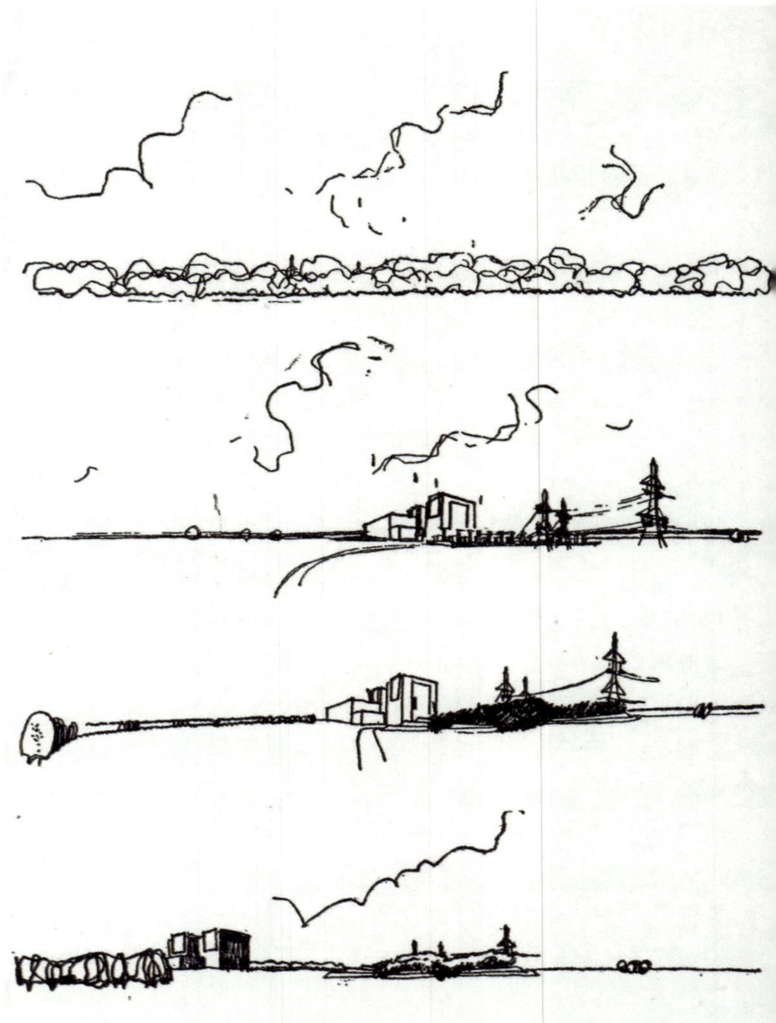

5

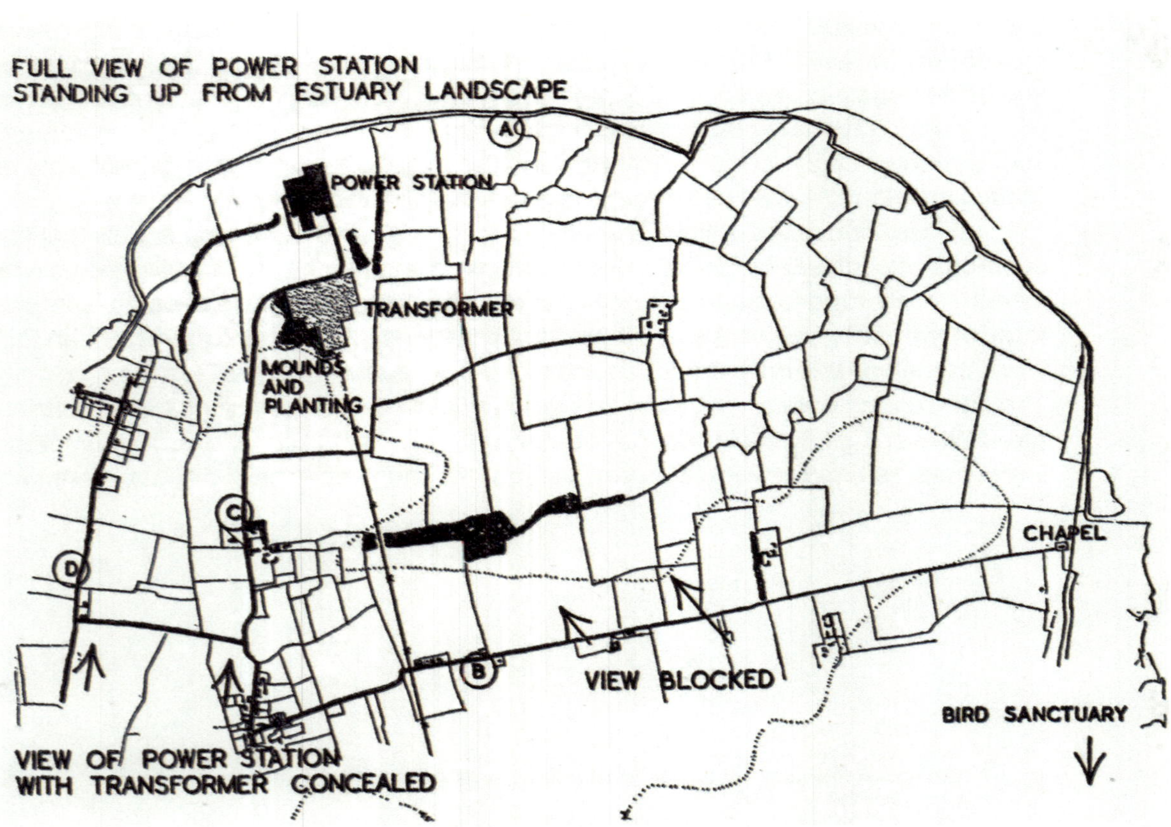
FULL VIEW OF POWER STATION
STANDING UP FROM ESTUARY LANDSCAPE
A
POWER STATION
TRANSFORMER
MOUNDS
AND
PLANTING
C
D
B
VIEW BLOCKED
CHAPEL
BIRD SANCTUARY
VIEW OF POWER STATION
WITH TRANSFORMER CONCEALED

6

and bond with the earth. The scale is cosmic rather than terrestrial, a representation of universal forces exerted in the service of the earth, according to Crowe. She was fascinated by the gigantic white spheres of the nuclear power stations in the French Chinon and the Scottish Dounreay, which represented the superhuman power in their most futuristic form.

7
Crowe, S. (1958). The landscape of power. London: Architectural Press.

8
The Machine in the Garden. Technology and the Pastoral Ideal in America is a 1964 work of literary criticism written by Leo Marx and published by Oxford University Press.

Nothing can humanize the scale of some of the modern power structures, Crowe wrote in 1958[7]. In order to reconcile them with their environment they demanded large, uncluttered and visually strong landscapes. This design strategy became known in the United States as the naturalization of the 'machine' by locating it in the 'garden'[8]. Crowe sought inspiration in eighteenth-century English landscape gardens, where functionality and aesthetics came together in one grandly designed landscape. The eminent eighteenth-century landscape architects Capability Brown and William Kent had clumps of trees, hills and even villages moved until their clients' gigantic mansions stood as if they had never been otherwise, much like film set designers did in Crowe's own time. Crowe also tried to give energy infrastructures a privileged place in the English landscape through hefty but site-specific design interventions. Her inspiration from the English tradition of garden design was not limited to aesthetics but also embraced the Arcadian ideal, in which people, as stewards of the landscape, should take special responsibility.

A perfect example of this attitude is the integration of 55 new nuclear power stations in Great Britain at the end of the 1950s. The British Energy Act of 1957 required the involvement of designers in this immense expansion of the energy supply. Landscape architects like Crowe, Brenda Colvin, and Geoffrey Jellicoe and architects, including Giles Gilbert Scott, Basil Spence, and Frederick Gibberd were hired as advisors. Exemplary is the landscaping around the now decommissioned Bradwell Nuclear Power Station, designed by Crowe in the late 1950s. She made a phenomenal redesign of the area around the power station, with on the one hand a sensitivity to the historically developed characteristics and on the other the courage to make far-reaching interventions. Fences around the power plant were recessed in a ha-ha, a design solution coming straight from the English landscape garden. Strong steep edges hid the messiness at ground level and led the eye to the imposing towers of the reactor. Not only the views up close, but also those from afar were carefully orchestrated. Her design extended for miles around the nuclear power plant. Seen from the seaside, the power plant stood confidently on the flat land. Here, Crowe only expanded the typical willow planting along the dykes. Inland, the view was framed and accentuated as the approach road came out from the leafy exit of the village and 'opened out into space and sunlight', with the giant reactor as a focal point → fig. 4-6[9].

9
Crowe, S. (1958). The landscape of power. London: Architectural Press, p. 66.

The same attitude, but with a slightly different approach, gave rise to the design of the gas storage facility in Langelo in the north of the Netherlands, designed around 1995 by the office of Dutch landscape architect Alle Hosper and Cor Kalfsbeek Architecten, commissioned by the Nederlandse Aardolie Maatschappij (NAM). It is a typical Dutch design, that is in itself a very strong design, and also sits perfectly in the flat landscape. Above ground, installations were needed that would cover about 25 hectares, in the delicate landscape of a characteristic stream valley near a small Dutch 'esdorp'. The NAM wanted to spread the buildings out and camouflage them with

4–6 A sample of Sylvia Crowe's work to reconcile the forms of energy technologies with the surrounding landscapes. The drawings show the case of the Bradwell Nuclear Power Station Station where the landscape architect used land formation and planting to emphasize the clean bulk of the main structure. The study was conducted from four points of view A, B, C and D (1958, p. 64–65).

vegetation, but the designers had a different idea[10]. They bundled the energy infrastructure into one elongated strip, anchored in the landscape by linking up with the direction of a historic route. The contrast between the strong architectural form combined with the respectful treatment of the vulnerable landscape made the gas storage a positive addition—a machine in the garden—rather than a poorly hidden intruder→fig. 7.

The garden in which the machine sits and has to reconcile with can also be an urban one. The hydro-electric power station in the German river Iller in the medieval town of Kempten was designed in 2010 by Becker architects. Hydropower here supplies electricity for 3000 households. The technical installations are hidden under a carefully kneaded, continuous concrete mass, which refers to the river-washed rock formations near the power plant. The shapes are a representation of the water dynamics, which change from a calm state at the inlet to the churning and pitching of the water near the turbines, before returning to a calm state after the electricity generation. The power station thus belongs to the turbulent nature of the Iller River, while at the same time respecting the existing building assemblage of the former spinnery mills on the banks of the river[11].

To reconcile energy and environment requires both space and a visually strong landscape—whether organically grown, enhanced or fully created. There is a clear limit to the capacity of such landscapes to take in further 'machines'. Consequently, this approach is not usable everywhere, and perhaps not much at all in the current energy transition. The illusion of a machine in the garden is difficult to maintain when solar panels and wind turbines will make the energy supply visible, audible and palpable in everyone's daily living environment. As a historical design attitude is it very interesting though, because is stems from a less dogmatic understanding of landscape as a flexible realm that is able to visually absorb all kinds of alien structures and forms.

INTEGRATE

The third attitude identified in the past and relevant for the engagement with today's energy transition is to *integrate.* Its proponents dismiss the idea that energy infrastructure is autonomous and has nothing to do with our lives—that it needs to be isolated somewhere, out of sight, out of mind. Instead, it can be beneficial, not only to a power company, but also to a region, a community or a family. Already in *The Landscape of Power*, Crowe advocated a 'complete landscape', something that is only possible if attention is paid to both hard and soft, to technique and beauty, to machine and landscape.

One of the earliest examples of this attitude is the Tennessee Valley project from the 1930s. This American region the size of England was characterized by a rampant Tennessee river, eroded farm lands, depleted forests and industries. One organization, The Tennessee Valley Authority, was given the task of bringing the derelict region back to life in 1933. Central to the development strategy was the generation and distribution of electricity through an impressive system of dams, power stations and reservoirs. The electric powerlines were seen as a blessing of modern times: '[they] extend into every city, fan out over the countryside and penetrate remote mountain coves to bring the miraculous working energy of electricity to farms, homes and factories'[12]. In addition, the Authority launched multiple programmes to limit soil erosion, support farming and

10
Van Dooren, N. (ed.). (2003). Alle Hosper. Landschapsarchitect 1943–1997. Rotterdam: nai010 publishers, p. 166.

11
Argyriades M. (2011). Hydroelectric Power Station by Becker Architects. Yatzer.com, visited December 2021.

12
Frincke, H.C. A new regional landscape: the Tennessee Valley Authority. In: Crowe, S. and Miller, Z. (1964) Shaping Tomorrow's Landscape. Volume II. Amsterdam–Djambatan, p. 97.

7

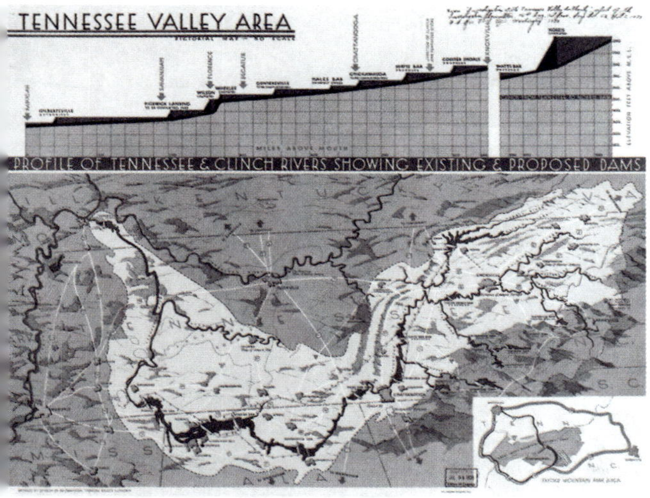

8

9

13
Interview with Dirk Sijmons, 26th January 2022.

forestry, and develop sites for recreation along the river. Making the area look beautiful was an equally important goal, also to persuade the American public of the efficacy and usefulness of this publicly funded and administered massive project. Landscape architects and architects were employed by the Authority from the very beginning. They collaborated on many fronts with their technical colleagues and situated the power plants and dams in 'reservations', designed landscapes that erased the scars of construction and provided the public with visitor centres, overlooks, and sites for recreation such as picnicking, fishing, and boating →fig. 8.

Although The Tennessee Valley project was exemplary in its time, interweaving infrastructure and landscape, ecology was totally overlooked. From the 1960s several publications helped bring the dark side of our ever-growing energy demand and associated environmental concerns into broad public awareness, like marine biologist Rachel Carson's *Silent Spring* (1962), *The Limits to Growth* by the Club of Rome (1967) and landscape architect Ian McHarg's *Design with Nature* (1969). Designers became activists. They started experimenting and took the theme to universities and design studios. Instead of merely mitigating the impact of energy structures, they started designing 'complete landscapes' themselves, introducing alternative energy resources like solar or wind power.

Dutch landscape architect Dirk Sijmons is one of those activists. Through the years and in many roles, as state government advisor for landscape, professor, author and one of the founders of H+N+S Landscape Architects, he tries to convey the message that today's energy transition is unprecedented both in size and implications. Crowe wrote her book in the blessed post-war years, Dirk Sijmons says, an optimistic era powered by fossil fuel and nuclear power[13]. A lot has changed since then. The energy challenge became more complex and more political. With the transition from fossil to renewable energy sources, technologies can no longer all be isolated, nor camouflaged or reconciled. According to Sijmons, today's energy transition is no longer just a technical task for professionals, but should be primarily a cultural challenge that touches everyone.

Similarly, Italian landscape architect Lorenzo Vallerini was active in many roles, as a practitioner, regional government advisor, author and researcher at the University of Florence. Between 1995 and 2005, he coordinated a study for the ENEL, the Italian National Agency for Energy, to draw up criteria for the locations of new geo-thermal plants and their infrastructure in the Amiata region. Vallerini based his recommendations on research into the existing landscape values. From these values he distinguished criteria for different landscape types, which were more or less suitable for housing power plants and infrastructure corridors. For the landscape directly surrounding the power plants Vallerini provided a set of design principles, in which the simultaneous amelioration of the local landscape and the interweaving of cultural and ecological functions was of vital importance.

Another excellent example of the third attitude is the 'Solar Strand' for Buffalo University. In 2010, American landscape architect and Berkeley University Professor Walter Hood won the design competition to integrate 5,000 solar panels with a typical 1960s modernist campus landscape. The ambition of the university board was to transform a simple utility field into a land art installation, and for the energy infrastructure

7 Model of the gas storage facility in Langelo, The Netherlands, designed by landscape architect Alle Hosper and Cor Kalfsbeek Architecten, 1995 (Source: Bureau Hosper).

8 Pictorial map of the Tennessee Valley Area, by the Tennessee Valley Authority, 1939 (Source: Library of Congress).

9 Design proposal for the Buffalo Campus Solar Strand by Walter Hood, 2010 (Source: Studio Walter Hood).

to function as an accessible landscape where people can 'thrive'[14]. Hood not only visually embedded the solar panels in the landscape, but also connected them to the history, geography, ecology and educational focus of the campus. On the Solar Strand, the PV-panels are arranged in three long lines with footpaths between them. Groups of panels have a different height, the lowest referring to that of a human being. From the outside, you don't see a monolithic structure, but staggered heights, scaling up and down. From the inside, one has multiple views and perceptions. Two of the largest panels form the walls of a public square, used as an outdoor classroom. The cobbled brick and flagstone paving is made of recycled materials from campus renovation projects, while the mowing regime reflects a more ecological and sustainable approach to maintaining the campus landscape →fig. 9.

14
Scognamiglio, A. (2013). The Solar Strand. Domusweb.it, visited December 2021.

PERSPECTIVE

In the next chapters of this book a new attitude seems to arise, building comfortably on the legacy of the three historical design attitudes described above. Its proponents aim to *enrich* landscapes visually, socially, economically and environmentally. The key characteristic of this attitude is perhaps to challenge everything. In their search for nature-inclusive and socially-just solutions, designers strive to affect more and more decisions, also the ones that were previously outside their sphere of influence. They still design the actual site, nowadays in coproduction with local stakeholders, but also participate in the actual search for sites and the choice of energy technology. They even start to provide engineers with directions about the looks of the technology itself, for example printed solar panels. All along, they must not forget their most important, historical challenge: making designs that, as Sylvia Crowe said, connect people with the poetics of landscape.

Questioning the Present

Critical Examination of Energy Landscapes: An Introduction

2.1

DAN VAN DER HORST

This book exhibits a number of evocative case studies of energy landscapes in which common technologies are used, but which are displaying unique visual and narrative vignettes. Accepting to write this essay felt like I was offered a preview of a new exhibition, but without help from the curator to frame my expectations and guide me through the exhibits in a structured sequence. You, the reader, are invited now (as I was then) to meander around the next chapter's exhibits—these energy landscape case studies—in whichever order you prefer, absorb the information at a leisurely pace, and then at the end, reflect on what insights you gained from this experience.

As for my own perspective, in my quest for commonalities, I take the liberty to speak of 'atmo-powers' (solar and wind) and 'geo-powers' (hydro and geothermal). Geo-powers are much more geographically concentrated and can have a much longer local history of human utilisation. The iconography of the Hoover Dam brings to mind that a great power is being controlled and the fame of Dante's *Inferno* (inspired by Devil's Valley in Tuscany) speaks of a landscape that is old. The recent growth of atmo-powers comes with a much lighter footprint, but more widely distributed—we might think. The landscapes of Eggebek (wind, solar and biomass) and Gemasolar (concentrated solar) remind us of the impact atmo-powers can have too. The domineering 'eye of Sauron' and its army of bowing mirrors are a futuristic iconography, silent but violent in the complete obliteration of the landscape that was. These new concentrated forms of atmo-power seem to go hand in hand with spatial exclusion and exclusivity forged by the blunt tools of land appropriation, or in the case of Eggebek, a repurposing of an old military land grab.

THE MATURING OF GEO-POWERS

Canales Village reminds us that large-scale hydro has led to the forcible eviction of local residents, a major social impact it shares with surface mining of bituminous coal—arguably the worst fossil fuel. Also reminding us of coal but in a more positive way, both the Hoover Dam and Larderello illustrated how the long-term labour demand associated with the mining of energy has led to the creation of new local communities. What perhaps sets aside Larderello and Boulder City from many other mining 'company towns' is that they were early beneficiaries of the electricity production: a public service was provided at a time when electricity was not yet widely spread in such relatively rural areas. But the local benefits also come in the form of water pipes. The Larderello power plants also provide district heating to a number of neighbouring villages, whilst Lake Mead behind the Hoover Dam provides about 90 per cent of the water for Las Vegas, some 30 kilometres away. It is inconceivable that Las Vegas would have grown to its current size without this abundance of cheap water and electricity. Similarly we can assume that many of the Hoover Dam's one million annual visitors will visit Las Vegas. Many people working and living in this city that sells leisure, have boats on the marinas dotted around Lake Mead. The megadroughts, linked at least in part to anthropogenic climate change, that have affected much of the western USA in recent decades and have led to the extremely low levels of water visible in the photograph, thus threaten this regional leisure industry both directly (the lake shrinks, the marinas become unusable) and indirectly as less water is available for city parks, golf courses et cetera. Accidentally, Boulder City was nick-named Nevada's Garden City, which of course implies the use of abundant irrigation water for the city's parks. There is another climate link here. The town thanks its unusual design to Saco Rienk de Boer, a Dutch architect who had moved to the USA for climatic reasons; he suffered from tuberculosis in the damp and cold climate of the Netherlands and came to Denver to visit the Bethesda Sanatorium. He eventually became the city's landscape architect and had a distinguished career; the American Planning Association's annual awards programme is called the DeBoer Awards for Excellence in Planning.

The case studies of geo-powers tell stories of long-term and perhaps irreversible landscape change. The resource base is not static; rainfall varies, geothermal resources can be exhausted. Demand for district heating will fall as Italy warms up, but demand for the water from the Hoover Dam and the Canales Dam will only increase. These dams were never built for the single or primary purpose of generating electricity; irrigation, flood control, local job provision and rural (infrastructure) development were also of great importance at the time. Leisure and tourism were later beneficiaries rather than early drivers. Growing in size and (economic) significance, locally observable through visitor numbers, leisure facilities and urban expansions, their expanding water and energy footprints can attain monstrous proportions as their role as electricity generators shrinks.

But more strictly as an industrial activity, the harnessing of renewable energy can also 'thrive' in landscapes largely devoid of other economic activities or popular cultural significance. Salton Sea is a peculiar story of an accident featuring the same actors as with the Hoover Dam: the 'wild' Colorado River and the engineers seeking to control its waters. This led to a leisure economy around the resulting lake in Imperial Valley. The Hoover Dam put an end to natural floods that would occasionally refill the lake, but flood irrigation by farmers continued to generate run-off into the lake. It is a depressing story reminiscent of the Aral Sea; as water became scarcer and more valuable, and agricultural irrigation practices became less wasteful, the lake shrunk dramatically, leaving a dry bed of dusty sediments full of salt and agricultural chemicals, at the mercy of the wind. Leisure resorts like Bombay Beach became ghost towns, leaving behind only a handful of the poorest residents to tell the first-hand tale of California's greatest environmental disaster. It provides a sobering down-stream counter-narrative to the modernist engineering feats scripted with tall concrete at the Hoover Dam and embellished by architects and artists.

The rusty pipes of the geothermal powerplants in the flat and featureless agro-industrial space of Imperial Valley (a fertile plain of alluvium from the Colorado River), stand in stark contrast with the shiny pipes amongst the conifers and evergreen trees on the hills surrounding Larderello, Tuscany. We read that these Californian geothermal plants are expanding their operations, but this economic success cannot be reconciled with this picture of desolation. Presumably, the power companies are under no pressure to improve the looks and landscapes of these plants, as there are no concerned local residents with the clout to complain. This desolate, dystopian space, shaped by environmental catastrophe and evolving forms of corporate extractivism (first large-scale mechanized irrigated agriculture, now geothermal plants), is so very different from Tuscany's living landscape where green trees and shiny pipes sprout from the ground to provide key benefits to local people; a green environment and warm homes. The area around Larderello must have ongoing tensions between technology and ecology (e.g., bio-physically, aesthetically) but these are perhaps internalized within local communities that share both burdens and benefits.

Surely there must be ways to start healing the land and bring back people (at least visitors) to this now desolate corner of Imperial Valley? The huge, square, empty fields around the power plants could host experiments in eco-innovation and restoration ecology. Perhaps growing native desert plants in the shade of those pipes or of new solar panels, fixing soil with their roots and carbon as they grow, and providing new habitat opportunities so that nature, long banned from this 'non-place' can slowly regain a toe-hold? Perhaps the semi-ghost town of Bombay Beach could host a museum and festivals about California's fraught environmental history, simultaneously drawing attention to the natural history of this rare and unique geothermal area with its tiny volcanoes that have been recently active. For a landscape of meaning and value to (re-)emerge, I think that we need nature and humans to act and interact in that space continuously for a long period. The model of humans moving in, stripping nature and moving on, has no place in the twenty-first century on our small and precious planet. This case study challenges us to not look away, but rather to re-engage with such spaces of depletion and desolation. If healing is a journey, then what better places are there to start our efforts to repair?

THE MAKING OF NEW ATMO-POWER LANDSCAPES

Humans have used atmo-powers for millennia, through technologies as diverse as sundials and sails. Even before the use of electricity, wind power has shaped some landscapes in profound and irreversible ways. Wind-driven water pumps allowed the Dutch to create and inhabit polder landscapes by removing excess surface water, and allowed European settlers to occupy and farm in arid parts of the Americas, Australia and Southern Africa by providing access to scarce ground water. There is some sense of thematic continuity and poetic justice in the observation that the linear features of the 'new land' in the Dutch Flevo-polder, now provide such suitable sites for modern wind turbines. The province of Flevoland is an entirely and explicitly artificial space, planned by the state, designed by engineers, and created with huge machines. And yet it is also very much a living landscape, fully embraced by its new residents and many daytrip visitors, recognizing how the story of its creation is deeply rooted in the culture and collective identity of the Dutch people and the 'old land' provinces around Flevoland.

The Dutch landscape, immortalized by its many painters, has often been displayed as a dynamic interaction, or at least a balancing act, between large bodies of water, some thin wedges of low-lying land, and a big sky ruled by the wind. In the old days, the wind was both a foe and a friend; during storms it powered the sea to destroy valuable land and through windmills it helped people to remove the water, thus restoring land again. Now with improved dykes (flood protection technology), the old foe has less power, and with better turbines, the old friend is returning, even offering to make a contribution in mitigating anthropogenic climate change and limiting sea level rise. The Dutch who have generated huge amounts of wealth and created a lot of environmental damage from the rapid depletion of their domestic supplies of peat and gas, in both cases creating subsidence: they were drowning their own land. In recent decades the Dutch have been comparatively unambitious in the deployment of renewable energy. As the country now needs to step up its efforts how many wind turbines will the Dutch allow their land-and-waterscapes to absorb? What 'landscape protection' arguments can stand up to the sobering expectations that parts of this land will eventually be claimed by anthropogenic sea-level rise?

Now let's go back a bit from the landscape specific, to the techno-generic. Early experimentation with electricity generation through photo-voltaics (PV) and through wind turbines dates back to the nineteenth century, so long before the electricity grid was developed. In much of the twentieth century it became confined to very small-scale niche applications, from low-tech turbines for off-grid rural places to high-tech PV for space craft. Geo-powers were concentrated enough in various places to compete with fossil fuels. Atmo-powers have now reached the same stage, thanks to significant government aid for technology development, motivated by climate change concerns.

In technological terms, we can see in these case study energy landscapes two trends of deployment: scaling up of units and scaling up of projects. In simplistic terms, we can think of this as two different aspects of geometry affecting the landscape; bigger projects have a bigger (horizontal) spatial footprint, whilst bigger units are taller, and thus have a stronger (vertical) visual presence in the wider landscape.

PV panels have evolved in terms of efficiency but have remained small, modular units, suitable for projects of all sizes. However Concentrated Solar Power (CSP) represent much bigger units, which have grown over time. The (horizontal) spatial footprint of the heliostats (the tracking mirrors) is quadratic in relation to tower height, hence the need for flat, abundant and cheap land. The comparison between Gemasolar CSP (near Seville) and Las Gabias PV park (Granada) is fascinating because both are placed in agricultural landscapes and are operating tracking platforms (of mirrors and PV panels respectively). Whilst Gemasolar completely disrupts the existing landscape, providing a flat alien, barren, high tech backdrop that attracts commercial visual exploitation, Las Gabias appears to be much more integrated within the existing undulating landscape, following the shape and patterns of local orchards. Not only is Las Gabias referred to as 'an orchard', its panels oriented towards the sun in the same way as the leaves of trees, but the 'roots' of the trackers appear to host more wildlife and greenery than those of the adjacent olive and almond trees. So why is nature erased at Gemasolar? What herbicides are being used and do they affect the surrounding area? There is irony in the observation of a local wildfire, which disrupts the harnessing of solar heat, and in doing so, makes the light beams visible in the cloudless mid-day sky.

Like the moving trackers in the 'solar orchard' of Las Gabias, Gemasolar's 'eye of Sauron' is shut for the night. However, unlike the orchard, this mighty beast does not sleep. Gemasolar's metabolism is attuned to our nocturnal cravings, its belly of molten salts yielding electricity for our 'peak demand'. Gemasolar is perhaps an unusual illustration of how energy storage technologies can make the spatio-temporal links between production and consumption more tangible in the landscape.

Gemasolar and Eggebek would appear to have little in common, but they both represent a spatially concentrated effort to produce renewable energy, with high levels of investment and curtailed accessibility to a site that is likely to remain in use for a long time. Both host synergistic economic activities, serving perhaps as regional hubs to promote green technologies or low-carbon futures. One key difference remains. Gemasolar is a greenfield site for a high-visibility, high-status demonstration project of a new technology. Eggebek is a brownfield site, providing a more low-key setting for a collection of established renewable energy technologies. Taken out of agricultural use by the military decades ago, Eggebek is still 'gated' but at least there is evidence of healing and local reintegration; the biogas installation provides a reconnection with the local agricultural economy and community.

For wind, both forms of scaling up (unit and project) have been continuous over time, yielding larger turbines and bigger wind farms. Again, we find a quadratic relationship, now between turbine height and the area of wind capture by the blades. Since the wind blows stronger at higher altitude, 'bigger is better' remains the dominant techno-narrative. Super-sized turbines have a much more imposing visual presence, require bigger access roads and construction sites. For this reason, and the fact that the wind blows harder at sea, more and bigger turbines are now destined for off-shore deployment. On land, where wind farms (with small turbines) started to emerge in the 1990s, we now see them replaced with fewer but much taller turbines, generating much more kWh, individually and collectively.

At the famous early adoption landscape of Zahara de los Atunes (Andalusia), a huge number of wind turbines have been inserted into the landscape—seemingly at will. Some are 'organized' in parallel rows, reminiscent of a farmer ploughing the field. Others are planted more organically. On Google Maps their access roads are much more visible than the turbines themselves; they remind me of a vine, crawling through the landscape in regular, elegant twists and turns, without a single sharp angle or straight line. Wind turbine design has become so standardized and their presence so ubiquitous that whilst looking at the pictures, my attention is first drawn to the colour of the cows or the emerging crop in the tilled field in the foreground, before noting the turbines. Both observations suggest the same: that this is a multi-functional landscape where mining the wind, growing crops and grazing cattle can go hand in hand.

But Google Maps (my go-to tool for exploration in Covid times) provides a very different visual encounter, with each turbine appearing twice: a short white and a long black version, like two pins stuck at different angles in the same spot; off-centre in a white rectangle of barren soil. The latter version is the shadow of course, but it is much more clearly drawn and visually arresting against the colour of the land, and much taller than its whitish material counterpart. After some searching, I spot two different sizes of turbines, sprouting like black flowers from the same elegantly rambling vine. Repowering seems like harmonious progression from above; the larger turbines are twice the size of the small ones, but the relative distance to one-another remains the same and the width of the access road does not change. Indeed, it is now very visible how many more roads have been added to the landscape, causing damage no doubt, but also opening up the landscape for recreational activities; more functions and stakeholders is surely a good thing? The Viticuso case study speaks of exactly the same benefits of improved access to the countryside, but represents the opposite scale of wind energy landscape development. Viticuso is sized for the village, internalizing costs and benefits through spatial proximity and social capital, yielding a new, positive shared narrative of place and identity; not something one could ever spot from above.

To end my reflection, I wonder if I have taken too much interpretive liberty by adding a vertical view? Or is my partiality to the 'Google gaze' already becoming a majoritarian landscape experience? And if so, to what extent might this (re)shape societal perceptions on and debates about ongoing landscape change?

Present-day Energy Landscapes: A Journey through Europe and the United States

2.2

PAOLO PICCHI, DIRK OUDES and SVEN STREMKE

PREPARATIONS

Have you ever considered visiting an energy landscape? When we travelled through Europe and Northern America to visit some of these intriguing places, our focus was not technology itself but the whole landscape. We were driven by curiosity for the geology and geo-morphology, those physical forms of the landscape that influence the availability of renewable energy sources. We were looking for the local history and traditions, the real local knowledge you can get to know only by being in a place. We wanted to experience the sounds, colours and weather conditions in those landscapes. In one sentence: whenever possible we wanted to immerse ourselves into the landscape in its entirety.

'After lunch you can take the road just beside the hotel and walk along the valley towards *Colle Aquilone*. They constructed that road for turbines maintenance,' said the man. 'From there you will start seeing the turbines on the mountain ridge, you keep following the road, climbing the dense beech forest and the wind turbines will be disclosed to your eyes together with a wonderful view towards the *Mainarde* peaks.' This was what the proud police officer of the village told us while Mrs Assunta, owner of the local hotel and restaurant, was preparing our lunch. This chapter is inspired by personal traveling experiences, part of our continuous attempt to better understand the complex phenomenon of 'renewable energy landscape'. This chapter reports on a decade of intermittent curiosity-driven fieldwork. Not every trip was planned ahead in time, some landscapes were casually encountered during holidays, and the chapter is thus admittedly incomplete in terms of types of landscapes—an ongoing journey.

We share these experiences to demonstrate how curiosity for the 'whole' can bring about a different and successful approach in renewable energy development. Curiosity may be seen as a motor for three means of investigation in earlier explorations, which for us represented a strong inspiration: to see and interpret the relationship between different landscape elements across scale; to understand how energy sources and development shaped people and landscapes; and to document the spatial co-evolution of energy and landscape.

Those readers confident with landscape geography and the study of flora in particular, the so-called geo-botanics, will be familiar with the 18th-century explorer Alexander van Humboldt. Whenever he visited a new landscape, he was attentive to the smallest characteristics of the smallest plant yet—according to Goethe—with the capacity to place that small characteristic within the entire *cosmos*. In a similar attempt we understood that a small plant of *Limoniastrum monopelatum* in Andalucia is growing undisturbed at the verge of the wind farm road because the wind development made large strings of formerly cultivated land available to pioneering ruderal plants. Later, in the 1950s the French human geographer Maximilian Sorre in his definition of *geography of energy* was not focusing on energy itself but on how energy shapes both communities and landscapes in their development. The availability of different energy sources, Sorre found, influenced the local potential of human activities and the resulting landscape. More recently, the work of renowned photographer Edward Burtynsky comes to mind. When depicting the artifacts of oil development, he did not focus on the energy carrier itself but on those landscapes co-evolved with the practices of oil extraction, refining and consumption.

As our colleague and travel companion Rudi van Etteger affirms in his PhD thesis[1], landscape experiences can be either phenomenological or ontological in nature. The former is exclusively based on visual experience and aesthetic qualities based on other senses like smelling and hearing. The latter experience is based on awareness of the landscape origins. The origins of a landscape, in other words the complex of natural and human dynamics that shaped the current physical structure, influence the way we perceive it on a phenomenological level. Visiting those landscapes already aware of their ontology, or with the aim to learn about their development, can make a difference in how they are experienced. Yet in our landscape explorations we followed on the stimuli coming from the phenomenological experience, like in a novel landscape explored by Humboldt, following our intuitions and interpretations of reality, whenever possible engaging with locals, and we only investigated the complete landscape origins afterwards.

The means we use to communicate about our journeys are landscape maps, sections, photographs and written narrations merging the phenomenological and ontological. We created maps and landscape sections to represent our interpretation of the landscape ontology in its most valuable landscape physical structure. We use photographs and text to report on the trips' most salient facts, and the phenomenological dimension—seeing, smelling, hearing and tactile stimulus.

Each landscape is described according to the spatial and temporal dimensions from Pasqualetti & Stremke[2]. The *spatial qualification* indicates whether the renewable energy source or the technology can be qualified as a landscape entity or a landscape component. For example, a woodland providing primary biomass is an *entity energy landscape.* A row of wind turbines or PV arrays, on the contrary, are considered *landscape components*. The *temporal qualification* indicates whether these energy landscapes are dynamic, which means they exist only for a relatively short period of time. For example, due to the short lifetime or substitution of energy

1
van Etteger, R. (2016). Beyond the visible: prolegomenon to an aesthetics of designed landscapes. PhD thesis. Wageningen: Wageningen University.

2
Pasqualetti, M.J. & Stremke, S. (2018). Energy landscapes in a crowded world: A first typology of origins and expressions. Energy Research and Social Science, 36, p. 94–105.

technologies (think about the replacement of wind turbines with more powerful ones). If an energy landscape has a more permanent character, the infrastructure has longer life-time, think about a dam and its water reservoir. In addition to the temporal qualification we examined the energy landscape in terms of reversibility, in other words the possibility to return the landscape to the former condition after energy technology is decommissioned. A synthesis on technology and energy output data is provided for each landscape description.

The objective of this chapter is to cultivate readers' imagination and vocabulary with regards to energy landscapes, to encourage them to interpret and gain knowledge on these landscapes, especially for those currently involved in the assessing and designing of new projects. The map below shows the location of the landscapes visited during our journey through Europe and the United States →fig. 1.

1

1 A map of the energy landscapes visited in Europe and the USA.

A Hydropower energy landscape of the Hoover Dam
B Hydropower energy landscape in Canales
C Geothermal energy landscape of Larderello
D Geothermal Energy Landscape in the Imperial Valley
E Solar energy landscape in Las Gabias
F Solar energy landscape near Sevilla
G Wind energy landscape in Zahara de los Atunes
H Wind Energy Landscape in Lelystad
I Wind energy landscape in Viticuso
J Hybrid energy landscape in Eggebek

Hydropower Energy Landscape of the Hoover Dam, Arizona & Nevada, USA

We approach the Hoover dam from the west, on Route 93, after an extremely warm night at the Boulder Beach Campground. The campground is near Lake Mead but, unfortunately, not right next to the lake as the water table was considerably low. Lake Mead is the name of the artificial lake that was created by the construction of the Hoover Dam in the 1930s, fed by the Colorado River → fig. 1.

We drive through the Desert Mountains, nearing the eastern border of Nevada that is demarcated by the Colorado River. On the other side of the river lies Arizona and one enters a different time zone when traveling across the Tillman Memorial bridge. We immediately experience that the Hoover Dam is a major tourist attraction. Parking is scarce even though it is early in the morning and temperatures are already soaring. We walk along the Hoover Dam access road, spiralling down to the dam, looking for shade. The first sight is a set of electricity pylons. They sit at the verge edge of the steep valley cliff at 45 degrees and seem to fight gravity successfully. They are great eye catchers that make us wonder how this energy landscape was built in such a hostile desert environment → fig. 2.

The next memory is that this energy landscape conveys a sense of design thinking, both at the larger scale of the entire Hoover Dam area and the architectural detailing. Once we arrive on the crest of the dam, we admire the Art Deco penstock towers designed by Los Angeles-based architect Gordon Kaufmann. The architect was also responsible for the hiring of Denver artist Allan Tupper True, who designed walls and floors incorporating motifs of the local Navajo and Pueblo tribes, and artist Oskar Hansen, whose sculptures can be found in several spots on and near the crest → fig. 4.

For this case, the visual link between the energy source—hydropower—and affiliated energy landscape consisting of both the Hoover Dam and the lake Mead is clear. The Hoover Dam is an iconographic representation of how humans store and harvest energy. Engineers refer to this dam as a 'concrete gravity arch dam' that has a height of 221 metres and length of 379 metres. The reservoir behind the dam serves to collect gravitational potential energy that is then transformed into electricity by means of water turbines (2.080 MW capacity). These turbines are located in two power plants on either side of the Colorado River, one on the Nevada side and one on the Arizona side, and together generated 3,6 TWh electricity in 2015 (varies per year) The footprint of the actual Hoover Dam in itself is only a few hectares but its construction created Lake Mead, which has a maximum size of 340 square kilometres. The Hoover Dam with both its power plants and electricity infrastructure and Lake Mead together present a clearly distinguishable entity energy landscape. The boundaries of that energy landscape, however, vary depending on the water level in the lake → fig. 5.

The spatial dominance of the energy infrastructure in this landscape is clearly visible in the Hoover Dam area and less so around Lake Mead. The power plants, power lines, pylons and transformers dominate the appearance of the Hoover Dam area. Hardly any traces of energy infrastructure can be found in the larger Lake Mead area, though, while the reservoir is the means to collect the water and thus accumulate potential energy. In that sense, recognizing Lake Mead as part of a larger energy landscape presuppose knowledge of the fact that the Hoover Dam with its power plants is the reason the lake exists at all. The Hoover Dam and Lake Mead, indisputably, can be considered a relatively permanent energy landscape. This landscape is almost 100

1

2

Scale	Regional
Landscape	River canyon, arid climate
Year	Constructed between 1931 and 1936
Technology	Concrete gravity arch dam, different sets of turbine generators
Power	max. capacity 2.080 MW (since 1993)
Size	Dam height 221 m, length 379 m, Lake Mead 340 km^2
Yearly output	3,6 TWh (2015, varies per year)

years old and bound to persist for at least another few hundreds of years. Either way, the landscape transformation that came with the creation of the dam and the reservoir is irreversible; the original state of the environment cannot be restored.

It is important to remember that the Hoover Dam, in the first place, was built to control floods and to collect irrigation water for the larger region. Renewable energy, quite similar to some more recent energy landscapes, was originally generated to pay for the construction and maintenance of other-than energy infrastructure. The Hoover Dam was constructed between 1931 and 1936, the last turbine not placed until 1961. Environmental concerns, at that time, were limited and mostly focused on safety issues and irrigation capacities downstream. The general superintendent of the Hoover Dam construction—Frank Crowe—shares his family name with the British landscape architect Sylvia Crowe who, one generation later, wrote the seminal book *The Landscape of Power*.

Not unfamiliar to the development of fossil fuel energy landscapes such as coal mines, this hydropower energy landscape came at the expense of people's health and even lives. Between 100 and 200 workers died during the construction of the Hoover Dam and there is a monument at the site for those who lost their lives in the 1930s. Since 1985, the Hoover Dam has been listed as a National Historic Landmark of the United States. Each year, the site is toured by one million visitors and experienced by a much larger number of unregistered visitors and others passing the Hoover Dam on the Interstate 11 just a few hundred metres to the south.

3 → 72–73

4 → 74–75

1 A view of Lake Mead from Boulder Beach Campground (Photo by Sven Stremke).
2 The pylons sitting at the edge of the valley (Photo by Sven Stremke).
3 Map of the hydropower energy landscape of the Hoover Dam.
4 The Penstock intake towers emerging form the lake Mead water (Photo by Sven Stremke).

5

5 Hoover Dam, the colour of the rock shows Lake Mead's maximum water level (Photo by Sven Stremke).

6 The three penstock towers, the visitor center and electricity pylons in the background (Photo by Sven Stremke).

6

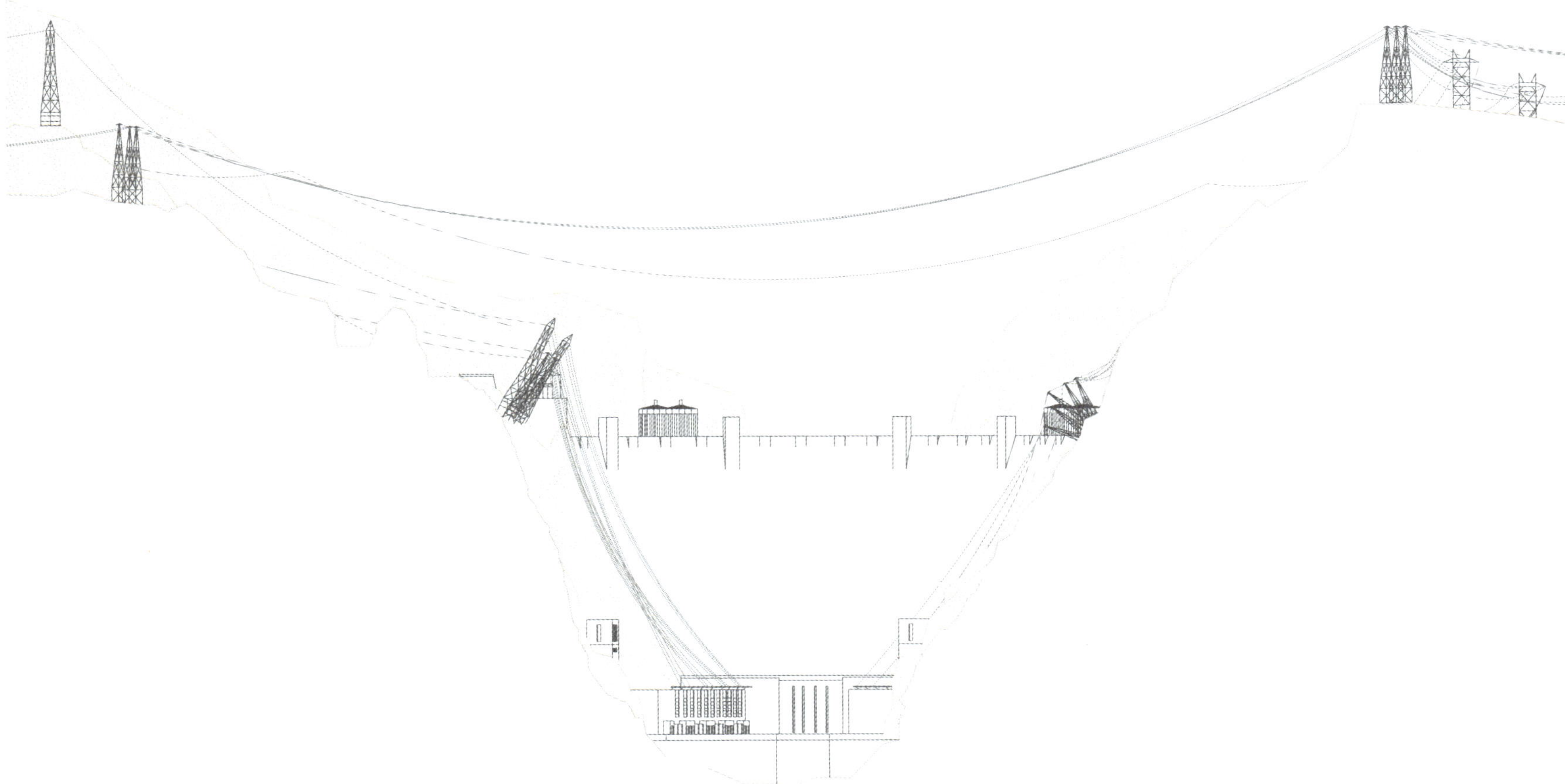

500
500
500
400
300
500

400
400
500
300
400
0
100 m
N↑

1

2

Scale	Regional
Landscape	Mountainous landscape
Year	Constructed between 1975 and 1989
Technology	Rockfill dam
Power	Max. capacity 8.5 MW
Size	Dam height 146 m, length 340 m, Canales Reservoir 1,52 km^2
Yearly output	Unknown

Hydropower Energy Landscape in Canales, Andalusia, Spain

East of Granada in the south of Spain lies the mountainous landscape that will eventually culminate in the Sierra Nevada. The road we take follows the River Genil upstream. This river is the second longest river in Andalusia. It originates in the Sierra Nevada and runs all the way to Palma del Rio, just north of Gemasolar (another energy landscape described in this chapter). The slopes are so steep that you can hardly see the river from the car. The small villages Cenes de la Vega, Pinos Genil and Güéjar Sierra are strung like beads along the Genil. Up until the 1980s, the original village of Canales was part of this string. Today, Canales refers to the large reservoir created for flood protection, electricity production as well as for the supply of irrigation and drinking water: *Embalse de Canales*. Arriving from the west, the dry side of the dam catches our eye first, though it is rather inconspicuous in design [→fig. 1].

Instead of smooth concrete, the dam is constructed from local rocks, making it look similar to the surrounding mountains. Power lines jumping over the valley on account of the steep slopes announce the site as a node in the electricity grid. This somewhat chaotic convergence of power lines on the dry side is contrasted by the still and calm atmosphere when we reach the crest of the dam [→fig. 4].

In this mountainous landscape, the Canales Dam is one of the few flat spaces that invites us to experience the surroundings at a slow pace. Despite the steep climb on the road and the next villages being at least 2–3 kilometres away, we find that we're certainly not alone: locals are taking a stroll here, enjoying their (brought-along) dinner or doing yoga [→fig. 2].

A closer look at the crest of the dam makes it clear what draws these people here: the dam constitutes a public park offering stunning views both across the reservoir and the canyon [→fig. 5]. The park on the crest has vantage points, walking paths near the edges, benches, and lampposts. In spite of the hiking trails around the reservoir, the park itself is rather isolated. In fact, the paths on the crest end abruptly at some rock face, on the southern end of the reservoir.

Walking along the east side of the dam gives us a view across the length of the reservoir, with the control tower and a large rock formation as two striking elements. The latter is called *el Pulpito de Canales* and harboured one of the three castles that guarded entrance to Güéjar Sierra. The original village of Canales used to be at the foot of this formation. The 64 inhabitants of this village were forced to move to Granada and other nearby villages when the reservoir was created. Despite this social displacement, the site is now attracting locals, as well as hikers, kayakers, and cyclists. Guillermo Bravo Guillén was the lead engineer for the dam, although it is unclear whether he was also responsible for the park.

Although both the reservoir and the dam were created to produce electricity, this landscape transformation was motivated by many other necessities, among which (drinking) water supply and flood protection. For the local inhabitants of the Canales village, the landscape transformation and the relocation of their houses must have been drastic. For contemporary visitors, the dam presents itself as a sober, yet carefully designed place, used and cherished by landscape users enjoying the stillness of the reservoir and the surrounding mountain landscape. Although there are a few examples of dismantled hydropower dams, the multitude of functions that the Canales hydropower landscape has for Granada and the nearby villages suggests a high degree of permanence for this specific energy landscape.

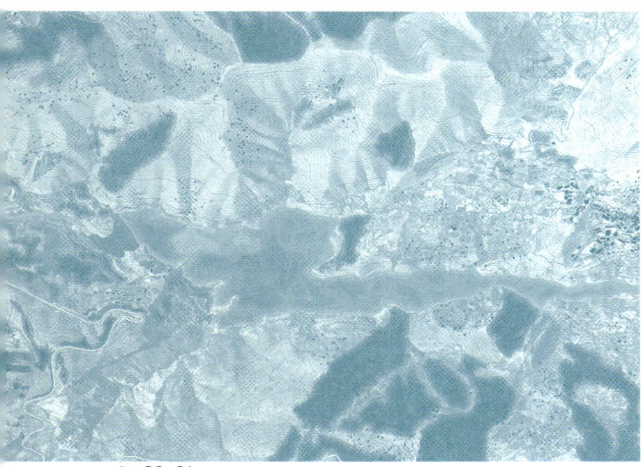

3→80–81

4→82–83

1 Approaching the rockfill dam from Granada (Photo by Dirk Oudes).
2 Local people enjoying a picnic on the top of their dam (Photo by Dirk Oudes).
3 Map of the hydropower energy landscape in Canales.
4 Local people take a walk on the crest of the dam (Photo by Sven Stremke).

5

6

7

5 The calm and peaceful atmosphere when looking at the lake form the crest of the dam (Photo by Dirk Oudes).

6 View of the valley with the village Pinos Genil in the background. In this mountainous landscape, the crest of the dam is one of the very few flat surfaces (Photo by Dirk Oudes).

7 The public park on the crest of the dam (Photo by Dirk Oudes).

1300
1200
1100
1000
1000
1110
1200
1300
1400

1400
0
100 m
N↑

Geothermal Energy Landscape of Larderello, Tuscany, Italy

During the summer of 2021, we were in Italy visiting various energy landscapes. At the end of July, we met with colleagues in Florence, in the Torrigiani gardens, to prepare the 'cultivating energies' Atelier for the Uniscape Conference later that year. What better occasion to visit the famous geothermal energy landscape of Larderello together? By chance, we met Matteo Baroni in the Torrigiani gardens, a Florentine artist and great-grandson of Piero Ginori Conti who, in 1904, came up with the idea to generate electricity in Larderello by exploiting the fumaroles steam through turbines.

On a very hot afternoon, we left Florence southwards through the Chianti region, to reach the so-called *Colline Metallifere* (Metal-bearing Hills). Those hills are rich of different metals such as silver and copper, they are well-known for their thermal waters and have been exploited since the antique Etruscan and Roman times. Larderello is set at circa 400 metres above sea level. The surrounding hills reach around 600 metres and are covered with forest and Mediterranean garrigue with blooming weaver's broom (*Spartium junceum*) and scattered downy oak (*Quercus pubescens*), denser oaks and ash forest mixed with cultivated conifers (*Pinus sylvestris*), pastures and olive groves, depending on the altitude and exposure of the slopes.

Mid-afternoon, we reached the Devil's Valley from south, so called since the Middle Ages for the presence of fumaroles (this valley inspired Dante in his description of *Inferno* in the *Divine Comedy*). Bend after bend we arrived from the south until we saw a stunning view beneath us: the first two cooling towers emerging form the woodland just beside the beautiful medieval tower of Castel Nuovo val di Cecina. The sight actually made us quite emotional after having studied this landscape exclusively from our desks →fig. 1. Above the valley of Larderello, you have a wonderful overview of the complex energy landscape and its recognizable features: cooling towers and the networks of pipes shining in the summer sun.

The five geothermal power plants of Larderello are part of a larger network of 34 geothermal plants with a cumulative power of 761 MW →fig. 7. Closed by the geothermal plant of *Valle Secolo* a solar plant on ground is also contributing to the power output. This network supplies all the electricity used in the provinces of Pisa, Siena and Grosseto, so these provinces use 100 per cent renewable electricity. In total, this network supplies 30 per cent of the electricity in the whole of Tuscany, as well as the heating for the surrounding villages of Pomarance, Castelnuovo Val di Cecina, Monterotondo Marittimo, Santa Fiora, and Monteverdi Marittimo.

Apart from the imperative presence of the cooling towers, the spatial character of this landscape is clearly dominated by the steam pipes crossing roads with arches that looks like landscape portals welcoming you the garrigue and the denser forest →fig. 3.

The pipes connect the steam extraction sites with the energy plants and distribute heat to the settlements →fig. 6. Their network is complex and visible with clear tracks cutting through forest and other vegetation. The combination of the shiny pipes and the blooming weaver's broom, downy oaks and pines gives a unique character to the landscape. Indeed, the metal pipes transecting the landscape invite visitors to follow their paths to unravel new places and forest clearings as if they were secret gardens →fig. 5.

Larderello itself is a typical example of an industrial village. The village we see now is the result of the work of the architect Giovanni Michelucci (the modernist architect of Florence central station), who made the city-garden plan with public buildings,

1

Scale	National
Landscape	Upper hills with woodlands and olive groves
Year	Started in 1904
Source	Geothermal
Technology	Steam turbines
Power	761 MW
Size	34 geothermal plants
Yearly output	4800 GWh

schools, the church, and open spaces planted with domestic pines. Notably, the church—according to the architect—was modelled after the first cooling towers.

The energy landscape of Larderello is more than 100 years old and is still changing. It seems that this exploitation will last for some hundreds of years to come. Recently, new plants have been inaugurated by Enel Green Power (the Italian State Company): the new approach is to limit the length of pipes and allocate smaller-scale plants closer to the extraction sites. These plants employ new cooling systems that no longer necessitate large cooling towers. The landscape transformation that started more than 100 years ago in Larderello can be considered irreversible. In fact, this energy landscape is considered cultural heritage and has a museum dedicated to it. Furthermore, these landscapes are visited by nature lovers and the trail 'le Biancane' recently won the Tripadvisor Travelers' Choice Award in 2021.

With respect to the longer history of this energy landscape, it is important to remember that it was during the Middle Ages that the exploitation of materials associated with geothermal events started, especially the boric acid. These activities then flourished during the Renaissance. In Montecerboli in 1818, a merchant of French origins, Francesco de Larderel, started the first industrial plant for the production of boric acid. To increase the boric acid production, new steam drilling techniques were experimented with in the surrounding landscape, which later proved useful for the geothermal energy industry. De Larderel had a new settlement built for the factory workers with houses, a church, a theatre and a pharmacy, and called it *Larderello*. In 1904, Piero Ginori Conti, director of the Larderel and Co. society, connected a steam-powered engine to a dynamo to produce the first electricity from geothermal energy → fig. 4. This led to the construction of the first geothermal power plant with steam turbines in 1913. Its capacity was 500 KW and the first cooling towers were installed in 1937.

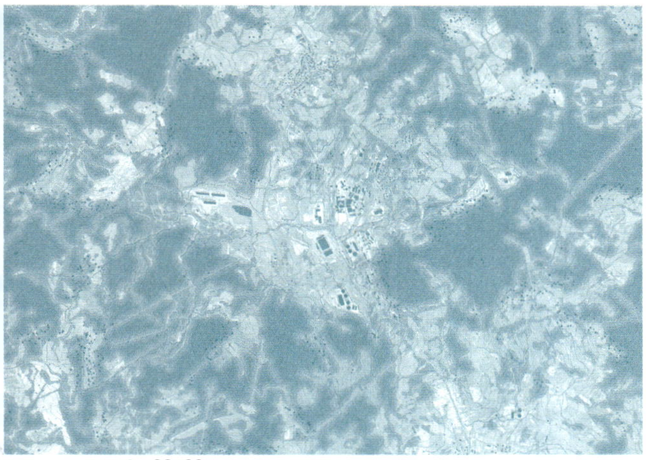

2 → 88–89

3 → 90–91

4

1 View of Castel Nuovo Val di Cecina medieval skyline and le Prata geothermal plant in the back (Photo credit Musei Val di Cecina—Geothermal Museum Larderello).
2 Map of the geothermal energy landscape of Larderello.
3 A pipe arch crossing the regional road 349 connecting Larderello to Castel Nuovo Val di Cecina (Photo by Sven Stremke).
4 Pietro Ginori experimenting with the first dynamo powered by steam to generate electricity in 1904 (Photo credit heirs Ginori).

5

6

7

5 A steam pipe crossing the green of the garrigue and the blue sky of the Tuscan summer in the back (Photo by Paolo Picchi).
6 The shining pipes interweaving the other infrastructures and creating ecological corridors (Photo by Paolo Picchi).
7 A map showing the network of pipes and the geothermal power plants in Larderello's area.

A Geothermal power plant Le Prata
B Geothermal power plant Larderello 3
C Geothermal power plant Larderello 2
D Geothermal power plant Farinello
E Geothermal power plant Valle Secolo
F Solar energy landscape near Sevilla
G Wind energy landscape in Zahara de los Atunes
H Wind Energy Landscape in Lelystad
I Wind energy landscape in Viticuso
J Hybrid energy landscape in Eggebek

500
400
500
600

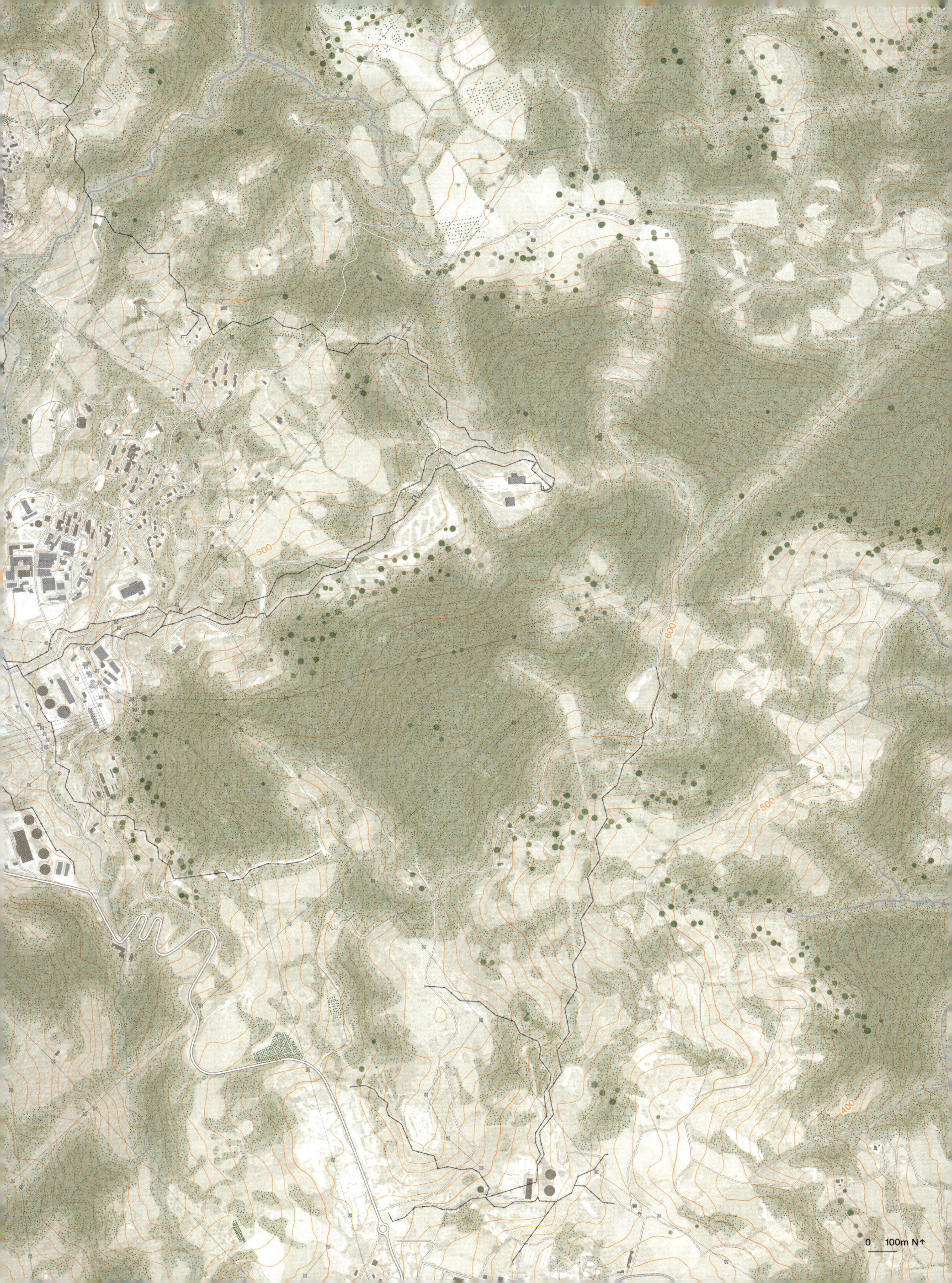

500
600
500
400
0 100m N↑

Geothermal Energy Landscape in the Imperial Valley, California, USA

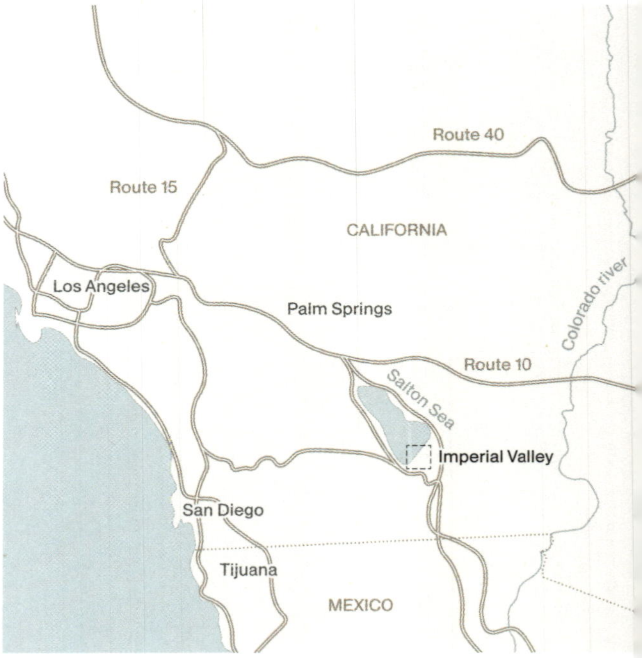

The introduction of energy technologies into the landscape is often described as one of the largest drivers of landscape transformation. More often than not, at a global scale, this landscape transformation is for a single purpose: energy development. The Salton Sea in the Imperial Valley (south-eastern California) is possibly the largest landscape transformation without *any* purpose. This lake came into existence by accident, due to faulty engineering. In 1905, while working on a canal to bring water from the Colorado River to the Imperial valley, the river started to take another course and, over a period of two years, created the Salton Sea with a surface of 900 square kilometres that dominates the Imperial Valley.

On our way to the Imperial Valley, we smell the water before we have even caught a glimpse of the lake. The Salton Sea has little to no water inflow and massive evaporation in the arid climate, resulting in declining water levels and increasing water pollution. We first stop in Salton Sea Beach, which, we soon realize, no longer has a proper beach→fig. 1. There are more abandoned houses here than inhabited ones, more fisher boats than fishers. Great numbers of dead fish occupy the muddy shoreline. Moving further South along Interstate 86 we soon enter the geothermal energy landscape of the Imperial Valley. We see the cooling towers on the horizon, and pass a number of geometric and irrigated fields, following straight asphalt roads for several miles→fig. 3, 4.

A huge transformation occurred here during the early twentieth century when the landscape was converted from a desert ecosystem into an irrigated agro-ecosystem through irrigation water supplied by the Colorado River. The primary land use is irrigated crop agriculture, otherwise, the Imperial valley is rich in different landscape types with extensive wetlands close to the Salton Sea southern coastline, riverine vegetation creating large and sinuous ecological corridors that interrupt the monotony of the geometric agriculture parcels. Those water courses originating from the Salton Sea have in turn created other small lakes and wetlands. Wetlands are also important habitat for bird species such as pelicans and cormorants, wading birds, waterfowl, shorebirds, and gulls and terns.

The sight of the cooling towers is soon accompanied by large pipelines and power lines on either side of the access road. In appearance and scale the geothermal power plants look much like coal or gas power plants and the clouds from the cooling towers signpost each of the 11 power plants. Once we get closer, we realize that the buildings and other structures are rusty and worn out by the sun and salty air→fig. 5. If the Hoover Dam is a true tourist attraction with appealing architectural details and interesting narratives, the Imperial Valley geothermal energy landscape is the antidote, a non-place ruled by function optimization and a complete lack of attention to the human senses. This energy landscape shares many characteristics with fossil fuel energy landscapes; it can easily be mistaken for one.

In this energy landscape, there is no visual link between the energy source—geothermal heat—and the affiliated energy technology: 11 power plants. This is because the energy source is hidden in the underground and no efforts have been made to create visual cues, to 'daylight' geothermal energy. If looked at from above, one can see that the power plants are located next to main roads but, other than that, are irresponsive to any other landscape feature. What is interesting and partly visible in the landscape is the fact that the Imperial Valley lies at a fault line between two tectonic

1

Scale	Regional
Landscape	Flat desert
Year	Constructed between 1982 and 2023
Technology	Power station with 14 units dry steam turbines
Power	max. capacity 432 MW (14 existing units)
Size	11 power plants
Yearly output	1741 GWh (2018, varies per year)

plates. Five, more or less inactive underground volcanoes are present in the area and several so-called buttes can be found. The Obsidian Butte and the Rock Hill Butte, approximately 30 metres high, lie within the geothermal energy landscapes at the shore of the Salton Sea and reward courageous hikers with wide views over the otherwise flat landscape.

The Imperial Valley geothermal energy landscape comprises 11 power plants with 14 turbine units, next to the extensive network of above-ground pipelines and overhead electricity lines. The footprint of each of the power plants is no more than 10 hectares, but their spatial appearance in the widely open and flat landscape is both dominant and contrasting with the irrigated agricultural fields that are so typical for the southern shoreline of the Salton Sea. Altogether, this renewable energy landscape is possibly the least discernible from fossil-fuel energy landscapes. If anything, the trains are missing that usually transport coal to the power plants.

This part of the Imperial Valley with its 11 geothermal power plants can be considered a relatively young energy landscape. In fact, another power plant is under construction and scheduled to start generating electricity in 2023. The landscape transformation that came with the creation of the power plants, in theory, could be considered reversible. We state 'in theory' because we are not aware of any agreements between the companies and the authorities regarding the dismantling of the power plants, pipelines and overhead power lines at the end of their lifecycle.

2→96–97

3→98–99

1 A view of Salton Sea from the north-western coast (Photo by Sven Stremke).
2 Map of the geothermal energy landscape in the Imperial Valley.
3 Crossing the irrigated fields and a geothermal plant in a distance (Photo by Sven Stremke).

4

4 Crossing the irrigated fields and a geothermal plant in a distance (Photo by Sven Stremke).
5, 6 Getting close to the power plant we notice a plant of big saltbrush (Atriplex lentiformis) growing in between two pipe lines. This is a typical southwestern California and northern Mexico plant growing in dry and salty soils (Photo by Sven Stremke).

5

6

0 100m N↑

255133
CRUISEAMERICA.com
7RUD276

1

2

Scale	Local
Landscape	Hilly Mediterranean intensive agriculture landscape
Year	Constructed in 2008
Technology	Dual axis tracker and fixed tilt PV
Power	max. capacity 18 MW
Size	35 ha (for the north part)
Yearly output	ca. 40,3 GWh (varies per year)

Solar Orchard in Las Gabias, Andalusia, Spain

Our efforts to reach the solar energy landscape of *Las Gabias*, near Granada in the south of Spain, make it clear that renewable energy is a recent driver of landscape transformations: we cross the completely deserted highway A4 that will soon serve to bypass traffic around Granada. The abrupt transition from the brand-new bridges over the highway to local dirt roads shows that landscape patterns have yet to 'heal' from this incision. The energy landscape is quite difficult to reach. This power plant is deeply embedded in the agricultural landscape around Granada, which is characterized by a slanted mosaic of olive and almond groves and grassland. Steep and irregular dirt roads prove cumbersome even for the 4×4 that is tasked to take us there. The poor accessibility emphasizes the productive and pragmatic character of this landscape: this is an area that serves many but is seen by few.

This photovoltaic power plant was built in 2008 and was at that time the largest photovoltaic plant in Andalusia. In the local media this solar power plant is referred to as 'macro huerto solar', which means 'large solar orchard'. We understand why when we see the power plant from 2 kilometres away: it is hardly distinguishable from the almond groves. Only the attentive eye notices the difference in fractality between the edgy solar trackers and organic almond trees. The individuality of the solar trackers, compared to long solar arrays, certainly helps in making the plant look like another type of orchard within the larger landscape patchwork. This is enhanced by the fact that the shapes of most plots on which the trackers are located have been kept intact; only some of the former agricultural plots have been combined into larger ones for the plant. Moreover, the plots are not all clustered, plots of grassland or olive groves are still part of the patchwork. This patchwork design and the singular solar trackers give a sense of familiarity of the energy technology in this landscape [→ fig. 1]. The power plant is divided into two parts, with the southern part located roughly 1 kilometre below the one shown in figure 3.

When we move closer, the scale difference between the solar trackers and trees becomes apparent. Each solar tracker consists of 63 PV modules and is approximately 6 metres high and 11 metres wide. The soil around the trackers has been excavated in a circular way to enable an optimal orientation towards the sun throughout the day, emphasizing their solitary character. Paradoxically, while the solar trackers have their feet in a lush green and flowering grassland, the almond and olive trees are standing in arable clay for intensive cultivation [→ fig. 4].

We also discover that this energy landscape entails more than just solar trackers: the relatively flat parts of the landscape facing south have been accommodated with fixed tilt PV arrays. The pragmatic and productive character of this solar energy landscape is underlined by grazing sheep, some broken PV panels and others being replaced with different models (e.g. different shades of blue) [→ fig. 2].

The solitary character of the solar trackers makes this energy landscape quite 'transparent' with a discontinuous spatial boundary, compared with solar landscapes with ground-mounted and fixed tilt PV panels. As with most solar power plants, this plant is in theory relatively dynamic: mechanically, the trackers can be removed rather easily. The trackers even allow for a larger part of the soil to receive sunlight and water, thus keeping the soil relatively healthy. The existing connection to the electricity grid, meanwhile, may support repowering of this solar landscape in the future.

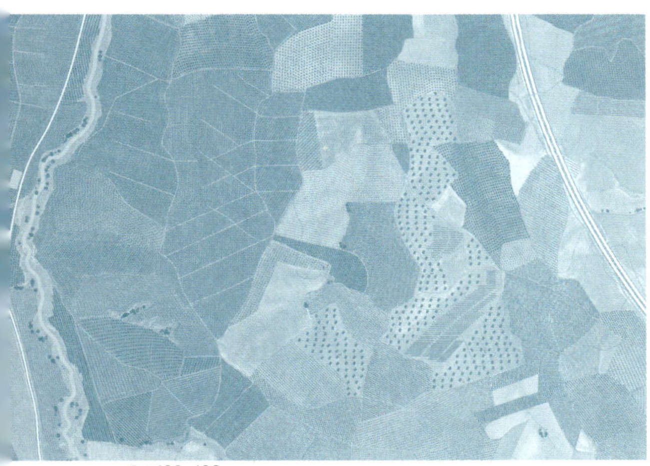

3 → 102–103

4 → 104–105

1 The large solar orchard seen from a distance of 2 km is hardly distinguishable from the almond groves (Photo by Dirk Oudes).
2 A view of the relatively flat parts of the landscape with fixed tilt PV arrays (Photo by Dirk Oudes).
3 Map of the solar orchard in Las Gabias.
4 A closer view of the trackers reveals the scale difference with the trees in the back, almonds on the right and olives on the left (Photo by Dirk Oudes).

700

0
100 m
N↑

Solar Energy Landscape near Sevilla, Andalusia, Spain

We are on the A4 motorway traveling from Granada to Sevilla after having visited the inconspicuous hydropower energy landscape in Canales. That hydropower dam is an invisible giant, folded within the mountain topography, where locals enjoy their dinner watching the calm water. Although we are aware that Concentrated Solar Power Plants (CSP) can be quite conspicuous, we are not prepared for the ornate central receiving tower of Gemasolar that is visible from over 17 kilometres away. Some user reviews on Google describe the tower as 'something out of a science fiction movie' and others even refer to 'the great eye of Sauron' from *The Lord of the Rings* [→ fig. 1].

We stop several times along the highway to observe the iconic landmark. As the central receiving tower is visible from far away, it is a good thing that this tower was carefully designed. Compared to other CSP towers that look like oil rigs, the sleek and light design of this tower conveys a clear message of genuine innovation *and* design. For the landscape user unfamiliar with CSP towers, the tower looks to be much more about *broadcasting* than *receiving*. This is especially the case from a distance when the heliostats are not yet visible. Heliostats are large mirrors that reflect and concentrate solar irradiation to the central receiving tower [→ fig. 5, 6].

When we get closer to this CSP, a nearby fire causes large smoke clouds to cross the CSP and presents us with a mesmerizing view as the otherwise invisible light beams between heliostat and the tower become visible. We take the exit from the motorway and arrive in a landscape with arable fields, edged by strips of flowers and specked by trees. The surrounding organic landscape contrasts starkly with the sleek tower and the unusual field of heliostats [→ fig. 7, 8].

Near the entrance is a small car park right next to the substation that connects the CSP to the electricity grid. From this point, the central road through the field of heliostats provides a clear and uncanny view of the lighting tower. As all mirrors are oriented towards the central tower, the striking and neat design of the supporting structure of the heliostats—the frame—is clearly visible [→ fig. 9]. This is reflected by the barren soil underneath the heliostats. Right up to the perimeter fence, vegetation reflects the power of heavy rainfall in spring, while the area inside the fence only exudes an air of tidiness and technology. Gemasolar breathes cutting-edge technology. In the central receiving tower, molten salt (at 290 degrees Celsius) is heated up to 560 degrees Celsius by the concentrated sun light. The steam produced in this process powers a turbine that generates electricity. The molten salt—a phase change material—allows the power plant to store up to 15 hours of production, tackling the intermittent character of solar irradiation between day and night.

1

The sharp boundaries and the complete transformation of the original landscape of Gemasolar make it evident that this is an example of an entity energy landscape. The spatial expanse and the accompanied landscape transformation resemble a form of centralized electricity production that is somewhat comparable with conventional power plants. Where the latter are situated near transportation infrastructure to bring in coal or gas and cooling water, CSPs are situated in remote areas where labour is cheap and solar irradiance abundant. In contrast to most PV power plants that are considered 'temporary', the expensive technology and the involved landscape transformation of CSPs makes them more permanent. In this specific energy landscape, the presence of the CSP also attracted a second energy facility.

Scale	Regional
Landscape	Hilly Mediterranean intensive agriculture landscape
Year	Constructed in 2009; operational in 2011
Technology	Concentrated solar power with up to 15h storage using molten salt heat storage system
Power	max. capacity 19.9 MW
Size	195 ha, 140 m tower
Yearly output	80 GWh

The high-tech allure of Gemasolar has drawn the attention of actors not usually associated with renewable energy. In 2011, Mercedes-Benz used this energy landscape as backdrop for an advertising campaign. In 2013, the power plant was featured in the popular videogame Gran Turismo 6. In this simulation game, players can drive through the field of heliostats. And in 2015, model and fashion show producer Jessica Minh Anh used the central road as a fashion runway →fig. 4. The power plant even gets 4.7 (out of 5) stars on Google Reviews. Gemasolar is an example of energy landscapes that are being appropriated by people and companies outside the field of renewable energy. Or, put differently, companies are increasingly aiming to be (visually) associated with a post-carbon future. While this solar energy landscape clearly represents an inert object in the larger surroundings, with loss of historic landscape patterns and biodiversity, Gemasolar also provides a vision of what future energy systems can look like.

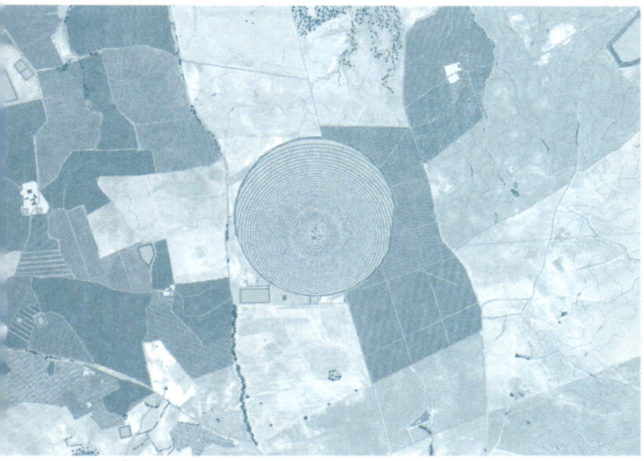

2 → 110–111

3 → 112–113

4

1 The central receiving tower seen from a distance of 17 km along the A4 (Photo by Dirk Oudes).
2 Map of the solar energy landscape near Sevilla.
4 The fashion show producer Jessica Minh Anh in Gemasolar (Photo credit Stephanie Louise Taylor, Media @ JMA Global).

5

6

7

8

9

5, 6 We could gain a closer view on the heliostats climbing a pylon (Photo by Dirk Oudes and Sven Stremke).
7 A view of the surrounding landscape contrasting starkly with the sleek tower and the field of heliostats (Photo by Dirk Oudes).
8 Getting closer to the receiving tower along a countryside road (Photo by Dirk Oudes).
9 The design of the supporting structure of the heliostats (Photo by Dirk Oudes).

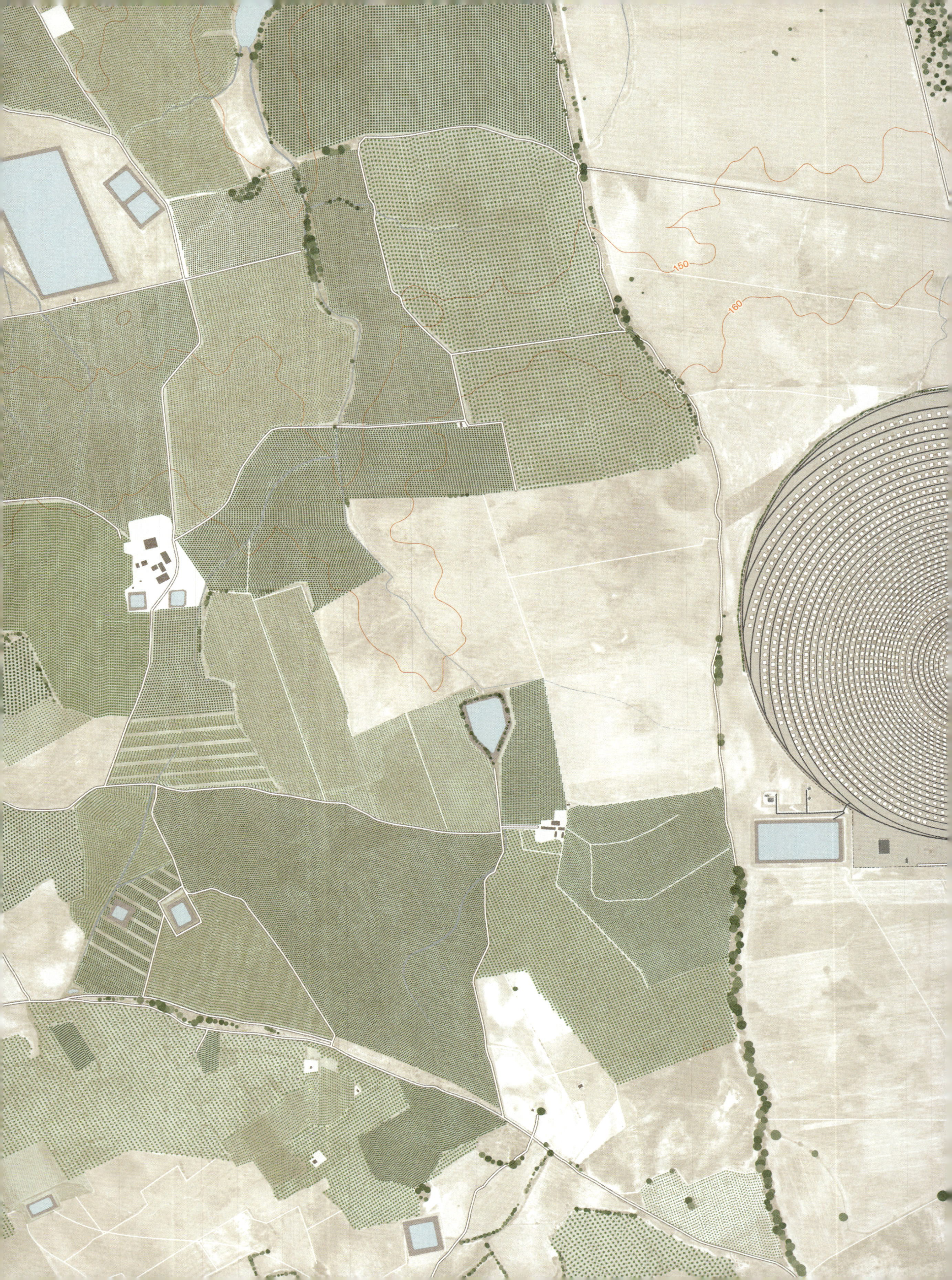
150
160

160
150
140
130
0 100m N↑

Torresol
28
29

1

2

Scale	Regional
Landscape	Open landscape with intensive arable land and pastures
Year	First plot in 1993
Technology	Wind turbines
Power	80 MW
Size	40 wind turbines by 0,3 MW and 34 wind turbines by 2 MW part of two different wind parks
Yearly output	Unknown

Wind Energy Landscape in Zahara de los Atunes, Andalusia, Spain

In May 2018 we were sitting at the terrace of café Con horizonte, a *Bar-Asador* serving local food in the village called La Zarzuela, in Zahara de los Atunes, in western Andalusia. We enjoy our cortado coffee while contemplating the local horizon, dominated by the presence of wind turbines. We are still wondering today if the name of the bar was inspired by the peculiar wind energy horizon →fig. 1. The toponyms Zahara in ancient Andalusian Arabic meant a rocky place, referring to the geological formations. Historically those landscapes have been described as rocky and windy; located at the mouth of Gibraltar, winds are strong throughout the year. La Zarzuela is not a well-known village, a few houses and a tiny chapel, that's it. Tourists only visit it to rent a house for less than they would have to pay at the nearby coast. Wind turbines now characterize the landscape, a common story in the Iberic peninsula. Those wind turbines are part of the grand wind energy development project of Tarifa, along the route E50 from Gibraltar to Cádiz. Traveling along the route after Facinas, you pass the village of Tahivilla. There, towards the west, where you see the highest concentration of turbines, set in a valley descending to the seaside, is where La Zarzuela is located.

The landscape is characterized by arenaceous rocks and *matorral* vegetation (*Rhamnus spp*, *Cistus spp*) with cork oaks (*Quercus suber*). The white-coloured deep and narrow valleys (*canutos*) with perennial water courses contrast with the more open landscape featuring intensive cultivation of cereals and seasonal creeks. The coastline features beautiful beaches facing the deep blue ocean. The wind development started in 1993 with the installation of 250 turbines near the settlements of Algeciras, Tarifa and Facinas. At the time, this was the largest wind energy landscape in Europe, both in spatial extent and energy generation. At present, the energy landscape of Tarifa comprises numerous wind parks of different ages. In line with developments elsewhere, the number of turbines will decrease as a result of repowering with larger models. The wind energy landscape is composed of groups of turbines set on the top of the surrounding Sierras (part of the Los Acornocales Natural Park), and groups placed in the open and gently undulating landscape descending to the shore of the Atlantic Ocean on the west as in the case of the landscape we visited →fig. 2.

In between the two small villages of La Zarzuela and El Almarchal, wind turbines are part of two distinguished wind parks located in the middle of intensive agriculture with cereal fields →fig. 5.

The abundancy of new maintenance roads created a new pattern in the landscape, and led to new agricultural activities. Those new roads interrupt the intensive agriculture pattern and represent continuous corridors for biodiversity; indeed we could appreciate a huge variety of herbaceous plants and flowers →fig. 7.

In this energy landscape, turbines and maintenance roads are evidently a landscape component, not in conflict with agricultural land use, even though the turbines density is very high compared to other wind farms. The temporal scale is relative dynamic: as mentioned before, wind turbines are replaced with turbines with a larger capacity.

3 → 118–119

4 → 120–121

1 The landscape descending towards the ocean (Photo by Dirk Oudes).
2 The view from the café Con Horizonte (Photo by Dirk Oudes).
3 Map of the wind energy landscape in Zahara de Los Atunes.

5

6

7

5 The wind landscape seen from La Zarzuela outskirts (Photo by Dirk Oudes).
6 Hardly any views from outside the villages are without wind turbines (Photo by Dirk Oudes).
7 Blooming meadows with Crysanthemum leucathemum, Crysanthemum segetum, Echium vulgare, Hedysarum coronarium, Centaurea pullata and others, along one of the turbine maintenance roads (Photo by Dirk Oudes).

300
200
100

100
0 100m N↑

Vestas
Vestas
Vestas

1

2

3

Scale	Regional
Landscape	Open polder landscape
Year	1996
Technology	Wind turbines
Power	16.8 MW
Size	28 wind turbines
Yearly output	147 GWh

Wind Energy Landscape near Lelystad, Flevoland, the Netherlands

In June 2021, traveling back to Amsterdam after an afternoon walk with the family in the historical gardens of Het Loo Palace, we took an alternative route through Flevoland, the newest land and province in all of Europe. We started our journey through Flevoland by crossing the Drontermeer in Elburg. Nice to see here the original coastline of the former Zuiderzee with fields above the sea level, a rarity in this part of The Netherlands. Flevoland has its own landscape character; whenever you cross the threshold of this new land, the perception you have is of a very ordered and functional landscape. The Flevoland landscape was built to increase food production and to create housing for the growing Dutch population. Flevoland was created form the Zuiderzee (Dutch for southern sea) in phases in the 1950s and 1960s and the name comes from the antique lake that the river Rhine was creating here, *lacus Flevus* as the Roman Geographer Pomponio Mela called it in the first century BCE. The lake was first destroyed during the Saint Lucy storm in December 1287 (Sint-Luciavloed), when the North Sea erased most of the dune systems and transformed the lake into the Zuiderzee. Some Zuiderzee dunes are now covered by woods, and visible from the wind park we visited that day, the Irene Vorrink wind park, to the northeast of Lelystad, built in 1996. Flevoland seems to host wind turbines quite well in a perfect composition with the well-ordered parcels of scattered woods and predominantly arable land with the famous tulips, as well as cereals, corn and vegetables, especially spinach, endive and cabbage—the base of popular traditional dishes like *stamppot*. This landscape also reflects the *genius loci* that enabled the social acceptance of the installation of the highest number of wind turbines in the Netherlands. However, the more recent wind development on the initiative of private farmers created an overpopulation of wind turbines, without a proper landscape design that follows the existing alignments [→fig. 2]. Differently for those arriving from the south, having crossed landscapes with seemingly unplanned wind turbines, it is immediately evident that the Irene Vorrink wind park was developed in concerted ways employing strong design thinking. Indeed, the wind park is one of the first and maybe most famous in the Netherlands for its spatial design: the turbines stand a few meters offshore from the *IJsselmeer* dyke and follow the coastline in one long row, a well-known landmark for people that frequently travel along the A6 motorway [→fig. 1, 3]. Each turbine is connected with the land by a small bridge.

We parked the car and went for an inspiring walk between land, water and wind, three fundamental elements to cultivate both food and energy. It was a Sunday afternoon, and that road is quite popular for recreational activities, some people were testing new motorbikes on the dyke, for example. We wandered along the dyke in the breeze watching the sparkling waves and fluttering turbine blades. This landmark is even a popular site for marriage shootings [→fig. 4].

This landscape perfectly represents the component energy landscape type. As in Het Loo, baroque parterres are frequently replanted. In the wind park, the original 28 wind turbines will be soon replaced by new 24 more powerful turbines. This means that the energy landscape is relatively dynamic in nature.

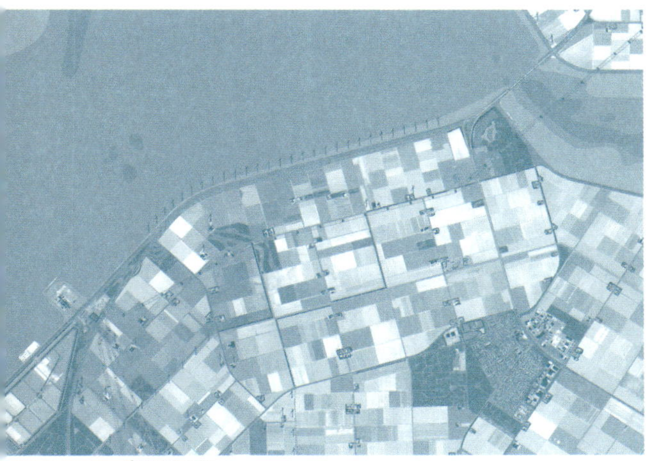
4→124–125

5→126–127

1 The Irene Vorrink wind park seen from the dyke (Photo by Paolo Picchi).
2 The Irene Vorrink wind park seen from a rest area along the A6 (Photo by Paolo Picchi).
3 The marriage of Sam and Ruben immortalized in front of the Irene Vorrink wind park (Photo credit Patricia Pietersen).
4 Map of the wind energy landscape near Lelystad.
5 Bird view of the Irene Vorrink wind park and the ordered agriculture parcels of Flevoland (Photo courtesy: Robbie van Heijningen, SkyFoto NL).

0 100 m
N↑

Wind Energy Landscape in Viticuso, Latium, Italy

I first encountered the wind park of Viticuso while traveling by train between Rome and Naples: my eyes were attracted by a row of wind turbines, proudly standing on the ridge of a beautiful and rugged mountain[→fig. 1].

With this memory in mind, we travelled here especially for this wind park. We arrived at Viticuso late September 2020. Italy was still in partial COVID-19 lockdown, the landscapes colours were starting to turn as autumn approached. The road to reach the village passing by Cervaro is very panoramic, yet very narrow and it took some time to climb the steep western versants of the mountain. The mountain of Viticuso is called Mount Aquilone (literally Mount *Kite*, 1268 metres high) which is a local antique name for the north-easterly wind. It is the southbound relief of the Mainarde group in the Apennine chain, part of the National Park Abruzzi Latium Molise, the first Italian national park, established in 1928, although the wind farm is not part of the Park. The south-western slopes and the ridges are rugged and have almost no vegetation. There are visible remains of calcar stone paddocks from the traditional silvo-pastoral economy, now playing in composition with the turbines. The north-eastern slopes, on the other hand, are rich in forest. The landscape on this side is a typical high Apennine landscape: cooler slopes enable woodlands climbing up to 1600–1800 metres while dry grasslands, rockeries and calcar-dolomitic walls reach up to 2000 metres (Mount Meta, the Mainarde peak is 2241 metres high). Above 1000 metres, the forest is entirely composed of beech trees (*Fagus sylvatica*) with just a few maples, rowans and ashes in clearances (*Acer pseudoplatanus*, *Sorbus aucuparia* and *Fraxinus excelsior*)[→fig. 5, 6].

The village is set at the border of a small plane, a fertile former lake, where traditionally residents grow crops such as corn, using its flour to prepare a local polenta dish mixed with fresh vegetables and summer herbs. Indeed, the history of Viticuso dates back to the sixth century, the time of the Longobardian domination and it is related to the powerful Abbey of Montecassino. After the Second World War, a great many villagers emigrated to Canada because of the bad economic situation. They were unable to sustain themselves through cattle and forest management and the cultivation of corn and a few other crops in the small plane south of the village[→fig. 2].

That day we decided to stop for lunch in one of the few hotel-restaurants of the village. On the way to the wind farm, we found a hotel called Aquilone, which means kyte—everything here refers to that wind. Some locals were sitting in the bar, the summer was over and the majority of holidaysmakers had left. The owner of the restaurant, an elderly lady named Assunta, welcomed us and reserved the entire lunch room for us. While serving some starters she started a conversation, asking about the reasons of our visit. The lady asked her husband to join the conversation: when Signor Aldo was vice-mayor, now almost 20 years ago, he had been a strong supporter of the wind park project. While she was preparing some wonderful *gnocchi*, Assunta suggested I quickly pop into the town hall, just a few doors down, and ask for Amerigo, the local police officer to obtain the necessary information, included the contact details of Romeo, the well-known caretaker of the wind farm. After lunch we started our walk towards the wind park. When approached from the village, the wind park looks almost like a theatre, the wind turbines are placed in such a way that they are in harmony with the terrain. The turbines crown Mount Aquilone and seem to reach the top of the mountain[→fig. 4]. The wind park was initiated by local entrepreneurs based in Cassino, the EOLO srl,

1

Scale	Local
Landscape	Mountain landscape with dry pastures and beech forest
Year	2002
Source	Wind
Technology	Wind turbines
Power	9 MW
Size	15 wind turbines
Yearly output	Unknown

with strong local support. At a certain point, at the turn of the new millennium, while the village was approaching its 1000th birthday the wind park was seen as a driver of economic development and a means for the village to have an impact on history once again. According to the people we spoke to, the local community is really proud of their wind park, affirming that this is the first and only wind park in the region, and just like for many others European cases (Eggebek, Canales or Zahara de los Atunes in this chapter) it drew attention to the village's history and traditions. The plant was built in 2002 and consists of 15 turbines of 50 metres height, each one with 600 kW capacity amounting to a total output of 9 MW. The spatial qualification is a typical component energy landscape, wind turbines and the maintenance road are the lonely new components of this energy landscapes, while the power line connecting to Viticuso is very small and hidden in the woods and hedges, so you can barely see it → fig. 7.

The temporal component is very dynamic, the 19-year-old turbines will be repowered very soon with more powerful generators, augmenting the capacity with 10 MW. The wind park pays the municipality an annual rent to re-invest in services for recreation and tourism. The wind energy landscape enabled some economic development without compromising other landscape functions, such as pastures or woods. It also enhanced other functions, such as eco-tourism thanks to the construction and maintenance road. This road was made on the footprints of an antique path and is now a popular mountain bike and hiking route → fig. 8.

2

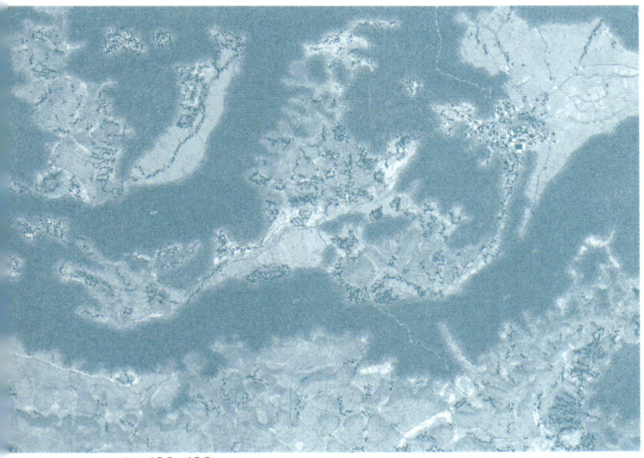

3 → 132–133

4 → 134–135

1 Mount Aquilone and Viticuso wind park seen from the valley along the high speed train line linking Rome to Naples (Photo by Paolo Piccchi).
2 The village of Viticuso with wind fam in the back (Photo credits Regione Lazio).
3 Map of the wind energy landscape in Viticuso.
4 From the road from the village, the wind farm looks like a theatre, a natural coronation of the valley (Photo by Paolo Picchi).

5

6

7

8

5 The eastern terminal of the wind park as seen from the rugged versant of the mountain (Photo by Paolo Picchi).

6 The same turbines emerging from the dense forest on the opposite versant (Photo by Paolo Picchi).

7 The power line serving the village of Viticuso runs along the maintenance road to then go into the woods, climbing a hill and reaching the village from the plane side (Photo by Paolo Picchi).

8 Mountain bikers on the maintenance road of the wind park on the ridge of Mount Aquilone (Photo credit MTBVolturno).

900
1000
1100
1100
1200

900
1000
0
100 m
N↑

Hybrid Energy Landscape in Eggebek, Schleswig-Holstein, Germany

Some early afternoon late September 2019, we were driving from Oslo to Amsterdam in a friend's Tesla, we decided to travel by electric car instead of flying. We were returning from the joint Conference of the European Council of Landscape Architecture Schools (ECLAS) and the University Network for the European Landscape Convention Implementation (UNISCAPE). There, we had presented our research and education on energy landscapes. After crossing the border between Denmark and Germany the landscape was gently undulating along the A7 motorway towards Hamburg. This is a tiny stretch of very windy land between the North Sea and the Baltic Sea. We knew we would cross the municipality of Eggebek, where a hybrid and vast energy landscape has been created at a former airfield: what an intriguing premise. The windiness of those landscapes determined the traditional landscape: parcels with pastures and cereals, lined with pedunculate oaks trees. Eggebek's coat of arms even features such an oak (*Quercus robur*). The village origins date back to the creation of the Romanesque church in the twelfth century. The name *Eggebek* comes from ancient Danish and means the edge on the creek, the creek Treene flowing south of the energy landscape. The community of Eggebek hosted a military airfield that was closed in 2003. The airfield was then opened to the community to use it for a business park, agriculture and silviculture.

Upon arrival in Eggebek, the dominant and recognizable landscape elements indeed turn out to be former airfield hangars emerging from the flat landscape, with green roofs full of blooming flowers. The landscape is a balanced composition of agriculture and energy development →fig. 1, 4.

PV arrays are partly hidden by a hedge with local shrubs such as rosehip (*Rosa canina*), hawthorn (*Crataegus monogyma*), blackthorn (*Prunus spinosa*) and German greenweed (*Genista germanica*) →fig. 1.

Once you climb on top of one of the hangars and stand among the dandelions (*Taraxacum officinale*), you can finally experience this hybrid energy landscape in its full spatial expanse: this blue lake of photovoltaic arrays; the green domes of the biogas plant; the corn fields for biogas; the pastures with cattle; and the wind turbines.

1

Scale	National
Landscape	Partly open landscape lined with trees
Year	2011
Source	Solar, wind and biomass
Technology	Fixed tilt PV, wind turbines, Biogas plant powered by corn
Power	83.5 MW from solar, 20.5 MW from wind, 0.72 MW biogas
Size	130 ha PV panels, 10 wind turbines, 1 biogas plant
Yearly output	917 GWh

2

3 →138–139

4 →140–141

The landscape was very quiet, almost metaphysical. Besides the renewable energy development, the former airfield is now the set of various other local economic activities, but the energy landscape is enclosed by fences and not accessible. Anyhow, we entered to familiarize ourselves with this hybrid energy landscape.

The last 20 years, the windiness of those landscapes resulted in political support for several new wind parks in Schleswig-Holstein. Ten wind turbines were installed east of the airfield area in the early 2000s. Later the community of Eggebek opposed the installation of additional wind turbines in the airfield as they considered it to be too close to the village. Therefore in 2011, they agreed on the construction of a solar park, at that time the largest ever built in Germany. The Eggebek energy landscape has a 100 MW capacity connected to the national grid and provides biogas for local use. It is a hybrid energy landscape composed of wind, solar and biomass energy sources. At the local scale, wind turbines are spatial components of the landscape, not interfering with the agricultural activities, while the vastness and density of the solar arrays make them a spatial entity of the landscape. The temporal scale of wind turbines is relatively dynamic with a lifespan of around 25 years. The solar park can be considered dynamic, as it was simply placed at the location of the former airfield without transforming its infrastructure; the runway, for example, is still there, beneath the arrays.

1 A picture of the combination of hangars, agriculture and renewable energy generation (Photo by Dirk Oudes).
2 The lined hedge between the runway and the parallel service road (Photo by Paolo Picchi).
3 Map of the hybrid energy landscape in Eggebek.
4 Agriculture, hangars and a wind turbine (Photo by Dirk Oudes).

0 100m N↑

Back Home, Enriched by Our Experiences

In December 2021, a wall of the Academy in Amsterdam was full of pictures from the energy landscape we visited. The wall helped us reflect on our trips and what we had learned from them. A very simple anecdotal question came to mind: would you prefer to listen to your favourite music played by an orchestra in a concert hall, together with people sharing the same interest, or would you rather listen to it alone at home, streaming it from some music platform? Indeed, we think that in the former case you can probably learn more from the experience and form a more sophisticated opinion about the concert. Even when you appreciate a single orchestra component, for example the oboe player, you are conscious that the whole orchestra components make the symphonic music. In the same way even when we appreciate the technology as a single landscape element, for example a wind turbine, we are conscious that the whole elements combined constitute the landscape. From our journeys we can deduct at least three important learnings.

The first thing we learned—we beg the pardon of landscape professionals who certainly are aware of this—is the need to *immerse yourself in a landscape* and experience its colours, smells, touch and vistas. Immersing yourself in an energy landscape will change your attitude: fully comprehending the complexity of it will give you a more nuanced perspective on the landscape ontology as an energy landscape and not as a landscape 'degraded' by technology. Indeed, there is a relevant difference between those ontological perspectives. In the first two chapters of the book, we saw how, throughout history, energy development always generated landscapes. Nowadays, some of those are considered cultural landscapes, thanks to decades of studies, people's appreciation and expert opinions. No one, for example, would say the famous Kinderdijk UNESCO World Heritage site is a landscape degraded by windmills. Or take the Hoover Dam: for some this is a national monument, for others this may be a concrete dam that afflicted the natural monument of Colorado valley. To change your perspective on the landscape ontology, you need to immerse yourself and be curious, and let go of preconceived ideas that see the technology not part of the landscape. Indeed the curiosity we felt when we explored these landscapes should be the same when studying a landscape prior to renewable energy developments. Curiosity is the key here: curiosity about the landscape's smallest elements such as a single plant growing at the verge of some street, or a bench that was placed at a certain spot, curiosity about the particular in the *cosmos*, as we mentioned at the beginning of this chapter referring to Humboldt. A good example is our visit to Eggebek. The energy landscape of Eggebek is mostly unknown, there are no references in literature apart from scattered information you can find on a couple of websites. A personal journey to this landscape, an immersion, was the only chance to experience it and understand its ontology.

The second learning is that *we depend on our interpretation of reality*, our worldview and attitude towards the landscape. Critical here is to discuss the landscape with other people, such as locals, travel companions, and experts in the field. To turn the first interpretation into a more solid approximation of reality we largely depend on the exchange of different opinions and experiences about the energy landscape. This is easy to understand for those readers dealing with landscape in their daily practice. Whenever we approach a landscape there is a first interpretation. The way we look at it is influenced by the specific lens we use. Looking at energy landscape, for example, we immediately think that a main function of the landscape is energy generation. When we approach a woodland in the Alps, we look at it through the lenses of timber production and recreation. You could ask if a landscape function like recreation is not very different from that of energy generation or timber production. But we can answer this question with the example of Canales: we were looking for an energy landscape, yet once we arrived, our first interpretation was that of a recreational landscape and only then did we interpret it as an energy landscape as well. As for the aforementioned Alpine woodland, the recreation and production functions did not interfere with each other: we noticed that because we were visiting Canales as a landscape and not just as a rock-fill dam producing a certain amount of energy for Granada.

The third thing we learned is that *we always depend on knowledge,* to understand the landscape. The knowledge can be gained on two distinct levels. The first level is the knowledge you can get by engaging with the local community: having conversations and listening to the stories that locals will be happy to tell you. In support of this learning, we can mention the conversation we had in Viticuso in the Hotel Aquilone. The local residents revealed so much about the ontology of the energy landscapes. At that level you can obtain information that will be hard to find in any publication, such as the real trade-offs, people's desires and specific development challenges. The second level of knowledge comes from studying the local historical development of the landscape, the ecology, the culture and traditions through the existing literature. Here too, we can distinguish between national and international online sources and the sources accessible through no other means than physically going to local libraries and museums. In support of this learning, we can mention the precious information we gathered from the open-air panels of the geothermal museum in Larderello.

These three main learnings from our travel experiences can be projected to future energy landscapes, to better approach their planning and design. Immerse ourselves in the landscape; perceive it in its entirety, without specific lenses; interpret and discuss it as a future energy landscape with local residents and experts. Then gather all the possible knowledge, listening to the stories locals will be happy to tell you, go to the local museums and libraries and then read the literature in the field.

Since communities need to be involved when we design future energy landscapes, curiosity about local knowledge, for example agricultural practices, cherished vistas, and people's stories and activities in their landscape deserve more attention from those working on energy transition. If not, we will keep seeing mayors of coastal towns in the Netherlands opposing offshore wind energy developments, while we learned from Viticuso how the vice-mayor who promoted and sustained the wind farm now 20 years ago still enthusiastically tells that story of the area's new identity. During the COVID-19 pandemic, Viticuso illuminated its wind turbines with the colours of the Italian flag to spread the now world-famous message *andrà tutto bene.* With this, we conclude this chapter and say that indeed we travelled to learn, but at the same time we learned how to travel. Not unimportant, one could argue, as designing is nothing but travelling to the future.

1

Mainstreaming Innovation from Best-practice Solar Landscapes 2.3

DIRK OUDES

INTRODUCTION TO SOLAR DESIGN

In 1983, one of the first ground-mounted photovoltaic (PV) fields was built on Pellworm, one of the German islands in the North Sea. In the past decades, this solar field of not even 5 hectares has been repowered several times. It evolved to a hybrid energy landscape when wind energy and battery storage were added. The site has become a popular tourist attraction and includes a 'solar café'.

While a peculiarity in the 1980s, today the development of fields with PV panels is rapidly becoming a prominent industry. Solar fields are now found in plans of national, regional and local governments to achieve renewable electricity targets and mitigate climate change. This popularity is explained by rapidly declining costs, the modular character and the overall accessibility to solar irradiation. In 2050, up to two-thirds of global electricity production is expected to be provided by PV, with again a share of two-thirds for utility scale: PV on large (non-residential) rooftops, water and land[1]. As part of an industry, land-based solar fields are conceived as *power plants*, where technological and energetic efficiency prevail → fig. 1. The landscape is often merely considered to be the *backdrop* or *décor* for such a development. Consequently, design of solar fields is often limited to mitigation of (perceived) visual impact and / or compensation of habitat loss.

There is however, a substantial legacy with regard to design and solar energy. Already in ancient Chinese, Greece and Roman architecture, street plans, room orientation and the design of the house itself were optimized to enjoy the available warmth in the winter, while keeping the heat at bay in the summer. In the nineteenth century, principles of greenhouse design were transferred to housing by architects such as Humphry Repton. So-called conservatories became glassed-gardens attached to the houses[2]. Fossil fuel abundance took away the urgency of solar architecture, only to be revived by the energy crisis and the environmental movement in the second half of the twentieth century. Today, these movements are reaching their full potential, exemplified by zero-energy design[3]. PV integrated in windows and building facades

1
Breyer, C., Bogdanov, D., Aghahosseini, A., Gulagi, A., Child, M., Oyewo, A. S., Frafan, J., Sadovskaia, K. & Vainikka, P. (2018). Solar photovoltaics demand for the global energy transition in the power sector. Progress in Photovoltaics: Research and Applications, 26(8), p. 505–523.

2
Perlin, J. (2013). Let it shine: the 6,000-year story of solar energy. Novato, California: New World Library.

3
Dobbelsteen, A. van den, Ham, E. van den, Blom, T., Jansen, S., Bokel, R., Broersma, S., Gommans, L. & Fremouw, M. (2021). Zero-energy design. Amsterdam: Boom.

1 Sawmills Solar, United Kingdom (Photo by Dirk Oudes).

are becoming more and more common, with attention for colour, texture, transparency and architectural design. These examples show that for solar energy in urban landscapes, energy performance is balanced with other criteria, such as comfort and aesthetic quality.

Such efforts for solar fields are pale in comparison. To draw away from the dominant technological focus, solar fields in landscapes are often framed as a solar *farm*, a solar *park*, a solar *meadow*, and more recently, solar *garden* and solar *landscape*. Farm, garden or landscape: all terms refer to a concept previously not linked to power plants. Especially the terms park and garden seem to refer to something that is carefully conceived, or *designed,* while this is certainly not always the case for solar fields. The purpose of this framing is to transfer existing connotations carried by the terms garden and park to a solar field. The reality of constructed *solar parks* however, often fall short of the expectations generated by the term. As a consequence, confusion on what a solar field *is* or *can be*, results in confusion between governments, developers and local residents on what a solar field *should be*.

While wind energy landscapes have already drawn the attention of environmental designers since the 1980s[4], people have only begun to study solar fields recently. In a theoretical contribution, Scognamiglio[5] advocates the notion of 'solar landscapes'. In a solar landscape, PV is not *integrated* in the landscape, but rather *designed as landscape*. This chapter aims to expand this thinking on solar landscapes by presenting and reflecting on a number of real-world cases that exhibit early features of solar landscapes. This chapter draws from 20 cases studied and visited over the last years, of which a selection has been analysed and described elsewhere[6, 7].

4
Dobbelsteen, A. van den, Ham, E. van den, Blom, T., Jansen, S., Bokel, R., Broersma, S., Gommans, L. & Fremouw, M. (2021). Zero-energy design. Amsterdam: Boom.

5
Scognamiglio, A. (2016). 'Photovoltaic landscapes': Design and assessment. A critical review for a new transdisciplinary design vision. Renewable and Sustainable Energy Reviews, 55, p. 629–661.

6
Merida-Rodriguez, M., Lobon-Martin, R. & Perles-Rosello, M.-J. (2015). The Production of Solar Photovoltaic Power and Its Landscape Dimension. In M. Frolova, M.-J. Prados, & A. Nadaï (Eds.), Renewable Energies and European Landscapes: Lessons from Southern European Cases. New York: Springer, p. 255–277.

7
Oudes, D., Van den Brink, A. & Stremke, S. (2022). Towards a typology of solar energy landscapes: Mixed-production, nature based and landscape inclusive solar power transitions. Energy Research & Social Science, in press.

SOLAR LANDSCAPES IN EUROPE

When solar fields are designed in close relationship to the host landscape, the solar landscapes that emerge reflect the variety in the characteristics of the individual landscapes. Solar landscapes in urban areas contain functions that address needs of contemporary urban citizens. *Eco solar park 'T Oor* for example, is located on a residual piece of land between road and railroad infrastructure in the city of The Hague (the Netherlands). Here, locals are able to grow food in a permaculture setting and there is a direct supply of electricity to the nearby light rail connection.

In other cases, the characteristics of the host landscapes make it relatively easy to reduce the visibility of the solar infrastructure in the countryside. Notably in the undulating, semi-enclosed English landscapes, solar landscapes such as *Southwick Estate Solar Farm* [→fig. 1] or *Sawmills Solar* are only visible to the attentive observer, despite the high numbers of PV panels. But also in the German *solar park Hemau*, located within a wooded area, the PV panels remain largely inconspicuous [→fig. 2]. Dating from the early 2000s, the wooden support structure of the PV arrays has been built by local farmers. Contrasting these inconspicuous cases, German examples of brownfield reclamations actively proclaim their transformation to solar landscape. These cases are examples of solar infrastructure being used as place branding, aiming to attract a range of other technological, commercial activities. *Energielandschaft Morbach* for example, is a former munition depot that has been transformed to an agglomeration of wind turbines, PV panels and a biomass facility. The site is accessible and visitors

2

3

can book guided tours and go into 'education bunkers' to learn about renewable energy and the history of the site.

In the following, four specific solar landscapes in four different countries will be presented. These cases were selected as all four have a unique setting and narrative, and all received recognition by the environmental design disciplines in the respective countries (either by winning awards or being featured in a magazine). The Dutch solar landscape *De Kwekerij* is located at the edge of a rural village and functions as an actual park. In addition, this solar landscape includes water retention areas and aims to improve local biodiversity. Its innovative character has earned it an honourable mention in a regional spatial quality award competition.

Southill Solar (United Kingdom) won an award from the Landscape Institute for the way it engaged the community in the design of the solar landscape. This cooperative solar landscape is located in an area with substantial aesthetic qualities. The project aims to carefully balance renewable energy provision, ecological restoration and visual qualities.

Solarfeld Gänsdorf (Germany) is a large-scale solar landscape that already in 2009 aimed to be a modern cultural landscape, preserving soil conditions and safeguarding a combination of renewable energy and agricultural function in the future. In 2013, this project won an award from the German Landscape architecture association (BDLA).

Monreale (Italy) aims to bring back the heterogeneity of a landscape mosaic in an otherwise monotonous agricultural landscape. This project aimed to demonstrate that renewable energy can become an integral part of a landscape, together with olive production, an ecological corridor and agriculture. The project was featured in the magazine of the Italian association of landscape architects (AIAPP).

For each case, the general setting is described, followed by its unique characteristic that sets it apart from other cases. After this description, the case is analysed using an existing analytical framework for solar landscapes[6]. This framework consists of the analysis of the landscape patterns and solar infrastructure, visibility, multifunctionality and temporality. The first three are expressed in individual maps, the latter is expressed in the text and shown in the other maps.

2 Southwick Estate Solar Farm, United Kingdom. The semi-enclosed landscape hosting the 48 MW / 83 ha solar landscape is limiting the view on the solar infrastructure, both from further away (this picture) and from up close (Photo by Dirk Oudes).

3 Solar park Hemau (Germany). The former munition depot Hemau was transformed into a solar field in 2002. The enclosed landscape character that made the site suitable for a munition depot also turned out to make it suitable for a solar field (Photo by Frank Stremke).

The Early Adapter

'The monte at Gänsdorf serves as a cultural vista-landmark and its spiral pathway to the top symbolizes the shift from fossil to renewable energies.'

Helmut Wartner, Landscape Architect

1

In the south-eastern corner of Germany, enclosed by Czechia and Austria, the movements of the Danube have created a rich river valley landscape. North of the Danube, the landscape is characterized by alluvial forests and the mountains of the National Park Bavarian Forest that go up to 1000 metres in altitude. The area south of the Danube has been cultivated for agriculture with a large-scale and highly productive landscape as a result → fig. 5. In 2009, the second-largest solar power plant of the world started producing electricity in this landscape. The size of *Solarfeld Gänsdorf*, also called *Strasskirchen Solar Park*, is even roughly similar to the urban area of Strasskirchen, the municipality in which is it largely located. The landowner is a locally well-known entrepreneur who became interested in photovoltaics in an early stage of the energy transition. He immediately seized the opportunity to build the solar power plant when a large agricultural area became available for sale. The solar power plant was meant to produce enough electricity for the entire municipality.

Looking back, this landowner addressed issues in 2009 that are still critical in the development of solar fields: involvement of stakeholders, local financial benefits and a landscape-inclusive design of the solar field. First, local stakeholders and the municipality were included in a very early stage of the project. Because of this early involvement and the position of the entrepreneur in the local community, no objections were raised in the formal planning procedure. Second, local stakeholders were able to participate. Financial participation materialized in a separate 'community part' of the solar landscape. Also the municipality benefitted financially from the solar power plant. The landowner convinced the investors to pay taxes locally. For a small municipality such as Strasskirchen, this resulted in a doubling of their local tax income. Third, the landowner worked together with the landscape architect to develop a solar field different from others at that time. Key in the design is that from the start the perspective has not only been on the production phase, but also on the decommissioning stage. Existing plot borders were respected as much as possible and the landowner developed steel ground screws to support the arrays, to minimize soil disturbance. These measures are meant to keep the soil suitable for agricultural use once the arrays will be decommissioned. The landowner even has more specific plans: in due time, he hopes to convert the site into a combination of agriculture and electricity production: agrivoltaics. In this way, he aims to bring back the practice of strip cropping. Currently, there is a small experimental site that already brings these ideas into practice.

2

The configuration of the PV panels within the existing landscape plots seems strange at first, but at the time of construction, fixed-width arrays were standard. The result is that multiple 'left-over' spaces emerge in the design → fig. 6. These residual spaces are dedicated to ecological improvements → fig. 8. These biodiversity hotspots

3

Name	Solarfeld Gänsdorf
Location	Strasskirchen, Bavaria, Germany
Designer	Helmut Wartner, Wartner & Zeitzler Landschaftsarchitecten bdla (Raum+Zeit)
Nominal power	54 MWp
Size	180,9 ha
Year	2009

consist of a variety of weeds, plants and shrubs to provide a habitat for insects, birds and mammals. The regional authorities monitor the effect of the hotspots and have found that the site is beneficial for breeding birds[8]. The somewhat isolated location amidst large-scale agricultural landscape may limit its full potential, though, for instance for reptiles. In an early stage of the project, an innovative mowing regime was introduced between the PV arrays to improve biodiversity within the fenced area as well. This space was mowed in three stages, from more intensive in front of the panels to extensive at the back of the panels. Due to a change in investors, this more expensive ecological management was stopped. The design clearly offers two ways of experiencing the solar landscape: from the outside and from the inside→fig. 7. The experience from the outside aims to blend the solar infrastructure within the existing landscape and reduce the visibility as much as possible→fig. 1, 2. To this end, the outer perimeter of the solar landscape is planted with a discontinuous hedgerow. The gaps in the hedgerow make the solar infrastructure visible to the keen observer, but for most landscape users, the hedgerow belongs to the existing landscape. A solid hedgerow would have drawn more attention in this landscape type[9, 10]. The scale of the solar landscape and the fact that the plant is spread across multiple agricultural plots allows the landscape user to experience the plant from up close. The existing roads that cut through the solar landscape are flanked by broad vegetative buffers on one side, offering the landscape user a view of the contrast between nature and technology. While walking there, rabbits cross the road and deer use the buffer to traverse the site. Both outside and inside the power plant, the scale of the solar landscape remains hard to grasp. To this end, a small lookout (called: Monte) is located in the south part of the plant, that gives the landscape user a clear view over the entire project→fig. 3.

This innovative approach on a solar power plant was recognized by the German Landscape architecture association BDLA in 2013, when Solarfeld Gänsdorf was awarded the German Landscape architecture award in the category 'Infrastructure and Landscape'. The project is a clear mark in the development of solar fields, moving from energy-optimized systems to solar landscapes. It is, however, not the end point. With the eyes of today, one can easily identify some 'teething troubles' in this early prototype of a solar landscape. The fixed width of the arrays, for example, limited the design possibilities of the solar system layout within the existing plots. Although the residual spaces are used for biodiversity enhancement, the small-sized, sharp-angled plots contrast with the vast and rectangular plots of the river valley landscape. In addition, while the Monte and the roads between the different parts of the plant offer recreational opportunities, the question arises: for whom? The host landscape is largely agricultural, with small rural villages and no nearby recreational routes.

8
Gabriel, M., Scholz, A. & Stierstorfer, C. (2018). Ökologische Evaluierung des Solarfeldes Gänsdorf (Landkreis Straubing-Bogen, Niederbayern), p. 43.

9
Merida-Rodriguez, M., Lobon-Martin, R. & Perles-Rosello, M.-J. (2015). The Production of Solar Photovoltaic Power and Its Landscape Dimension. In M. Frolova, M.-J. Prados, & A. Nadaï (Eds.), Renewable Energies and European Landscapes: Lessons from Southern European Cases. New York: Springer, p. 255–277.

10
Apostol, D., Palmer, J., Pasqualetti, M.J., Smardon, R. & Sullivan, R. (2017). The renewable energy landscape: preserving scenic values in our sustainable future. Abingdon, Oxon: Routledge.

4 →152–153

1 View from the outside: solar infrastructure hardly visible (Photo by Dirk Oudes).
2 View from inside: patch with solar arrays clearly visible together with flowerbeds (Photo by Dirk Oudes).
3 The monte (lookout) provides clear views on the solar landscape (Photo by Dirk Oudes).
4 Overview of Solarfeld Gänsdorf (Photo by Frank Stremke).

5 Host landscape in 2008.

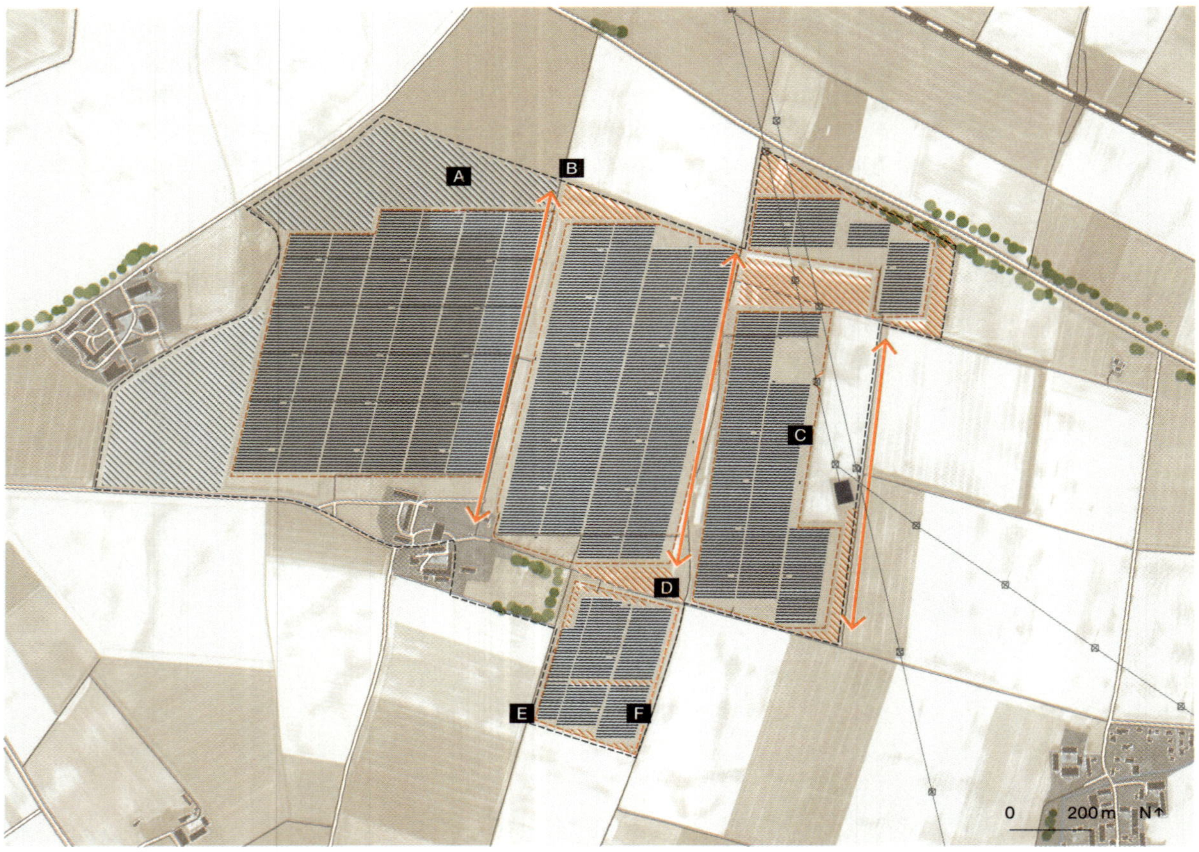

6 Landscape patterns and solar infrastructure of Solarfeld Gänsdorf.

A Original land use function (agriculture) maintained
B Original corridors and most of existing plot structure maintained for future agrivoltaic use
C 5 patches, each consisting of multiple arrays of 100m wide
D Left-over spaces used for additional functions
E Autonomous fence layout creates new (temporary) parcellation
F Seperate patch for community PV system

7 Visibility of Solarfeld Gänsdorf with a clear distinction between inside and outside. From outside, the solar system is hardly visible. Inside the large solar landscape, the PV system is clearly visible from the lookout and between the PV patches.

- A Single clear view from regional road
- B Larger trees planted close to the road
- C Between the patches, on one side a clear view of the PV system. On the other side a contrast between wildflowers and PV system
- D New discontinous hedgerow used for screening. Purpose of hedgerow is to mimic surrounding vegetation structure
- E Monte (lookout): clear views of the solar landscape

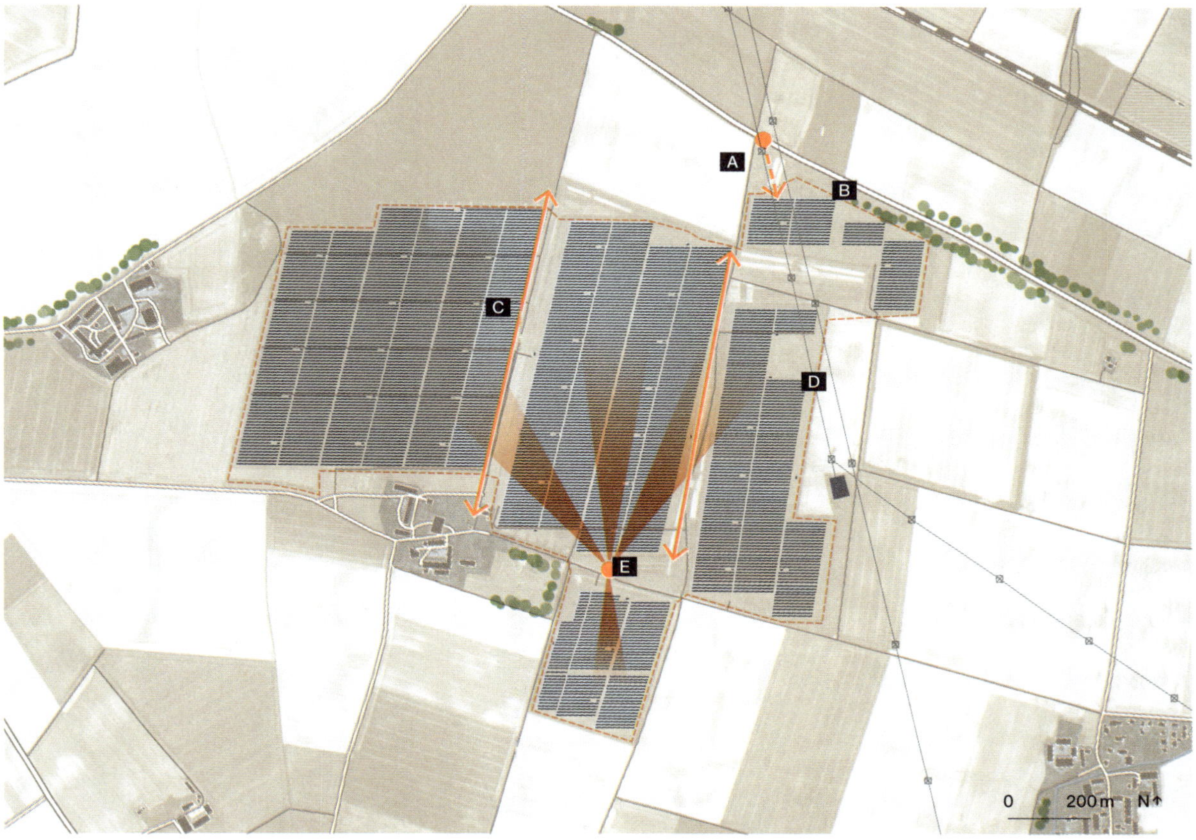

8 Multifunctionality at Solarfeld Gänsdorf.

- A Agricultural land use maintained
- B Wild grassland
- C Bee habitat
- D Fruit orchard
- E Demonstration site agrivoltaico
- F Grassland. Orginally with ecological management, but cancelled when investor changed
- G Monte (lookout)
- H Potential recreational paths. In practice hardly used. Area is not well connected to surrounding recreational network

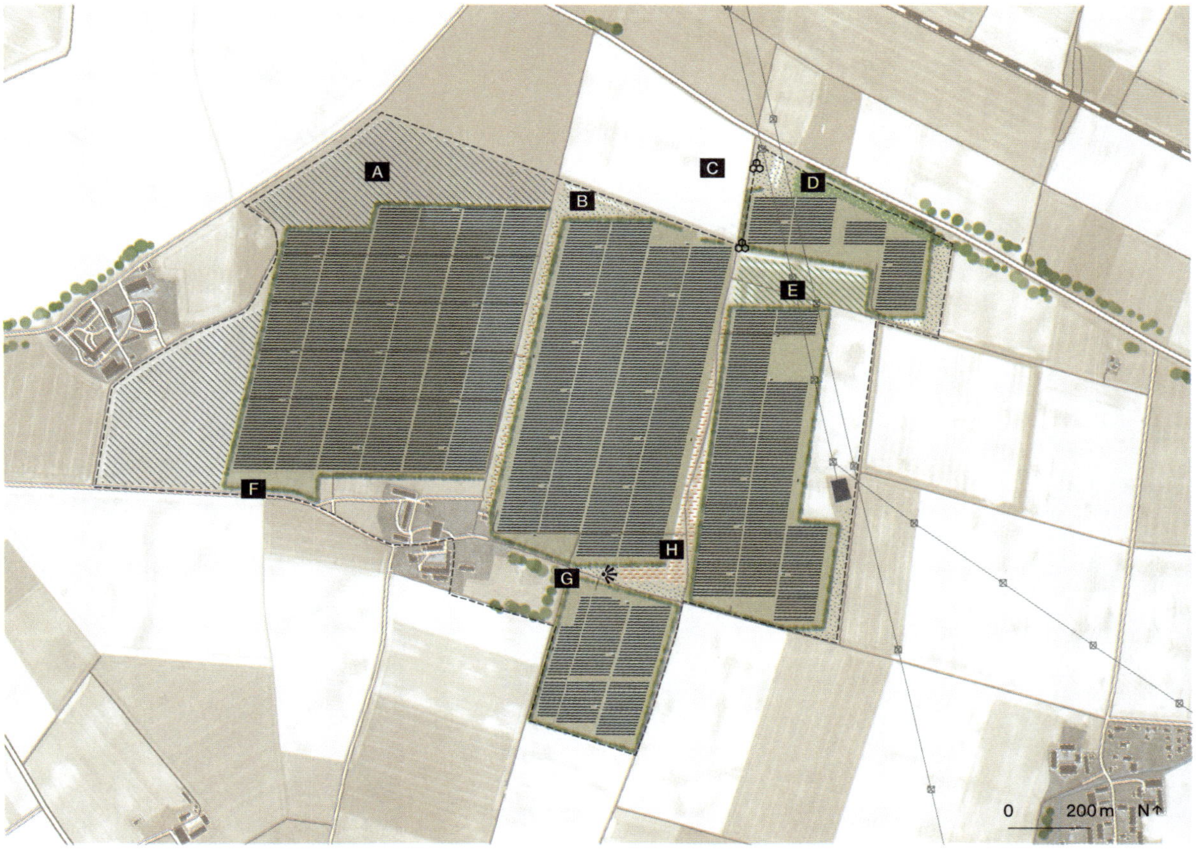

The Demonstration Project

'The idea was to test how a farm can produce extra-virgin olive oil, almonds, recover soil fertility through a permanent grassland, improve the ecological network and biodiversity and produce renewable electricity at the same time. The design recovers agricultural diversity, soil quality and nature in a landscape intensively exploited for cereal cultivation.'

Fabrizio Cembalo, Landscape Architect Progetto Verde

1

The Mediterranean landscape south of Palermo on the island of Sicily, Italy, consists of large-scale homogenous agricultural patches. These patches are organically cut off by so-called *fiumaras*, water lines that are dry in summer and turbulent in winter. The agricultural pattern consists of wheat cultivation, pastures and scattered olive groves → fig. 3. The village of Camporeale is located on a mountain ridge of roughly 500 metres in altitude, accompanied by a linear formation of welded steel lattice wind turbines In the plain 200 metres below, the wind turbines are joined in the provision of renewable energy by *parco fotovoltaico Monreale*. This solar landscape deliberately shares the name of the town 40 kilometres north of the site, famous for its cathedral's Byzantine mosaics, landscape views and mild climate. The site is delineated by a provincial road on the west side and the *fiumara* Ravanusa in the east, in an otherwise sparsely populated area. This pilot project was realized in 2010 by the region and aimed to demonstrate what a contemporary landscape mosaic that included solar energy, agricultural production and ecological restoration could look like. Compared to the previous state of the site, the project increased the spatial heterogeneity by dedicating zones to these functions. In this sense, the realization of the solar landscape was seized to demonstrate the potential of renewable energy as a multifunctional landscape development that could be exemplary for the surrounding region. The outer perimeter of the original agricultural plot remained intact and was further divided into three individual parts: a single-axis tracker solar system, an olive grove and a wet ecological corridor alongside the Ravanusa → fig. 1. The PV system is divided into seven patches of comparable sizes with the transformers located between the patches → fig. 6. The leftover spaces are planted with olive and almond trees → fig. 2, 8. The new olive grove east of the solar system gently slopes towards the Ravanusa, which is enriched with a newly planted riparian woodland. A drainage system beneath the single-axis tracker system collects rainwater and transports it to a water basin. These basins, or *Gebbias*, are typical for Sicily. The collected water is used to water young trees and for emergency irrigation in prolonged dry periods to avoid the loss of olive and other fruit production. A mix of perennials, including legumes capable of nitrogen fixation, was seeded beneath the arrays. This to improve both soil fertility and the pasture for the sheep. Except in the eastern part that contains the ecological corridor, a hedgerow with flowering shrubs was planted alongside the perimeter to increase biodiversity. This hedgerow simultaneously decreases the visibility of the solar infrastructure from the provincial road → fig. 7.

2

Name	Parco fotovoltaico Monreale
Location	Comporeale, Sicily, Italy
Designer	Fabrizio Cembalo Sembiase, Progetto Verde
Nominal power	5 MWp
Size	28 ha
Year	2010

The project is still clearly visible when descending from the village of Camporeale and the solar infrastructure remains clearly visible when one descends over the 5-kilometre-long provincial road towards the project →fig. 3.

This project received national recognition, notably in a special issue on energy of the Italian Association of Landscape Architecture (AIAPP) journal in 2012. The design presents a contemporary Sicilian farm, producing electricity and olive oil, which simultaneously increases the ecological and aesthetic quality of the countryside. Unfortunately, the project also demonstrates a lack of care after the realization and a mismatch in priorities. During the field visit, a decade the solar landscape was realized, carpenters are making sloped roofs on the transformers to match local architecture →fig. 4. In stark contrast with the attention to architecture, roughly half of the olive grove has already died from a shortage of water.

3 →158–159

4

1 The three main components of the design: the ecological corridor (left), the olive grove (middle) and the solar infrastructure (right). The olive grove is currently in poor condition, in the background, a larger sample of olive trees is still alive (Photo by Dirk Oudes).
2 Leftover spaces are planted with olive trees (Photo by Dirk Oudes).
3 Solar landscape 'Monreale' as seen from the nearby village of Camporeale (Photo by Dirk Oudes).
4 Sloped roofs are added to the transformers (Photo by Dirk Oudes).

5 Host landscape in 2006.

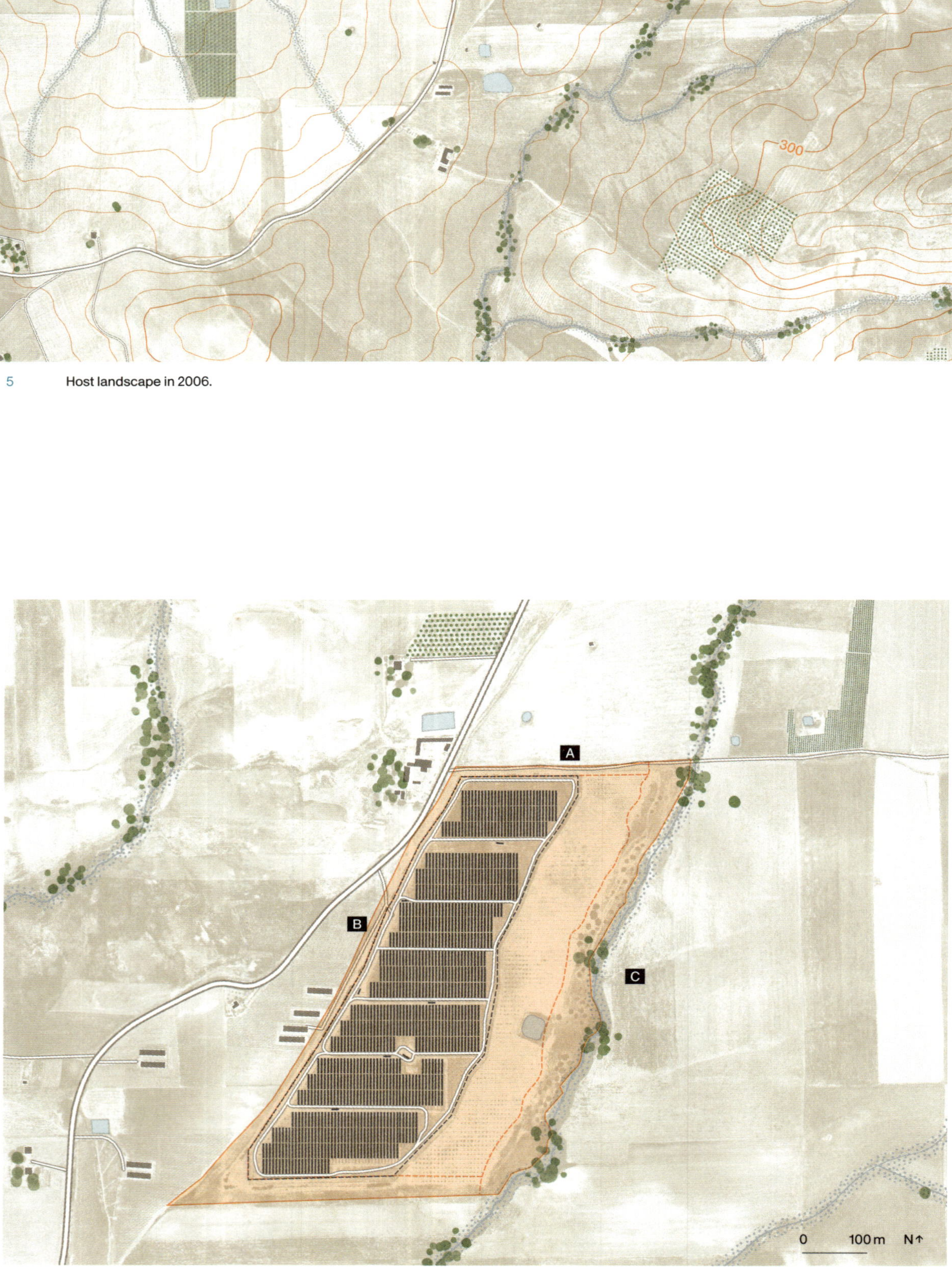

6 Landscape patterns and solar infrastructure of Monreale.

A Original plot
B Seven patches of east-west oriented PV panels. Shape and orientation of patches roughly match with surrounding plots
C Original plot split into four smaller plots with specific functions

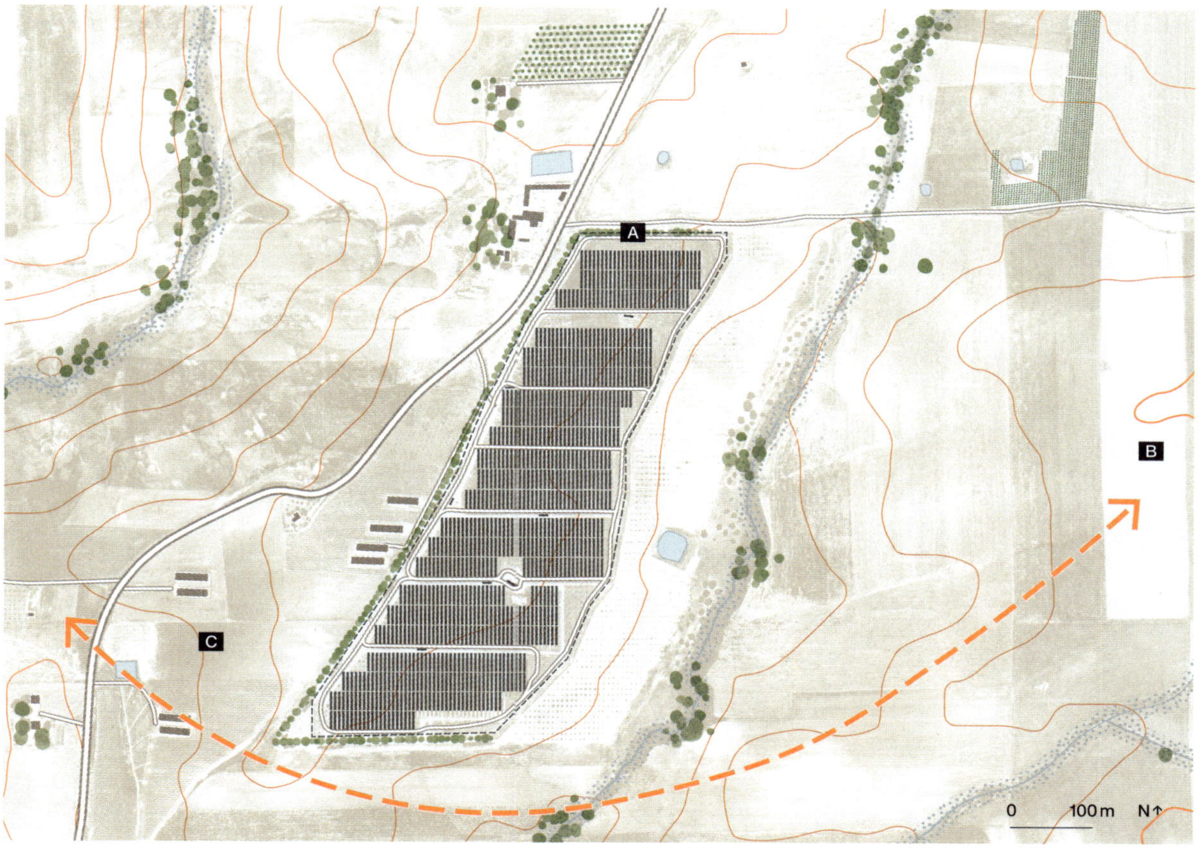

7 Visibility of PV system at Monreale.

A Discontinuous hedgerow to decrease visibility from main road
B Partial visibility from local road (at 1000+ m)
C Natural topography blocks view from main roads

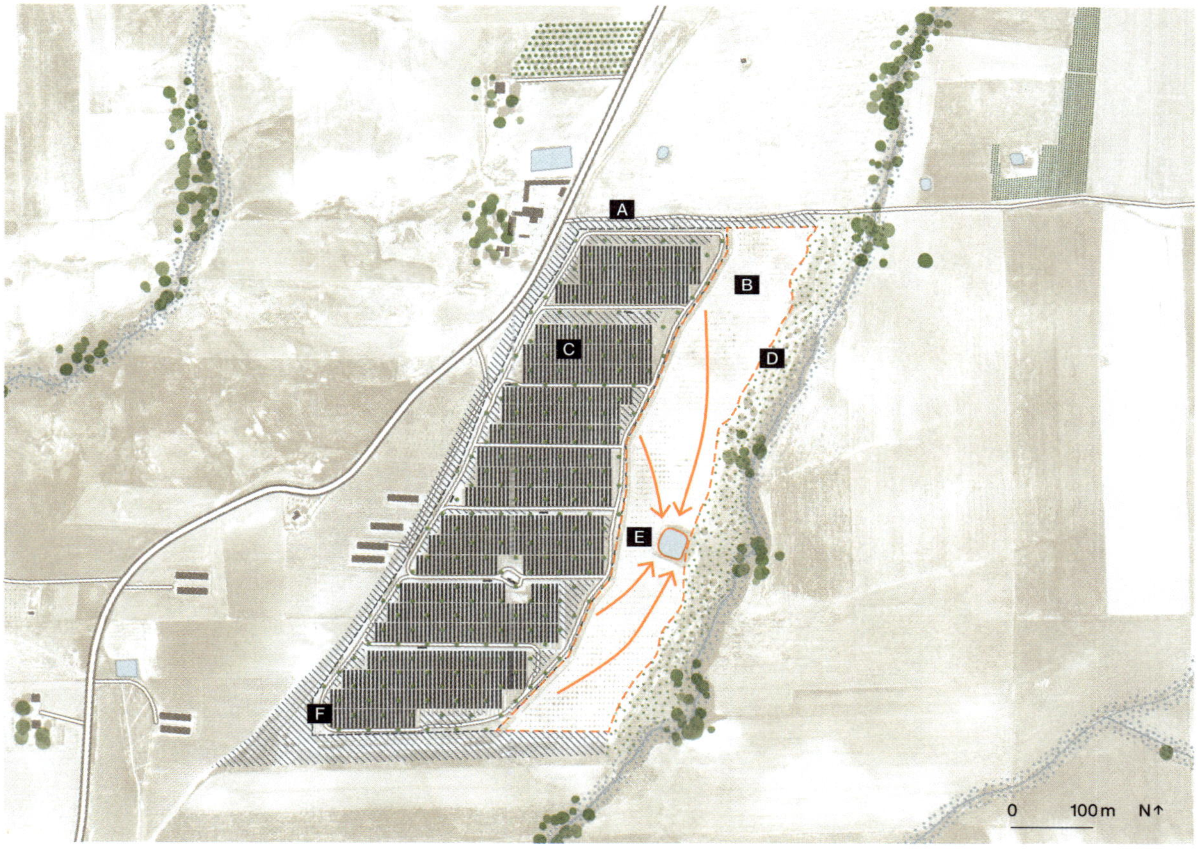

8 Multifunctionality at Monreale.

A Discontinuous hedgerow to decrease visibility from main road
B Olive grove for local olive oil production
C Enhancing soil fertility through mixed herbs seeding
D Enhancing biodiversity in ecological corridor of the Ravanusa
E Collecting rainwater from PV arrays collection in pond
F Enhancing biodversity through shrubs and trees

The Community Solar Landscape

1

> 'The new design that followed the 'Bring Your Brolly Day' addressed the visual impact and expressed community support, resulting in a successful planning application. The explicit community support was probably more important than the visual impact for the successful application.'
>
> Tim Crisp, Director Southill Community Energy

North-west of Oxford, United Kingdom, lies the Cotswolds, a designated area of outstanding beauty (AONB), characterized by small seventeenth-century villages and manor houses in a hilly landscape with medieval estates and ancient forest patches →fig. 3. The yellow Cotswald stone derived from the hills has been used in the low walls separating agricultural land and in local architecture, giving the villages their distinctive character. In 2012, the local sustainability cooperative of the village of Charlbury started a campaign to build a community solar power plant. The cooperative proposed to build on a large linear plot of grassland that undulates towards the river Evenlode, a tributary of the Thames. The people behind this sustainability cooperative had been inspired by a visit to the first UK community solar farm located 40 kilometres (25 miles) south: Westmill Solar farm. The plot of grassland is enclosed between a local road and railroad and consists of two parts, separated by a traditional dry-stone wall. Application for solar power plants usually involves substantial costs, such as for securing a grid connection, the design, and a landscape and visual impact assessment. This community initiative was the first in the United Kingdom to get financial support from the Rural Community Energy Fund to cover part of these initial costs. In the initial design, most of the site was covered with PV arrays in a low density. This planning application however, was refused on the basis of visual impact in the AONB. The cooperative decided to resubmit the planning application. To counter these objections, the sustainability cooperative organized a so-called 'Bring Your Brolly Day' (brolly is another term for umbrella). On this day, more than a hundred local citizens (on a population of less than 3,000) marked various layouts of the power plant with their umbrellas →fig. 1. The linear shape and the undulation towards the river were taken as a basis for a virtual grid on the plots. The surrounding area is rich with footpaths which are actively used. Five photographers were strategically positioned to capture the potential visibility of the panels, represented by the locals with their umbrellas. Once a signal was given, the line of locals moved on to the next line off the grid and the photographers would take another picture. The photographs gave a comprehensive insight into the visibility of the proposed solar power plant. Three design models followed from this event that were discussed during a community meeting. The community then decided to reduce the number of panels (going from 5.5 to 4.5 MWp) and move the PV panels to the lower part of the valley, favouring a lower visual impact over higher financial returns for the community. The well-supported, revised plan convinced the authorities to approve the project. Profits from the solar landscape are directly inserted into local projects that aim to reduce greenhouse gas emissions. For example, almost 70,000 pounds went to the local community centre to improve energy efficient lighting and ventilation.

Name	Southill Solar
Location	South of Charlbury, Oxfordshire, United Kingdom
Designer	Charlie Clews, ClewsLA
Nominal power	4,5 MWp
Size	18,1 ha
Year	2016

Yearly, 10,000–15,000 pounds goes to the implementation of Cotswold Conservation Board's Landscape Management Plan.

In the design, the original agricultural plots have been kept intact →fig. 4. A traditional stone wall separates the plot into roughly two even- sized plots. The shape of the PV system is, in line with the agricultural plot, longitudinal. The original dense hedgerows alongside the railroad and the regional road have been enhanced where gaps would have allowed a visual connection.

The cooperative did not only consider the visual impact, they also aimed to improve the ecological conditions of the site →fig. 6. Over half of the project area has been dedicated to increase biodiversity. The low-grade agricultural land now features nest boxes, a community fruit orchard and a field with sunflowers for wintering birds →fig. 2. The grassland beneath the PV panels, adjacent to the PV panels and the field margins have been seeded with different types of wildflower seeds to provide habitats for a variety of animals →fig. 7. Inspiration was drawn from Westmill Solar, one of the first solar farms in the UK to actively engage with biodiversity improvements alongside electricity production. Such knowledge exchange stresses the significance of capacity building and communities of practices. At some point, Westmill Solar even provided a start-up loan for Southill Solar.

Besides the colourful sign at the entrance →fig. 9, nothing draws the landscape user towards the site. The participatory visual impact assessment helped to carefully design the solar landscape so as to decrease visibility from the surrounding roads and walking paths →fig. 5. Where gaps in the hedgerows existed, they have been planted with new shrubs and in a few years the gaps will have disappeared. The transformer, easily the most conspicuous element of the PV system, has been located at the lowest part of the valley, keeping it almost completely out of sight. Although this solar power plant is not accessible to the general public, local groups help with weeding, harvesting and maintenance of the fruit trees, and other land management activities.

2

1 Bring Your Brolly Day at Southill Solar in 2014. Local residents standing on a line representing a potential layout of the proposed solar power plant (Source: Southill Community Energy).

2 Field providing winter foraging for birds at Southill Solar (Photo by Dirk Oudes).

3 Host landscape in 2012.

4 Landscape patterns and solar infrastructure of Southill Solar.

A Original plot with rare limestone grassland maintained
B Project boundary matches original plot shape
C Limestone wall divides the attenuated plot in two parts
D Shape of PV patch splits the plot along the long side of the plot

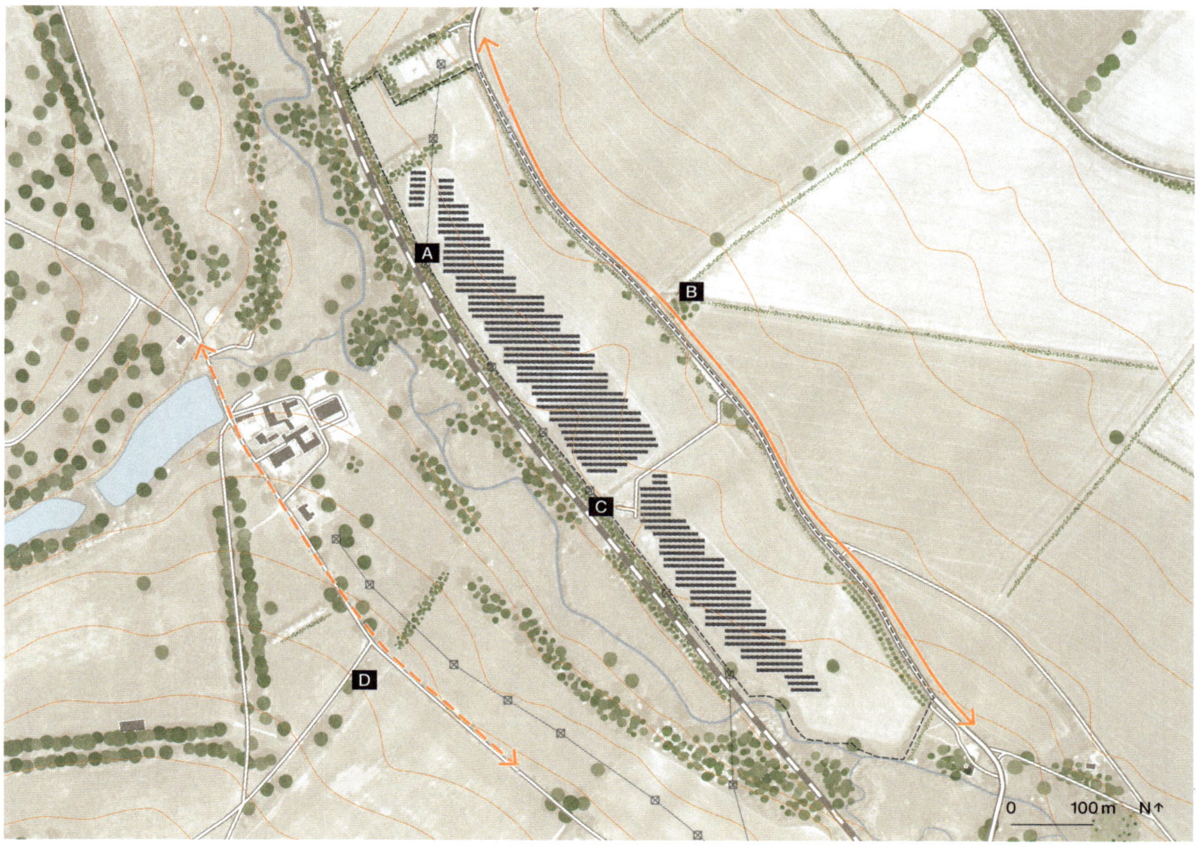

5 Visibility of PV system at Southill Solar.

- A Arrays located in lowest side of the valley
- B Existing vegetation used and enhanced for screening
- C Transformer located in lowest point of the valley
- D Occasional views from footpath

6 Multifunctionality at Southill Solar.

- A Original plot with rare limestone grassland maintained
- B Field margins with tussocky grassland, for nestling bumblebees and ground-nesting birds. Foraging, nesting and refuge for birds, mammals and invertebrates
- C Traditional grazing meadow with fine grasses and wild flowers
- D Community orchard with nuts and fruit trees
- E Pollinator area
- F Area sown with wild bird seed mix for winter foraging

7

7 Large wildflower meadow (Source: Southill Community Energy).
8 The PV panels have been located at the lowest part of the valley, next to the railroad (Photo by Dirk Oudes).
9 The sign at the entrance of Southill Solar (Photo by Dirk Oudes).

8

SOUTHILL SOLAR FARM
SOUTHILL COMMUNITY ENERGY
GENERATING 4.5 MW OF LOCAL GREEN POWER
OWNED & RUN BY THE COMMUNITY
DISTRIBUTING SURPLUS FUNDS TO THE COMMUNITY
PROMOTING NATIVE WILDLIFE AND HABITATS
DEVELOPED BY SOUTHILL COMMUNITY ENERGY
www.southillcommunityenergy.coop

9

The True Solar Park

'Solarpark De Kwekerij combines recreation, play, nature development and sustainable energy generation, creating a unique area for ecology and for people to enjoy. On the basis of these various functions, this solar park may justifiably be called the energy landscape of the future.'

Erik Mol, Policy Advisor municipality Bronckhorst and Co-initiator of Solarpark De Kwekerij

1

While the Netherlands is famous for its rigid and rational polder landscapes, Solarpark De Kwekerij is situated in a bocage landscape. This landscape in the east of the country is characterized by curvy roads with trees, forest patches and small rivers crossing through undulating agricultural patches. Right next to the town of Hengelo, a solar park was constructed that actually includes the key functions of a *park*: an accessible area that allows visitors to stroll, play, relax and meet other people. The financial crisis around the 2010s provided the opportunity for a unique solar park to emerge at a site previously designated for new housing development. There used to be arable fields and a tree nursery (*Kwekerij* in Dutch) here [→fig. 5]. From the start, the designers, the municipality and the developer involved local residents in the development of the site. Even in the operational stage, a group of residents manages the site. The project benefited from this approach when it became clear there were no formal objections in the permit procedure. The low energy density of the park made it difficult to provide an encompassing business case for both *solar* and *park* functions. Ultimately, the park function was legally separated from the photovoltaic panels and financially supported by the regional government. The accessibility of the site is a feature you rarely see in solar landscapes. In the first operational years of De Kwekerij, local residents opened and closed the park on a daily basis, an automated time lock was later installed for this purpose.

The existing arable plots and the tree nursery were aggregated into a single plot to make room for the solar landscape [→fig. 6]. Existing landscape structures, such as parts of the former tree nursery and an existing hedgerow, have been integrated into the design. Most parts of the perimeter have been planted with hedgerows to mimic the hedgerow structure of the surrounding bocage landscape. In contrast with the full panel-coverage of most solar power plants, the almost 7,000 PV panels in De Kwekerij are clustered as small islands. These islands are located in such a way that visitors are able to walk between the panels. This recreational function is a priority: there are also picnic benches, playgrounds and a community gathering space [→fig. 1, 4]. Once inside, the visitor is confronted with a wide spectrum of functions that can be combined with PV panels [→fig. 8]. Across the site, wildflowers, fruit trees and structures for roosting, nesting and hibernating show that another goal of the site is to increase biodiversity [→fig. 3]. Local relief is created for biodiversity purposes, but also to create large retention areas in times of heavy rainfall [→fig. 2].

While the accessibility of the site enables visitors to really experience the PV panels, the experience from outside the site has been dealt with differently [→fig. 7]. Retaining existing vegetation (for instance from the former tree nursery) and lowering the height

2 →170–171

Name	Solarpark De Kwekerij
Location	Hengelo, Gelderland, the Netherlands
Designer	NLGreenlabel (Nico Wissing and Lodewijk Hoekstra)
Nominal power	2 MW
Size	7,1 ha
Year	2016

of the PV arrays closest to surrounding houses reduces the visibility of the panels from outside. The solar landscape is located at the edge of town and is connected to a regional walking path. In that sense it functions as a node in a larger recreational network.

In the short timespan that this solar landscape exists, multiple aspects have changed to accommodate new wishes and updated insights. At first, a small flock of sheep was used for maintenance, but the sheep were relocated after several incidents of sheep getting injured because of the sharp edges of the panels. After a few years a vegetable garden was laid out in the solar landscape, with courses on organic farming for those interested. Such interventions in the operation stage of the solar landscape are possible because the site is accessible and they illustrate the potential of local landscape users to actively shape a solar energy landscape. Over a larger timespan, the panels may be decommissioned and local residents are left with a fully grown public park. Similar to many other solar landscapes with a temporary permit, the actual decommissioning of De Kwekerij as *solar park* and subsequent transformation into a (nature) park is still uncertain.

3

4

1 The solar landscape functions as a public park and community meeting area (Photo by Erik Mol).
2 Entrance to Solarpark De Kwekerij, with a water retention area in front of it (Photo by Erik Mol).
3 Wildflowers at Solarpark De Kwekerij (Photo by Erik Mol).
4 A lookout provides a clear overview of Solarpark de Kwekerij (Photo by Sven Stremke).

5 Host landscape in 2016.

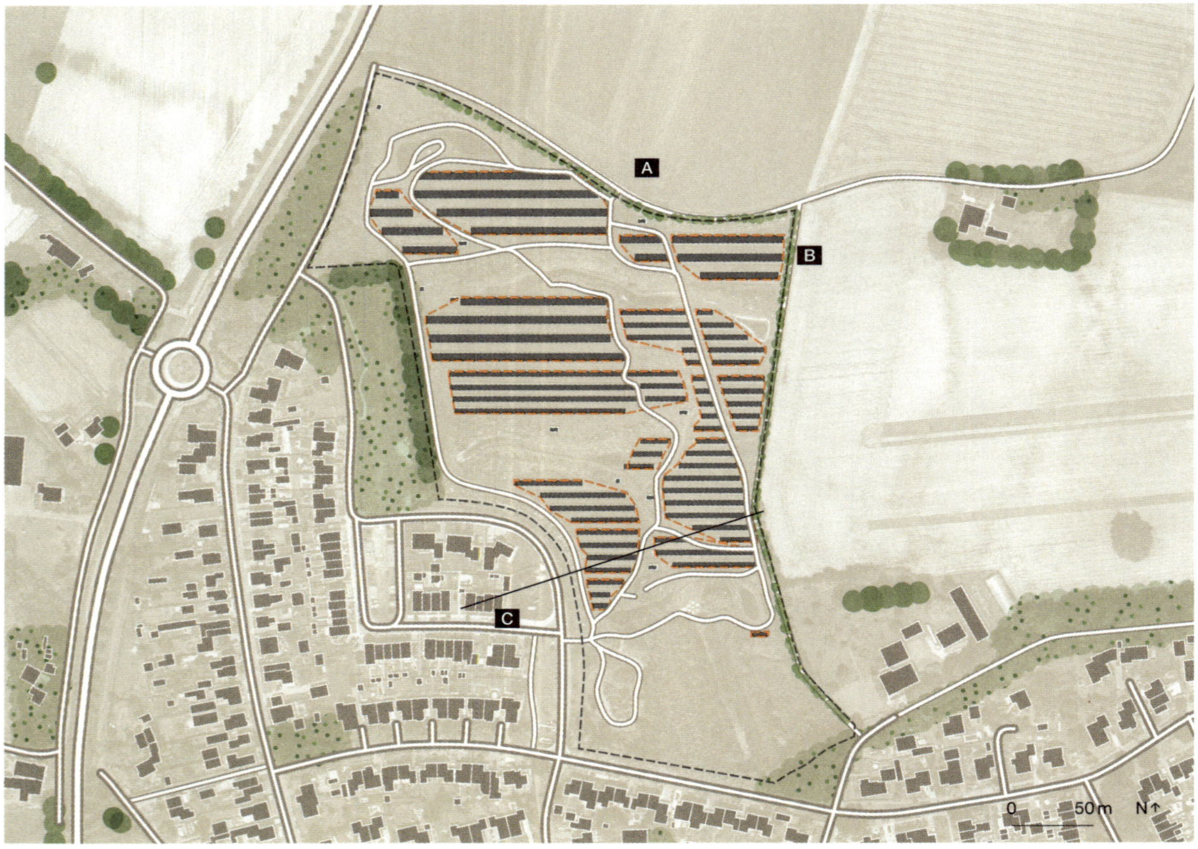

6 Landscape patterns and solar infrastructure at Solarpark De Kwekerij.

A New hedgerow to match surrounding pattern of bocage landscape
B Island configuration of 16 PV patches spread accross the plot, part of the overall 'public park' design
C Two plots of host landscape aggregated in single plot for solar landscape

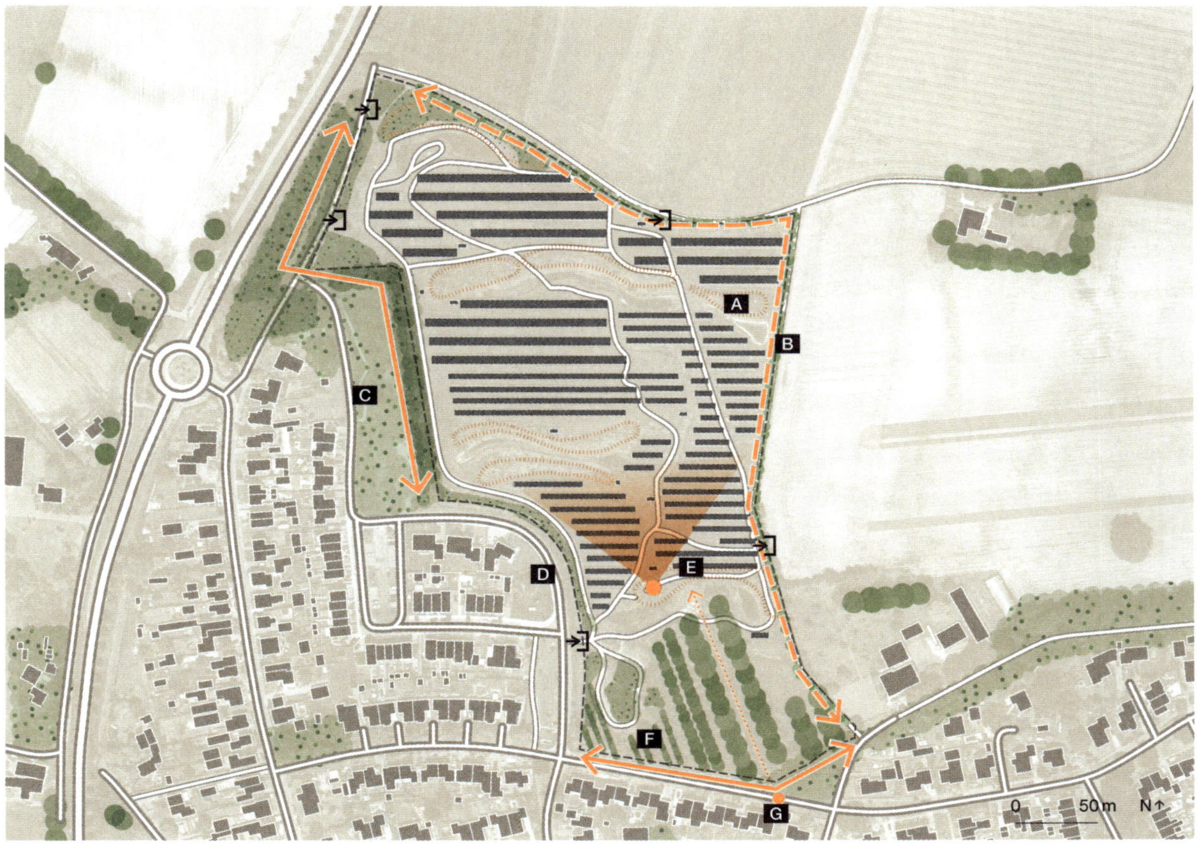

7 Visibility of the PV system at Solarpark De Kwekerij.

A Hills were created to reduce visibility
B New hedgerow used for screening
C Existing trees used for screening
D New hedgerow used for screening
E Artificial hill that gives the visitor an overview of the park
F Old trees of nursery used for screening
G Artificial hill visible, no PV arrays

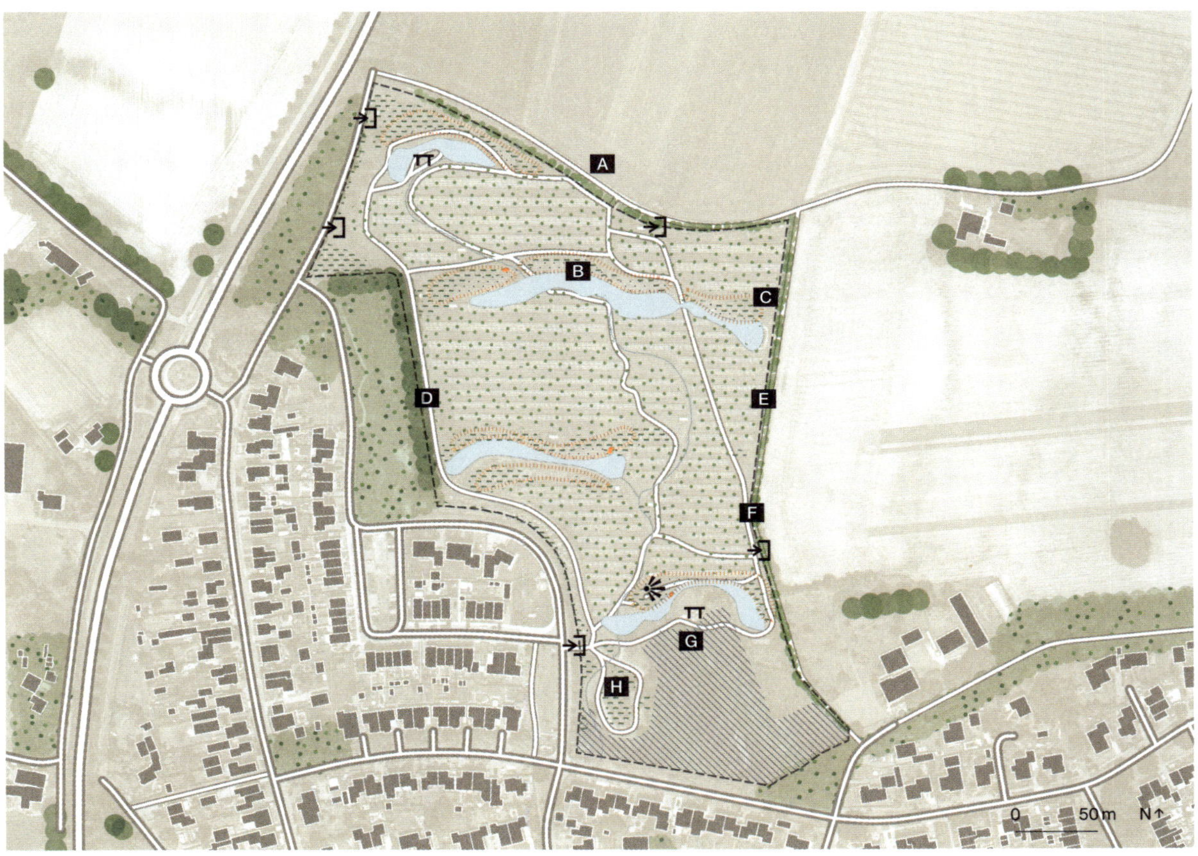

8 Multifunctionality at Solarpark De Kwekerij.

A Hedgerows for screening
B Water retention areas
C Artificial hill with shrubs
D Walking path network
E Hedgerows, wild flower beds, shrubs provide habitats
F Connection to existing network of footpaths
G Multiple locations to meet, eat and relax
H Car parking

1

Solar Landscapes: Understanding Landscapes and their Communities

Euphemisms such as solar park and solar meadow are word tricks at best most of the time, giving people the wrong idea of what to expect. In most instances, landscape users see a field of PV panels optimized for technological performance, generating economic profit and providing renewable energy.

Facing an expected increase in ground-mounted solar fields, landscape users are sceptical about their introduction in everyday landscapes—in many occasions, it means a transformation of the landscape they are accustomed to, no matter what the solar fields are called.

To deal with this landscape transformation—both the physical landscape and how it is experienced—requires a shift in the current conceptualization of solar fields. This chapter illustrated that designing solar fields *as landscapes* does not merely lead to an energy technology *in* a landscape, but to a *solar landscape*: a combined spatial arrangement of solar infrastructure and landscape.

In these solar landscapes, solar infrastructure interacts with existing landscape patterns, PV panels are hidden from view at some points, but highlighted at others, and multiple ecological, recreational or education features are added. Some solar landscapes even work with a timeframe that spans beyond the operation stage of the solar infrastructure: during the lifetime of the PV panels, the site is prepared for use after decommissioning. The presented four cases of 'solar landscapes' were conceived by frontrunner environmental designers, government officials and local communities that took landscape thinking to the world of PV. The cases show that the use of landscape patterns and elements leads to a variety of solar landscapes. The four cases are quite distinct, because they are all grounded in different landscapes and conceived by and for different communities. Genuine efforts to understand 'landscape'—both socially and physically—is thus a necessary first step in conceiving solar landscapes. Without this, the 'design' is easily reduced to the addition of many small, meaningless 'green' elements to solar fields, leading to uniformity across different landscapes.

This variety and site-specific solutions spurs 'local pride'—especially in the community-driven examples (Southill Solar and Solarpark De Kwekerij). These cases were built with no or few local objections and still receive active care as community groups are involved in the maintenance or redesign of the sites. In Solarfeld Gänsdorf and Monreale, the local community was not involved to the same degree and other 'larger players' were in control. In Solarfeld Gänsdorf, this resulted in poor ecological management. For Monreale, the decay of the olive grove indicates a lack of (local) commitment to produce olive oil at the site.

Despite these drawbacks, we must consider that these are only the first in line of a new generation of energy landscapes. New inspiring examples are currently being designed or constructed, hopefully further expanding and exploring the concept of solar landscapes. In many countries, however, there is a tendency to decrease financial support for solar fields, likely resulting in large-scale, economically optimized solar fields. How do we encourage the normalization of solar landscapes, help these become mainstream rather than exceptions? This chapter illustrated the key components of solar landscapes. These components may prove to be a first step for policymakers and decisionmakers to specify what a solar landscape is for *their* landscapes. An

1 Plant diversity and wooden support structure at solar park Hemau, Germany (Photo by Dirk Oudes).

exhaustive answer to this question requires more than best-practice examples. Nonetheless, all cases point out that genuine love for the local landscape is essential, and that a successful solar landscape requires real investment, both financially and in terms of care. This is not a limited nostalgic love for the present-day landscape, a topic further explored in the next chapter. Rather, a love and care for landscapes that are inherently dynamic, ever changing to meet the expectations of tomorrow.

Learning to Change: Climax Thinking and What Comes After

2.3

KATE SHERREN

1

1
Klosterman, C. (2016). What if we're wrong? Thinking about the present as if it were the past. New York: Blue Rider Press.

2
Le Quéré, C., Peters, G.P., Friedlingstein, P., Andrew, R.M., Canadell, J.G., Davis, S.J., Jackson, R.B. & Jones, M.W. (2021). Fossil CO2 emissions in the post-COVID-19 era. Nature Climate Change, 11(3): p. 197–199.

3
Sherren, K. (2021). From climax thinking toward a non-equilibrium approach to public good landscape change. In: Jacquet, J., Haggerty, J. & Theodori, G. (ed.). Energy Impacts: A Multidisciplinary Exploration of North American Energy Development. Logan, Utah: Social Ecology Press & Utah State University Press.

4
Sherren, K., Beckley, T.M., Parkins, J.R., Stedman, R.C., Keilty, K. & Morin, I. (2016). Learning (or living) to love the landscapes of hydroelectricity in Canada: Eliciting local perspectives on the Mactaquac Dam via headpond boat tours. Energy Research & Social Science, 14: p. 102–110.

5
Sayre, N.F. (2017). The politics of scale. Chicago: University of Chicago Press.

6
Elmqvist, T., Folke, Nyström, C.M., Peterson, G., Bengtsson, J., Walker, B. & Norberg, J. (2003). Response diversity, ecosystem change, and resilience. Frontiers in Ecology and the Environment, 1(9): p. 488–494.

7
Raymond, C. M., L. C. Manzo, D. R. Williams, A. Di Masso, and T. von Wirth, Changing senses of place: Navigating global challenges. Cambridge: Cambridge University Press.

Sven Stremke started this book by asking 'What if we were focusing on the wrong things?', echoing pop culture commentator Chuck Klosterman's book *What if we're wrong? Thinking about the present as if it were the past*. Klosterman writes, 'Before we can argue that something we currently appreciate deserves inclusion in the world of tomorrow, we must build that future world within our mind'[1]. But that is not how conversations about energy transition with those affected tend to start. Instead, the current landscape, and the livelihoods and lifestyles it might afford, get a privileged position in any vision of the future. We can all understand the urge to hold onto what is familiar, but if we act on that urge by rejecting local wind turbines or solar farms, it can slow, if not arrest, overall progress toward renewable energy systems. Given the pace of global climate change trajectories, we cannot spare such delays[2].

Since 2016, I have been describing the fallacious way of thinking about landscapes as being in their final or ideal state as 'climax thinking', and arguing for the need to foster a non-equilibrium way of thinking instead[3]. My first observation of this mode of thinking arose in a debate over the future of a hydroelectric dam in New Brunswick, Canada, that was failing early after its 1968 construction → fig. 1: the same families that had opposed the dam's original construction now vociferously opposed its potential removal[4]. My climax language borrows from the unfashionable concept of succession theory in ecology that hypothesized one plant community end point for any given set of conditions. This climax plant community was thought of as an 'equilibrium' state, returned to after disturbance if management was well done. In fact, the capacity of a site to 'bounce back' to that fated equilibrium was an indicator of good management, for instance in setting grazing stocking rates[5]. Since the 1990s, the equilibrium model that dominated ecology since the 1950s and 60s has been overtaken by non-equilibrium thinking that allows for multiple viable landscape futures[6]. Only very recently are we starting to see commensurate shifts in landscape science away from aspirations of stability. For instance, 'sense of place' research is starting to engage with the power dynamics and practicalities associated with normalizing stability in a changing world[7].

1 Mactaquac Beach, near Fredericton, New Brunswick, with the Mactaquac Dam and Generating Station in the background across its headpond. The early failure and potential removal of the Mactaquac Dam sparked controversy among the residents along its 100-km headpond. The houseboat we used for resident focus groups in Sherren et al. (2016) can be seen to left (Photo by the author).

I argue that it is not necessarily a sign of good management when built landscapes stay the same despite changing conditions, needs and / or value systems, or 'bounce back' after disturbance, instead of transitioning to new arrangements. I see climax thinking playing out in the face of a range of proposed sustainability transitions, often by those individuals with the most financial and political power. For instance, shifting to a more compact urban form enables active and public transit, but is often rejected by powerful single-family homeowners in the core who leverage heritage regulation, often with the impact of pushing development instead to peripheral sprawl[8]. Similarly, after big coastal storms in the United States, political careers depend on the speed in which neighbourhoods can be rebuilt and better protected, and it is often those with high property values who tend to be supported to stay put[9]. And in Nantucket, the first USA offshore wind development was opposed most vociferously by wealthy coastal residents, who seemed to be cynically leveraging environmental concern[10].

Support and acceptance are important areas of research in energy transitions contexts[11], but such work may lead to the illusion that options exist beyond large-scale change. The currently unacceptable will eventually become inevitable, but by that time likely also less effective as a solution. As mentioned earlier, social science research into resource management and landscape change has for many years been preoccupied with issues of place and attachment, even though the world is highly mutable and many of its occupants are quite mobile[12]. The status quo is often accepted as an ideal state, against which alternatives must compete. Prospect theory already tells us that's not a fair fight[13]: people are more averse to potential losses than they are attracted to equivalent gains. When making decisions under uncertainty, if people know what they are likely to lose from a change but don't know what they might gain, the potential loss will thus dominate their actions. On this basis, the status quo rarely needs to answer for itself or defend its inclusion in the world of tomorrow.

In situations across the developed world, many of those living near potential renewable energy sites believe they are entitled to landscape stability, and those anchored in fossil fuel-based towns that they are entitled to livelihood stability. The concept of just transitions has arisen to try to support the latter populations in the face of such commodity shifts[14], but the former is a more cosmetic challenge. We are often loathe to erase or overwrite anything for which we or our ancestors have laboured. Anthropogenic features from wooden lighthouses to cleared agricultural land and coal slag heaps are objectively useless when farms and mines are abandoned and navigation digitized, but often have passionate constituencies when change is afoot[15]. We are all capable of this kind of thinking, or 'motivated reasoning'[16], when our stories and cherished landscapes are threatened.

Renewable energy infrastructure must land somewhere, and we haven't got space to keep everything we've ever needed[17]. How do we decide what and where? Theorizing about climax thinking in the context of energy transitions, I hypothesized several causes and potential leverage points to disrupt our default settings[18]. My framework has temporal and spatial dimensions, but the two main drivers seem to be ignorance and exceptionalism. The past temporal dimension of that framework has been empirically un- or counter-productive so far. For instance, I wondered if climax thinking had something to do with a lack of understanding of how much change

8
Poppe, W. & Young, D. (2015). The Politics of Place: Place-making versus Densification in Toronto's Tower Neighbourhoods. International Journal of Urban and Regional Research, 39(3): p. 613–621.

9
Siders, A.R. (2019). Social justice implications of US managed retreat buyout programs. Climatic Change, 152(2): p. 239–257.

10
Marinakos, M. (2012). A mighty wind: the turbulent times of America's first offshore wind farm and the inverse of environmental justice. Earth Jurisprudence & Environmental Justice Journal 2:82.

11
Batel, S. (2020). Research on the social acceptance of renewable energy technologies: Past, present and future. Energy Research & Social Science, 68:101544.

12
Di Masso, A., D. R. Williams, C. M. Raymond, M. Buchecker, B. Degenhardt, P. Devine-Wright, A. Hertzog, M. Lewicka, L. Manzo, A. Shahrad, R. Stedman, L. Verbrugge, and T. von Wirth. (2019). Between fixities and flows: Navigating place attachments in an increasingly mobile world. Journal of Environmental Psychology, 61:125–133.

13
Kahneman, D. (2011). Thinking, fast and slow. New York: Macmillan.

14
Jasanoff, S. (2018). Just transitions: A humble approach to global energy futures. Energy Research & Social Science, 35:11–14.

15
Price, D., Coal cultures: Picturing mining landscapes and communities, (Routledge, 2020).

16
Kahneman, D. (2011). Thinking, fast and slow. New York: Macmillan.

17
Holtorf, C. (2015). Averting loss aversion in cultural heritage. International Journal of Heritage Studies, 21(4):405–421.

18
Sherren, K. (2021). From climax thinking toward a non-equilibrium approach to public good landscape change. In: Jacquet, J., Haggerty, J. & Theodori, G. (ed.). Energy Impacts: A Multidisciplinary Exploration of North American Energy Development. Logan, Utah: Social Ecology Press & Utah State University Press.

2

3

has already happened to a landscape, leading to the misconception that landscape is static. Our first test of this reminded residents of a nearby rural landscape in a survey about some of its previous iterations, but that did not have any impact on the acceptability of further wind energy development in a rural area of Atlantic Canada →fig. 2 [19]. This might be because having hosted the WWII-era Radio Canada International microwave towers for decades made them unconcerned about the impact →fig. 3. In a second test, we asked long-term coastal residents in focus groups to talk about how their landscapes had changed while they had lived there, but this seemed to increase their resistance to changes in the name of climate adaptation rather than decreasing it. Asking residents to recall earlier landscape versions might shift the reference point from which they measure local change backwards. Such a shift might illuminate the net scale of changes that had happened slowly and without them taking much notice (a phenomenon known as shifting baseline syndrome[20], making them averse to losing yet more[21]. It might be the case that better operationalizations of the past dimension could still be useful as a mechanism for understanding and manipulating climax thinking, but my sense for now is that looking backward is not helpful.

The hypothesized future and space-based dimensions of climax thinking have been more productive[22]. For instance, is our inability to conceptualize the future at the heart of climax thinking? Whether that is because we assume that our current landscape solutions will continue to work, or because we simply discount future generations[23]. Or is it an issue of space and privilege? Maybe people believe they cannot or should not have to adapt to landscape change. By finding a landscape change locally unacceptable, those with power can push (or hold) the implications of maintaining their status quo onto those more distant or less powerful. Those more physically, socially or temporally distant people are conveniently also less relatable, reducing our capacity for compassion. To be fair, we may also be unaware that our status quo has any remote impacts. It may be none or all of the above, but it adds up to the fact that when change is coming, we generally don't want it to come to our house.

Empirically, we *have* learned two things about how to move forward. First, we have learned that we need to make energy generation and transmission *more* visible not less, or at least making them *seen* differently and in different contexts (see chapter 2.3), tackling that 'ignorance' driver of climax thinking and shifting the status quo)[24]. The design practice of hiding energy infrastructure has been counter-productive for energy literacy—knowing what energy we rely on and where it comes from[25]. A Canada-wide survey showed that the strongest predictor of support for renewable energy was noticing any kind of existing energy infrastructure: basically, knowing it has and deserves a footprint[26]. Such awareness does not necessarily lead to willingness to bear that imprint, however the wind study mentioned earlier showed that once energy infrastructure was present it became part of what people saw as their local climax conditions—their status quo—making the prospect of more energy infrastructure less disconcerting[27]. In fact, in that work the two strongest predictors of support for energy infrastructure in view of the respondent's home were: 1) agreement that wind turbines provide a useful reminder of personal energy use; and, 2) support for wind energy as an exportable commodity like any other[28]. The latter speaks to a mainstreaming of renewable energy exploitation, putting it on par economically with conventional fuels rather than sidelining it as a

19
Chappell, E.N., Parkins, J.R. & Sherren, K. (2020). Climax thinking, place attachment, and utilitarian landscapes: Implications for wind energy development. Landscape and Urban Planning, 199:103802.

20
Pauly, D. (1995). Anecdotes and the shifting baseline syndrome of fisheries. Trends in ecology & evolution, 10(10): p. 430.

21
Kahneman, D. (2011). Thinking, fast and slow. New York: Macmillan.

22, 23
Sherren, K. (2021). From climax thinking toward a non-equilibrium approach to public good landscape change. In: Jacquet, J., Haggerty, J. & Theodori, G. (ed.). Energy Impacts: A Multidisciplinary Exploration of North American Energy Development. Logan, Utah: Social Ecology Press & Utah State University Press.

24
Linnerud, K., Toney, P., Simonsen, M. & Holden, E. (2019). Does change in ownership affect community attitudes toward renewable energy projects? Evidence of a status quo bias. Energy Policy, 131:1–8.

25
French, D. (2017). When They Hid the Fire: A History of Electricity and Invisible Energy in America. University of Pittsburgh Press.

2 The 14-turbine wind farm on the Tantramar marsh, on the border of New Brunswick and Nova Scotia, Canada, which was built in 2012 just before the nearby removal of a locally cherished WWII-era microwave radio transmission tower assemblage, inspiring the research of Chappell et al. (2020) (Photo by the author).

3 This Radio Canada International transmission tower assemblage was built during WWII to broadcast overseas, and were operational until internet replaced the technology in 2013; the towers were removed in 2014 (Photo: Col n MacKinnon, with permission).

boutique offering. It may be that we could all do with a conscious immersion in our energy landscapes, reflecting on how they affect us and, perhaps more importantly, how they affect others, as demonstrated in chapter *Present-day Energy Landscapes: A Journey through Europe and the United States*.

Second, we have learned that we need to tackle our sense of exceptionalism and learn to share responsibility for the changes we face. This tests our capacity for altruism and compassion for people who live far away or for future generations. For instance, people in China, Colombia and Venezuela supply the coal on which Nova Scotia, my home province in Canada, still largely depends, even though we have coal underfoot (see chapter *The Landscape of Others*, on the social and landscape impact of energy consumption in Europe on her home country of Colombia due to the coal trade). These impacts on people in the countries that supply energy are as invisible to most of us here as the impacts of climate change on future generations. Making this more tangible is admittedly difficult. In those coastal resident focus groups mentioned earlier, we used a wartime mobilization frame to prime discussions about duties to future generations and about the meaning associated with local sacrifices. Those who received this focus group treatment had a decreased climax thinking score in pre-post tests, while they also talked more urgently about the need for personal sacrifice in the face of coastal adaptation[29]. Similar results were found among those who were primed with discussions of duties to future generations. More recently, we were intrigued by local resistance in Nova Scotia to publicly available flood risk mapping, largely due to concerns about real estate value from a vocal few: buyers want it, but sellers do not. We used some climax thinking concepts to explore this phenomenon in a survey. A minority of respondents did oppose such flood risk mapping, citing concern for real estate, and these seemed to be in that climax bubble: they felt that they could not cope with significant landscape change and believed that their decisions would not have implications for others[30]. Even more surprising, however, being a parent did not seem to temper that opposition, despite the fact that their children might someday be in the position of buying property in a risky place as a result. As Krznaric[31] says, we need to learn how to be ‘good ancestors’. Rebecca Solnit[32] argues that we have unmet needs for altruism, but altruism may be a muscle that has atrophied from lack of use.

Since COVID-19 has hit, humbling our trust in the status quo, we hear more about smart recovery and green recovery. But we still think that we can control the climate, the ocean, or pandemics, rather than the other way around. The lessons above suggest some ways we can re-imagine our landscapes for a non-equilibrium future when global conditions are continually flouting expectations (otherwise known as ‘regressing to the tail’)[33]. I’m frankly not confident, however, that my generation or those before mine are going to be motivated to take the necessary steps. When resources and power are bound up in those who have the most to lose, materially, change will always be hard. This, too, has echoes of succession theory: ‘mature ecosystems appropriate more energy for maintenance’[34].

Thanks to older generations, younger generations have known less stability, which is their challenge, but also their superpower: they are thus highly adaptive in the face of uncertainty. Few of them assume or perhaps even aspire to a quality of life equivalent to their parents, and the status quo is being questioned and finally

26
Sherren, K., J. R. Parkins, T. Owen, and M. Terashima. (2019). Does noticing energy infrastructure influence public support for energy development? Evidence from a national survey in Canada. Energy Research & Social Science, 51:176–186.

27
Sherren, K., J. R. Parkins, T. Owen, and M. Terashima. (2019). Does noticing energy infrastructure influence public support for energy development? Evidence from a national survey in Canada. Energy Research & Social Science, 51:176–186.

28
Chappell, E. N., J. R. Parkins, and K. Sherren. (2021). Those who support wind development in view of their home take responsibility for their energy use and that of others: evidence from a multi-scale analysis. Journal of Environmental Policy & Planning, 1–18.

29
Sherren, K., K. Sutton, and E. N. Chappell (submitted). Climax thinking on the coast: a focus group priming experiment with coastal property owners about nature-based adaptation.

30
Howard, S. (2021). Understanding Resistance to Flood Risk Mapping: A Test of Climax Thinking in Southwestern Nova Scotia. Environmental Science, Dalhousie University, Halifax, NS, and online at https://dalspace.library.dal.ca/handle/10222/80416.

31
Krznaric, R. (2020). The good ancestor: how to think long term in a short-term world. Random House.

32
Solnit, R. (2010). A paradise built in hell: The extraordinary communities that arise in disaster. London: Penguin.

33
Flyvbjerg, B. (2020). The law of regression to the tail: How to survive Covid-19, the climate crisis, and other disasters. Environmental Science & Policy, 114:614–618.

34
Stremke, S., and J. Koh. (2010). Ecological Concepts and Strategies with Relevance to Energy-Conscious Spatial Planning and Design. Environment and Planning B: Planning and Design, 37(3):518–532.

asked to answer for itself: colonization, oppression, climate justice, identity. Everything is on the table. It is likely the role of my generation, and those before mine, to foster these new voices and give them more space to operate rather than continually narrowing their future options. We could adopt explicit processes to help us with such 'perspective taking' over space[35] and time[36]. The Long Time Project has 13 practical tools for how to reduce 'short-termism' in our thinking and decision-making processes[36]. Chapters such as *Poets of the Twenty-first-century Cultural Landscape* and *Energy Landscapes as Public Art* show just what these future energy leaders are capable of. Their ideas should help those of us who find it difficult to conceptualize a dramatically different energy future and instead find ourselves perpetuating current options and power dynamics rather than reducing our energy consumption and taking responsibility for it.

35
Ortiz-Riomalo, J.F., Koessler, A.-K. & Engel, S. (2021). Inducing perspective-taking for prosocial behaviour in natural resource management. Journal of Environmental Economics and Management, 102513.

36
The Long Time Project. (2020). The Long Time Tools: Tools to Cultivate Long-termism in Institutions online at https://www.thelongtimeproject.org/: EIT and Climate-KIC.

Imagining Alternative Futures

Poets of the Twenty-first-century Cultural Landscape

3.1

DIRK OUDES, PAOLO PICCHI and SVEN STREMKE

Signatories of the United Nations Climate Agreement from Paris 2015 agreed that global warming will be limited to less than two degrees Celsius compared to the pre-industrial era. In response, the European Union member states decided to reduce their greenhouse gas emissions by 55 per cent in 2030. In the meeting of the European Council on the 20th of June 2019, a large majority of member states embraced climate neutrality by 2050. To reach these objectives, the transition towards renewable energy sources is unavoidable.

Countries pursuing energy transition are currently confronted with two realities: a reality where the urgency of the global climate crises demands a fast and cost-efficient transition towards a zero-carbon energy system, and another reality of where local stakeholders oppose renewable energy projects that fail to engage with landscapes and communities.

Similar to many other countries, the Netherlands must accelerate the implementation of the energy transition in order to comply with international agreements. The National Climate Agreement, signed by more than 100 national stakeholders, renders pathways to reduce greenhouse gas emissions. Within Europe, the Netherlands is one of the countries with the highest population density and the scarcity of space results, in many places, in an eroding support for renewable energy projects. To paraphrase a recent manifesto from the Amsterdam Academy of Architecture: in the Netherlands we need 'more landscape'[1].

1
Kijne, H. (2018). More landscape, the need for a new perspective. Inaugural speech at the Amsterdam Academy of Architecture.

Here, the limited space demands integral and multifunctional solutions, perhaps more than in other countries, conciliating different transitions such as circular agriculture with multiple ecological and cultural objectives of communities for their living environment. Much in line with the European Landscape Convention (article 2), the practice of energy transition needs to engage with landscapes and communities. The great majority of initiatives such as the so-called regional energy strategies, however, continue to pursue energy transition in a sectoral manner, attempting to quantify the impact of this unpresented implementation of renewable energy rather than identifying utterly needed integral and multifunctional solutions.

1

2

2
Figueiredo, S. (2022). Spaces of resistance: the seeds of a renewed architecture culture. Archined, https://www.archined.nl/2022/04/spaces-of-resistance-the-seeds-ofa-renewed-architecture-culture/.

The development of wind turbines and solar fields, with few exceptions, is seen as an accounting problem instead of a socio-economic driver of spatial transformation and, potentially, cultural expression. This aligns with recent critique on Dutch 'architecture culture' that states market thinking stands in the way of a 'mindful relation to our built environment'[2]. The current discourse on energy transition revolves around economic feasibility, technological efficiency, and in some instances democratic legitimacy and preservation of our current living environments. These aspects, of course, are important to achieve climate neutrality. At the same time, they often lead to what we call 'analysis paralysis': progress in transitioning to renewable sources is hampered by the conviction that the status quo of our lifestyles and the landscapes that emerge from this way of living can be maintained.

This is an expression of what Roman Krznaric calls 'the tyranny of the now': The focus on the present at the expense of thinking about the future. His main message is that we should start behaving like 'good ancestors', giving future generations a voice and start thinking about the future again in images. In chapter 2.4 Kate Sherren poses the following relevant question: 'is our inability to conceptualize the future at the heart of climax thinking, whether that is assuming that our current landscape solutions will continue to work, or simply discounting future generations?' In line with the European Landscape Convention, we consider *landscapes* to be dynamic and *landscape design* to provide the common ground for both today's and future generations to discuss imminent sustainable transformations.

To mitigate the current paralysis of thinking in the present, to start educating and cultivating the discourse on imagination, we selected ten renewable energy related projects of talented young designers. All projects aim at carbon neutrality, exploring novel narratives for the future landscape of 2050. The designers studied either at Wageningen University or the Amsterdam Academy of Architecture, both in the Netherlands. While the designers come from many different countries, the projects are all located in the Netherlands. Based on the work of the young designers we explore three questions. First, we consider *who* these designers are. Not so much the designers personally, but what role they play in thinking about our future landscape. Second, we show the potential of *what* can be achieved if landscape is acknowledged as a fully-fledged part of the puzzle we call energy transition. Third, we illustrate *how* the energy transition entails much more than a change in energy sources and, because of that, can potentially count on more support in society. Can the two seemingly diverging realities—global urgency and local transformation—be reconciled?

WHAT ROLE DO DESIGNERS PLAY IN THINKING ABOUT OUR FUTURE LANDSCAPE?

The global energy transition requires local action. Realizing the energy transition without shifting the responsibility to other places or future generations requires many skills. In chapter 9 of his book *Poetics*, Aristotle points to the pivotal importance of historians and poets: historians use the *past* to better understand and interpret the *present*. Poets use the poem as a means of communicating about the *future*. Environmental design is one of the disciplines that need to connect past, present and future. In our teaching we therefore encourage environmental designers to become

1 A productive landscape that reveals energy provision combined with extensive agriculture and water retention (Source: Vincent Peters).
2 A sandy flat submarine landscape increases biodiversity and marine life by using well-designed wind turbine foundations (Source: Ziega van den Berk).

both historians and poets: this allows them to design the next generation of energy landscapes in strong connection with the past.

As *historians*, the energy transition requires designers to be sensitive to the characteristics and qualities of a place, of a landscape. A landscape is not only an area with all kinds of physical characteristics (open, enclosed, orthogonal, organic et cetera), but also an area to which people assign meanings and from which they partly derive their identity. The French landscape architect Bernard Lassus invites us to adopt an inventive approach to enhance our sensitivity, or 'going beyond first ignorance, with its feelings of absence or disorganized accumulations, in order to approach the site in its singularity' (1998, p. 57)[3] to read landscape layers in search of hidden or lost meanings. Such a view on landscape calls for the right of local landscape users to be engaged in the development of their direct living environment. Their landscape, although often not expressed in property rights, needs to be understood, especially in large-scale landscape transformations following from the energy transition. We noticed that young designers increasingly study and immerse themselves in landscapes, to understand how people appreciate their living environment. On land and offshore, designers and other professionals need to conceive ways of including the preferences of those who are not present at participatory workshops, because they are too young, can't join or haven't been born yet.

3
Figueiredo, S. (2022). Spaces of resistance: the seeds of a renewed architecture culture. Archined, https://www.archined.nl/2022/04/spaces-of-resistance-the-seeds-ofa-renewed-architecture-culture/

Vincent Peters investigated this in his graduation project *Recycling Energy Landscapes*, in which he uses the phasing out of natural gas extraction in the Netherlands to recycle fossil energy landscapes in the province of Groningen into landscapes with space for renewable energy, food production and water storage. His design is partly the result of an in-depth socio-spatial analysis of the meaning of natural gas extraction for locals and their landscapes →fig. 1.

Ziega van den Berk studied the qualities and characteristics of a landscape where residents do not easily get involved in the debate. In her project *Doggerland—the nursery of the North Sea*, she gives a voice to the underwater life in the ocean. From the design of the turbine foundations to the layout of the entire wind farm, stimulating the growth of marine life and boosting local biodiversity was central →fig. 2.

As *poets*, designers need to broaden the solution space of stakeholders and take them along to possible futures. Common technologies such as wind turbines and photovoltaic panels are highly industrial and standardized in nature, making it vital to come up with creative solutions. Alain de Botton, in his book *The Pleasures and Sorrows of Work* (2008), argues that we need creativity to change our current *opinion* about landscapes. He draws a comparison with the way in which sixteenth- and seventeenth-century Dutch and Flemish landscape painters influenced the appreciation for traditional windmills. Note that early windmills were denounced by the church and sometimes even set on fire by suspicious inhabitants. Now more than ever, there is a need for new narratives and inspiring examples that transform our aesthetic experience. In the twenty-first century this is no longer achieved by the work of a solitary painter with a white canvas, but by actively listening, questioning, and sketching among the great many different landscape users.

In his project *Not just another solar field*, Florian Becker shows how this can work in practice. His design research was part of an ongoing project to transform a former

3

4

5

waste dump in Mastwijk near the city of Utrecht. Together with a group of local residents, the landowner and initiator, he studied the redevelopment of the waste dump into a publicly accessible 'energy garden' for the local community →fig. 3.

Environmental designers work as historians and poets of the future, together with local communities, investors, farmers and all the required professionals as *good ancestors* of the twenty-first century.

WHAT NEEDS TO BE DESIGNED?

From the *who* we now look at the *what*. What needs to be designed? We argue nothing less than that the energy transition offers an opportunity to develop the cultural landscapes of the twenty-first century, expressing new responsibilities (including the climate), regained ownership and local pride. Please remember that many of the now famous European cultural landscapes were created with primarily economic and productive objectives. Think of the Kinderdijk energy landscape in the Netherlands, but also more anonymous, everyday landscapes that we now also appreciate for their beauty. Over time, we have started to view and appreciate these landscapes differently, sometimes even giving them the status of UNESCO World Heritage. We must therefore, together, join in the quest for the cultural landscape of the twenty-first century.

The project *The power of algae and insects* by Lieke Jildou de Jong is a good example of what the cultural landscape of the twenty-first century could look like. With insect farms in the dairy barns, 90 per cent of the pastures in the Groene Hart region in the west of the Netherlands become available for nature development, while the produced nutritional value remains the same. She proposes to use the remaining 10 per cent for renewable energy production in combination with soil restoration →fig. 4.

While creating a design takes relatively little time, (re)appraisal of cultural landscapes may take centuries to become part of culture. Time that is absent in the current climate crisis. Yet, time can be key in the development of energy landscapes. The relatively short (economic and technical) lifespan of for example solar- and wind energy technology provides opportunities as well, although not in the popular idea that these energy landscape become obsolete after 25 years. Renewable energy landscapes bring long-term strategies and short-term adaptations together. In the long term, energy landscapes can support natural processes that require time.

The project *Upgrade the polder* by Philippe Alignet is a good example of how renewable energy enables long-term strategies that support, in this specific case, soil formation. The young designer addresses the problem of soil subsidence in a rural polder landscape of the Lopikerwaard, in the province of Utrecht. Solar energy and thermal energy from the existing water bodies provide farmers with the financial leverage to realize soil formation: crop rotation includes resting part of the arable and pasture plots so that soil can be formed thanks to a hydrosere process (the process of open water turning into land through plant succession stages). Mobile photovoltaic arrays are part of the rotation and are placed in the resting plots →fig. 5.

Future generations will benefit from earlier decisions with high-quality landscapes as their outcome. On the short term, the lifespan of approximately 25 years offers the opportunity for each generation of landscape users to co-shape their landscape. Yingzi Wang makes this tangible in her project *Circular Urban Energy Park* for

3 Model of an energy garden information panel (Source: Florian Becker).

4 Algae farm in the peat landscape of the Lopikerwaard, a polder situated in the Groene Hart region, in the west of the Netherlands (Source: Lieke Jildou de Jong).

5 A conceptual landscape section showing the hydrosere process for soil formation and carbon capture (Source: Philippe Alignet).

6

7

an urban energy park in Amsterdam, part of a redevelopment of the former coal-fired power plant Hemwegcentrale. She proposes a staged development of the area using straightforward elevated structures with PV panels as a modern *tetris* to transform the area through time from energy park to urban park →fig. 6.

These examples show that the energy transition is an opportunity for decision- and policymakers to enable a societal transformation process. For environmental design practice, research and education, the energy transition provides an opportunity to develop a coherent approach, perhaps even a distinct *style*, to give rise to the cultural landscapes of the twenty-first century.

HOW CAN ENERGY TRANSITION CONTRIBUTE TO THE CREATION OF NEW CULTURAL LANDSCAPES?

Finally, we would like to consider the question of *how* energy transition can contribute to the creation of new cultural landscapes; which design attitude is needed for this? At the moment, the technology (for example solar panels) and the location (the landscape) are seen as two separate units: a solar field has an effect on the existing landscape and these are mitigated in order to comply with a set of standards. The danger of such an attitude, despite the efforts to maintain the status quo, is that landscape quality slowly diminishes. A new hedgerow may partly conceal a new solar park, but cannot conceal that the overall landscape quality, in the eyes of many, will decrease.

Although the focus on financial feasibility and current legislation are useful, they sometimes cloud the vision on the future of our landscapes. A larger solution space is needed to conceive the twenty-first-century cultural landscape, like the examples of the young designers illustrated. Technology and landscape should no longer be considered as two separate entities, but rather regarded as a whole: a *complete landscape*, to recall Sylvia Crowe mentioned earlier in chapter 1.4, or an *energy landscape in its entirety* as we experienced in journeys described in chapter 2.2. This holistic and integrative attitude provides the opportunity to interweave the different landscape layers, beyond the present-day instruments like buffer zones and smell circles that 'guide' landscape transformations. Creating synergies between *different functions*, paying attention to *landscape experience* and *time* are all means to improve the quality of a landscape.

Instead of *impact mitigation*, the emphasis then lies on *value creation*. This value creation starts with reasoning from the living environment and looks at how renewable energy can contribute to this environment. Locations are not selected because the *lowest possible negative impact* can be expected there, but because the *highest possible value* can be realized. The choice of technology, precise location and design is a result of existing and desired future spatial quality, and not the other way around.

Thinking in terms of landscape quality is not only at the heart of the European Landscape Convention (article 2), but has a long tradition in the Netherlands. Here, the concept of spatial quality is often divided into functional value, experiential value and future value. In the National Climate Agreement of the Netherlands (2019), striving for spatial quality is one of the 'spatial principles'. However noteworthy and important that is, the concept is yet to be operationalized for energy transition.

6 Artist impression on the elevated PV structures designed by Yingzi Wang (Source: Yingzi Wang).
7 Artist impression of the new island (Source: Changsoon Choi).

8

9

The project *The Blue Heart* of Changsoon Choi explores the *functional values* of an artificial island off the coast of South Holland. The island functions as coastal protection, provides energy for the city of Amsterdam and creates new habitats for seals. The location of the island is determined so it can function as an ecological stepping stone between the west-coast of the Netherlands and the Waddenzee, located to the north → fig. 7.

In the project *Land of succession*, Hester Koelman proposes to transform the Lopikerwaard landscape (Utrecht) with 30.000 oscillating vertical axis wind turbines that confer to the landscape a captivating structure and perception: they form a new grid, contrasting with the current polder structure → fig. 8. Urbanites can adopt their own turbine—capable of generating power for ten households—and use the polder as a recreational natural landscape. With this project, Hester studied an alternative way of increasing the *experiential value* of the twenty-first-century cultural landscape.

In the project *Solar Archipelago*, David de Boer investigates the *future value* of energy landscapes. He proposes to use the support structure of PV panels to create new islands in the IJmeer, north of Amsterdam. Solar energy is used to initiate the process of hydrosere and create hotspots for biodiversity and leisure. In time, the PV panels will be removed, allowing biotopes to settle and the panels to initiate a consecutive process of hydrosere in another place → fig. 9.

ILLEGAL, UNREALISTIC AND NOT SUPPORTED BY LOCAL STAKEHOLDERS?

The change in thinking we outline here, exemplified by the projects of young designers, may at first sight seem illegal, unfeasible, and possibly not supported by local stakeholders. The project of Philippe Alignet, for example, makes use of mobile units of photovoltaic electricity generation that rotate in time through the landscape. Alternating use of land for electricity (industrial land use) or food production (agricultural land use) is problematic in current legislation. We start seeing this policy challenge in the current debate about agriphotovoltaic systems. Ziega van den Berk proposes to create a rich variety of turbine foundations with local material in order to create a richer marine life. This proposal does not align with the current practice in the offshore industry that benefits from standardization. Lieke Jildou de Jong explores insect farms as a spatially more efficient form of food production. Yet at this moment, the societal demand for food made from insects is not great enough to justify such a landscape transformation.

The *value creation approach* proposed here is developed in response to the earlier mentioned *tyranny of the now*. The young designers show that thinking as *good ancestors* generates new ideas, inspiration and added value and go beyond standard solutions characterized by immediate feasibility and lowest financial costs.

Fortunately, we see that some of the ideas proposed by the young designers are already feasible, but not yet widespread. Think for example about the advanced radar systems on wind turbine 'De Ambtenaar' in the Dutch Wieringermeer. The turbine stops when large birds approach. Financial revenues of renewable energy projects are, as we speak, being used to create added value in some virtuous European cases. In Güssing (Austria) for example, biomass generation enables a sustainable form of cooperative forest management. Or in Sasso di Castalda, Basilicata, Italy, where financial

8 The value creation in Hester Koelman's design: the energy landscape new grid, contrasting with the current polder structure increases the landscape experiential value (Source: Hester Koelman).

9 The value creation in David de Boer's design: the PV structures start a process of soil sedimentation and natural habitat creation between the rows and the resulting landscape can be used for recreation (Source: David de Boer).

revenues from sun, wind and hydropower were used to realize a spectacular suspension bridge. Here, the community invites visitors to have a spectacular experience of the (energy) landscape from the bridge: "go for the landscape"[4].

When designing for *value creation*, the central point of departure is not so much the acceptance of a certain intervention, but the possibility for stakeholders to name and influence the qualities of their living environment. Shaping the heritage of the future together. A thinking framework such as landscape quality may be of help here: no top-down assessment, but a locally supported, coherent vision of spatial quality. This approach of energy landscapes helps to create places embraced by local communities.

In conclusion, we see young poets who bring new energy landscapes to life. Energy landscapes that may currently still be illegal, technically unfeasible and partly shaped without fully-fledged participation processes. In doing so, these designers oppose current practices where wind turbines and solar fields are realized through difficult and sometimes even painful processes, trying to mitigate adverse impact as much as possible. What is the effect for us and many other landscape users? We look the other way.

The alternative approach proposed by these young designers focuses on *value creation*. This approach, time and again, encounters resistance. Opponents might claim *what you are doing is not allowed,* or ask *who's going to pay for all this*? We argue that it is up to the *young generation* to break through this first reflex, to experiment, to learn from mistakes, and thus start to behave like good ancestors: contributing to the creation of the twenty-first-century cultural landscapes.

4
See the official video https://www.youtube.com/watch?v=793fMp4ojCc, and website http://www.pontetibetanosassodicastalda.com/

Energy Landscapes as Public Art

3.2

ELIZABETH MONOIAN and ROBERT FERRY

The common conception of power plants is that they should be segregated away from the surrounding landscape and public access because they are dangerous or toxic. This notion is mostly true for the power plants of the twentieth century, predominantly driven by dirty fossil fuels or radioactive materials. These kinds of power plants are noisy, polluting, ugly, and bad for public health. All of this is changing in the twenty-first century. Renewable forms of energy like distributed solar and wind do not pollute the surrounding landscape with hazardous fumes or toxic waste. By their nature, they can co-exist nearby or within different living environments. This simple distinction between old and new forms of energy provides an historic opportunity. For, as we integrate energy production into our daily landscapes the transition to carbon-free energy will begin to provide numerous social co-benefits. These benefits include energy democracy—placing people in control of the energy they generate and consume without reliance on centralized institutions and regulated monopolies.

Decentralized energy solutions such as community solar canopies can provide enhancements to the built environment by reducing urban heat island effects, collecting rainwater, and providing shade and shelter for public parks, river walks, reservoirs, markets, bus stops, parking lots, urban farms, and many other places around the city while enhancing urban landscapes. When designed well, city-integrated solar energy landscapes have the potential to be creative placemaking tools that support economic development and quality of life. Distributed renewable energy can improve local landscape identities while providing opportunities for new works of regenerative public art that use clean technologies as media for creative expression, giving back clean kilowatt-hours along with transformational human experiences.

Lastly, the co-benefits of distributed renewable energy landscapes include the conservation of cultural and ecological values. Placing energy generation near to the places where energy is consumed reduces the need for high-voltage transmission corridors and eases the conflict with rural land uses such as recreation, agriculture, forest preservation, land conservation, habitat protection, and visual resource stewardship.

As we make the shift from remote centralized power plants to distributed energy landscapes—taking advantage of the above stated opportunities—it will be important that we design these places with intention, being mindful of their relationship to nature, cultural heritage, place, and people. Communities are already reticent to accept the standard model of solar monocultural land development with endless rows of fenced-off dark blue modules. The shift in public perceptions can begin by providing alternative development models, demonstrating what a power plant can aspire to look like and involving community members in the planning and development of their renewable energy landscapes.

By designing and building our new energy landscapes as beautiful places for people and reflections of local culture, we can accelerate the embrace of new technologies by the general public and proactively respond to the concerns of 'Not In My Back Yard' objectors. Expanded public support for the implementation of renewable energy can help to drive more sustainable public policy and increase private investment.

A just transition will rely on inhabitants being engaged in the design process of local energy landscapes through co-design and other participatory processes. The legacy of these new landscapes should demonstrate that local communities were actively involved throughout decision-making and co-design processes and that the multifaceted benefits that accrue from renewable energy are shared equitably.

When we founded the Land Art Generator Initiative (LAGI) in 2008, we imagined large works of art in the landscape that were designed as cultural destinations and incorporated regenerative technologies as the media for creative expression. We imagined power plants as massive public artworks, feeding energy to the city through gigawatt-hours of clean electricity. These artworks would not only be functional solutions to the existential threat of climate change, but they would also be cultural drivers—inspiring reminders of the beauty and promise of a world that has moved beyond carbon and—as the editors of this book have framed—become important constituents of the cultural landscape of the twenty-first century.

After years of science communications focused on the gloom and doom of rising sea levels, mass migrations, extinctions, wildfires, droughts, and super storms, we felt that it was time to reframe the conversation by giving people something desirable to run toward, rather than something frightful to run away from. Our conviction has been that by persistently painting an inspiring picture of net-zero landscapes, we can help to build the political will to bring about their rapid implementation. Before change can occur, it must be imagined, and before new technologies can be deployed at scale, they must become universally popular. To this end, the goal of the Land Art Generator is to accelerate the transition to post-carbon economies by providing models of renewable energy infrastructure that add value to the built environment, inspire, and educate—while providing equitable power to homes around the world.

The following photo essay from the Land Art Generator illustrates the design opportunities inherent in renewable energy technologies when they are conceived as media for cultural expression. Six projects were selected from the over 1,300 that have been submitted to Land Art Generator Initiative design competitions. They were chosen for their grand beauty, their pragmatic function, their playfulness, and their ability to inspire. This new generation of power plants are places where you can take your family for a picnic. They are designed as destination landscapes, public parks, tourist attractions, and works of art that emanate a renewed responsibility for and embracing of energy in our lives.

Solar Mountain

Set in a remote corner of the Great Basin shrub steppe ecoregion of Northern Nevada, nestled between the rugged mountain ridges of the Granite Range and the barren Hualapai Flat lies a magical stretch of land in the Black Rock Desert that has come to be known as Fly Ranch. Replete with artesian hot springs, 100 native plant species, 90 types of birds, wild horses, deer, mountain lions, dozens of other animals, and pristine night skies, there is no other place like it on Earth. It is also far away from any public services and has no access to electricity.

Solar Mountain provides local electricity through an interactive installation with an organic form that blends in with this unique energy landscape. The spaces in and around *Solar Mountain* provide opportunities for people to connect with themselves, engage with other people, and strengthen their connection to nature. Complementing the solar cladding, visitors will discover a playscape where people of all ages can enjoy rock climbing or sliding.

Technology Solar photovoltaic
Yearly output 300 MWh of electricity per year
A top-ten submission to the LAGI 2020 design competition for Fly Ranch
By Nuru Karim, Aditya Jain, Divya Rastogi and Anuj Modi

Oscillating Platforms

Oscillating Platforms invites the waters of Copenhagen Harbour to create a flooded area within the Sonder Hoved Pier, once the site of an old shipyard. A series of free-form, floating platforms are anchored, reminiscent of ship's hulls and containing wave energy conversion equipment. Since the calm waters of the Copenhagen Harbour do not lend themselves to wave energy power generation, colourful masts and sails are integrated into the design. The sails catch the prevailing winds coming from the west and generate a rocking motion like that created by a wave.

Each habitable viewing platform—which visitors use as public park and meeting space—incorporates a pressurized air chamber, partially submerged in the water. The motion of the platform forces captured air through a Wells turbine at the top of the water column. As the water descends, it draws in air from the exposed top of the water column, also powering the turbine. *Oscillating Platforms* is playful as well as functional, inviting interaction with people of all ages at any time of the year.

Technology	Wind sails, oscillating water column, wells turbine
Yearly output	34,000 MWh

A submission to the LAGI 2014 design competition for Copenhagen
By Felix Cheong

Golden Roots

Golden Roots contrasts the urban environment of Copenhagen with the experience of the traditional Jutland rural landscape, suggesting a childhood walk through golden fields of rye. The installation recalls Denmark as a sparsely populated, agrarian country, where its inhabitants maintained a close relationship with nature. Across the remediated landscape of an urban brownfield, a system of paths and bridges guides visitors through a constellation of crop circles, bringing the calm countryside to life in the city.

The experience of being enveloped by nature is achieved through circular fields of rye, which have a natural maximum height of two meters. Red poppies, familiar in the region, provide a splash of colour and biodiversity. The fields are periodically harvested to generate high-energy biomass as well as to provide materials for the construction of observation towers that change every season. Rye bales are used to create towers of up to 18 metres tall when maximum crop yields are achieved. Paths and bridges allow visitors to walk within and to rise above the circles of rye. In addition to the energy production through biomass, each crop circle (connected by the paths) contains a piezoelectric floor, transforming the kinetic energy of moving people into electric energy.

Technology Biomass, piezoelectric paving
Yearly output 52 MWh
A submission to the LAGI 2014 design competition for Copenhagen
By Ronny Zschörper and Franziska Adler

Crack in the Ground

The largest public park in Masdar City, Abu Dhabi is a gateway entrance to the low-carbon city of the future. It is also the start of the green finger network of parks designed to ventilate and passively cool the urban desert landscape.

Crack in the Ground is a new kind of public space that is constantly changing as people experiment with different activities and uses within the shaded comfort of the new plaza, sometimes empty (in the morning) and sometimes full of water (in the afternoon). As a land artwork designed to allow the flow of air, *Crack in the Ground* demonstrates how the earth reacts to human impact. It is an invitation to reflect, a metaphor, and an architectural synthesis of landscape and change. The form of the artwork is an abstraction of the cracks that emerge from the lake beds that have dried due to global warming.

Photovoltaic panels and pumped-storage hydroelectric technologies come together to remind us that we are responsible for climate change while actively contributing to its mitigation. Thirty-two hundred square metres of solar panels are integrated into the south-facing planes of the sculpture. In the centre of the installation is an upper reservoir where water is stored with potential energy, acting as battery until energy is demanded after the sun has set. Energy flows down through hydroelectric turbines to a deep second reservoir to meet peak evening demand. During daylight hours, the solar panels provide energy to pump the water back up to complete the cycle.

Technology Solar photovoltaic, pumped hydro storage
Yearly output 1,400 MWh
A submission to the LAGI 2019 design competition for Abu Dhabi
By Fernando Landeros and Nicolas Vidal

Energy Duck

The common eider duck resides in great numbers in Copenhagen. However, its breeding habitat is at risk from the effects of climate change, which threatens the stability of food sources and increases the risk of nest depredation. *Energy Duck* takes the form of the eider to act as a solar collector, a buoyant gravity energy storage device, and a habitable tourist destination in the heart of Copenhagen's inner harbour.

Solar radiation is converted to electricity using photovoltaic panels attached to a spaceframe structure with ethylene tetrafluoroethylene (ETFE) weatherproof cladding. Some of the solar electricity is stored by virtue of the difference in water levels inside and outside the *Duck*. When stored energy needs to be delivered, the belly of the *Duck* is flooded through hydro turbines to generate electricity, which is transmitted to the grid by the same route as the solar-generated electricity. Solar energy is later used to pump the water back out, and buoyancy brings it to the surface. The floating height of the *Duck* indicates the relative cost of electricity as a function of city-wide use: as demand peaks the artwork sinks.

Inside, visitors will see the striking pattern of the mesh of solar panels in silhouette, backlit by daylight streaming through the gaps. Looking down they will see Danish seawater rising and falling within the pressure storage tanks.

Technology   Photovoltaic panels, hydraulic turbines
Yearly output   400 MWh
A submission to the LAGI 2014 design competition for Copenhagen
By Hareth Pochee, Adam Khan, Louis Leger and Patrick Fryer

Heliofield

Formerly a symbol of immense urban waste, Fresh Kills Landfill in Staten Island, New York City is nearing the completion of its transformation into a public park. When completed, Freshkills Park will be three times the size of Central Park. Its ecological restoration, which involves capping landfill mounds and placing layers of clean soil above, presents an opportunity to integrate renewable energy into the future landscape. It also presents a design challenge, since foundations are not permitted to penetrate the cap.

In response, *Heliofield* presents a network of three-legged modules that rise out of the prairie grass to collect the abundant solar energy that shines down on Staten Island. Large, heavy feet function as anchors below thin legs that elevate the photovoltaic (PV) panels above the head of parkgoers.

In addition to meeting technological needs, the system also serves flora and fauna with a set of interchangeable habitat components that address the inherent ecological challenges of the site, such as shallow soil depth and lack of trees. Functional amenities are designed for small mammals, birds, insects, and plants and supplement the limited habitat of the former landfill.

As the sun dips below the horizon across the water in New Jersey, *Heliofield* transitions from a solar power plant to a glowing night-time spectacle. The nocturnal ritual is designed to cultivate an appreciation for local ecology and biodiversity while presenting a beautiful, otherworldly display.

Technology Solar Photovoltaic
Yearly output 15,000 MWh
A submission to the LAGI 2012 design competition for New York City
By Michael Chaveriat, Yikyu Choe and Myung Kweon Park

Design as Dialogue towards 2050

3.3

JANNEMARIE DE JONGE

In the twentieth century, technological solutions were expected to resolve most of the environmental and societal problems. Even today this stance still gets lots of support. However, the idea that the current challenges society is facing can be completely resolved through technological solutions ignores the systemic character of these problems. This idea creates false expectations and tempts decisionmakers to take too narrow a view. We saw just such an instrumental focus during the first phase of the Dutch *Regional Energy Strategies* (RES 1.0, 2019–2021).

Although advisers had previously argued that *Regional Energy and Climate Strategies* (REKS) should be prepared, the policy instrument was narrowed down to just the energy agenda. There is, quite rightly, a sense of urgency in meeting the Paris climate targets, but the means—identifying areas for renewable solar and wind power—appears to have been elevated to an end in itself in the Netherlands and other countries. All too often, the proposed solution is 'integration into the landscape'. This approach not only denies the scale of the energy transition and the accompanying implications for our living environment, but also ignores the other major challenges, such as climate adaptation and the agricultural transition. In the decades to come these transitions will transform the landscape so radically that a holistic approach will be needed to guide the process.

For the purposes of the Regional Energy Strategies the Netherlands has been divided into thirty regions in which government authorities, residents, businesses, grid operators and civil society organisations work together. It is essential that the next steps (RES 2.0 and beyond) take a much broader view. The landscape that has to accommodate all these development agendas provides a suitable framework—it has the power—for integrating them into a coherent whole.

THE URGENCY PARADOX

The perceived urgency of the energy transition prevents us from giving ourselves enough 'free space' to take a more rounded view, while free thinking is needed now more than ever. This is the urgency paradox. As the Chinese saying goes: 'If you're in a hurry, take a detour'. The energy transition is a key challenge and it would benefit from a design dialogue that puts the landscape centre stage. Such a dialogue would bring together a steady stream of substantive inputs from practice, research, policy and design on all scales, resulting in new insights and practicable plans. This *free space* will foster unexpected linkages with other challenges and prove to be a valuable investment in cooperation and social capital, an investment that will pay for itself by creating a *bounded space* for political and business decision-making that can draw on widespread support.

Design dialogue plays two important roles in this process. The first is *opportunity-oriented*: discovering new approaches to smart thinking that can serve multiple objectives at the same time. The second is *confrontational*: for example, showing what adopting a narrow sectoral approach can mean. Combining the opportunity-oriented and confrontational roles can jolt regional players into a creative mode instead of them automatically digging their heels in and opposing proposed solar farms or wind turbines. It builds a bridge between the energy transition and other societal goals, bringing a much wider palette of solutions into the frame, such as additional energy savings, linking into wider social issues, innovative multifunctional land use and new economic drivers. This process will take us step by step towards a new reality in which energy generation will be seen as a logical part of the landscape of the twenty-first century. One insider called this 'intelligent muddling through'.

DESIGN DIALOGUE AS FREE SPACE

Designing is a thinking process in which you 'enter into dialogue' with the problem situation in search of principles for assessing the value of possible solutions[1]. This process consists of a continuous stream of exercises of the type 'if we did that, this is what we'd think of it'. The first step requires creative imagination (devising and imagining new solutions) and the second step involves reflective judgement. In this context, 'reflective' implies that there is no general rule, because we have to weigh up different things that are very unlike each other. For example, do we think—in a specific case—that renewable energy is more important than an unobstructed view of the landscape? Or, is a certain historic townscape compatible with modern solar panel technology? To find an answer, we drill down into our normative canon. The 'minutes' of this thinking process are a series of sketches, outlines, diagrams, cross-sections, partial designs, comparison studies, scenarios, et cetera. The process of co-creation can be supported by interviews, surveys and such like.

Design thinking therefore requires continuous integration of general facts and rules—often obtained from research—and social values and opinions contributed by participants in the design process, such as clients, landscape users and politicians[2]. The thinking process presupposes an inquisitive attitude capable of taking on board all matters that could be relevant. When faced with challenging problems it is this expansion of the solution space by incorporating unexpected ingredients that will open up opportunities for creative breakthroughs. A well-known example in the Netherlands is the incorporation of sand and clay extraction as an opportunity rather than a threat for nature restoration projects in the dyked floodplains of the major rivers. Since the

1
De Jonge, J.M. (2009). Landscape Architecture between Politics and Science. An integrative perspective on landscape planning and design in the network society. Wageningen: Uitgeverij Blauwdruk / Techne Press, 2009.

2
De Jonge, J.M. (2009) 'Ontwerpdialoog als integrerend gesprek / Design dialogue as an integrative discussion', in: M. Hajer (ed.), Sterke Verhalen. Hoe Nederland de planologie opnieuw uitvindt. Design & Politics #03. Rotterdam: Uitgeverij 010, p. 154–169.

1990s, this turnaround in thinking opened the way to new forms of large-scale habitat restoration. If the prevailing ideas about what could and could not be combined had been unquestioningly followed, the floodplains along the major rivers would now be much the poorer for it.

AN ENERGETIC ODYSSEY AS A UNIFYING NARRATIVE

An important step in the design process is developing a strong concept as a narrative to bring the parties involved together. A good example is *An Energetic Odyssey*. This multimedia installation shows how 25,000 10 MW wind turbines in the North Sea can meet up to 90 per cent of the electricity demands of the surrounding countries. The substantive input for the narrative was provided by experts and designers. The animation that was subsequently made transports the viewer to the year 2050 in steps of one year at a time. It depicts a scenario in which the North Sea undergoes a transformation and shows the development of cable landfall points, port areas and other infrastructure, but also biodiverse marine ecosystems. It is a hopeful story of cooperation between countries and organizations against the background of a long-standing stalemate in climate cooperation around the North Sea. The Paris climate agreement (December 2015) had just been signed when the design research was conducted, which considerably raised the profile of the initiative.

The core of the concept can be described as 'think big'. The *Odyssey* made it clear that in addition to a whole range of bottom-up initiatives, big market players, governments and the environmental movement also had to pull together in order to meet the climate targets in time. It showed that with a good plan it would be possible to combine electricity generation, spatial and technological innovation in port area development and ecological development. It is no surprise therefore that the first working title was 'Big Is Beautiful'.

The concept gained momentum during the 2016 International Architecture Biennale Rotterdam (IABR), using it as a free space for exchanging knowledge and inspiration, without the pressure of political agendas. This initial design dialogue was cleverly linked to the Dutch presidency of the Council of the EU in the same year. Responsible top officials recognized this as an opportunity for the energy transition and threw their weight behind it. A coalition of supporting parties was formed in a series of design sessions and workshops with a diverse group of stakeholders and specialists[3].

At the EU summit in the spring of 2016, a select group of about sixty European policymakers, business leaders and NGO heads met for an exclusive preview of *An Energetic Odyssey*, which was projected onto the floor. Two months later it was the turn of the European energy ministers, and in June 2016 the North Sea partners ratified their cooperation on offshore wind power[4]. The then Dutch minister of economic affairs, Henk Kamp, confirmed that showing *An Energetic Odyssey* had been very helpful in reaching this agreement. The concept had taken root.

FORDABLE PLACES

A design dialogue creates good conditions for developing a concept that can gain widespread support. Besides a joint exploration of ideas, it requires a sense of timing, recognizability, identifying the really important issues and using the right language

3
Substantive input and feedback on various concepts was given by the Port of Rotterdam, the Port of Amsterdam, Shell, Natuur & Milieu (Nature & Environment), Stichting De Noordzee, The Crown Estate, TU Delft, NSF, European Climate Fund, ENECO, Netherlands Environmental Assessment Agency (PBL), the Ministry of Economic Affairs and the Ministry of Infrastructure and the Environment. *An Energetic Odyssey* is a floor projection (6 × 8 metres) with a voiceover and was made by Maarten Hajer, H+N+S Landscape Architects, ECOrys and Tungsten PRO for IABR 2016, Next Economy.

4
Hajer M.A., Pelzer, P. (2018). 2050—An Energetic Odyssey: Understanding 'Techniques of Futuring' in the transition towards renewable energy. Energy Research & Social Science, 44, p. 222–231.

and images. It is like finding 'fordable places' where the three streams of urgency, public acceptance and conceptualization come together[5]. In this meandering reality, the conditions can be created at any time for a political decision that is both sufficiently robust and adaptable enough to stand the test of time.

A concept 'works' when key players take it to be logical and promising. In the Netherlands, for example, the concepts of the *Randstad* and the *Green Heart* not only encapsulated the urgency of the housebuilding programme in the post-war reconstruction period, but at the same time also recognized the value of retaining a large green lung between the major urban areas in the west of the country. This concept has remained intact for a long time as a guiding principle for contiguous urban development around protected agricultural areas[6]. Affordable housing and food production proved to be a powerful alliance of interests, and the growing demand for recreation could also be easily accommodated within the narrative.

In the case of *An Energetic Odyssey*, we can describe the fordable place as follows: the concept was able to bring the environmental movement and the business community together, and exploit the momentum generated by the Paris climate agreement and the EU summit to gain political traction, with the IABR as a 'neutral mediator'.

DIALOGUE APPROACH

'Thoughts without content are empty, intuitions without concepts are blind[7].'
A dialogue[8] is, in essence, an investigative conversation that leads to insight and understanding among its participants. This does not mean that it necessarily leads to consensus; rather, it means that everyone understands the logic and principles that underpin a particular vision. The aim of a dialogue, therefore, is *not* to bring about a political or other kind of decision, but to provide the indispensable ingredients for such a decision.

A characteristic of dialogue is going back and forth between concrete *experiences* and *reflecting on these experiences.* Personal experience provides the springboard for a joint investigative conversation, that can lead towards a shared reference and assessment framework.

Sticking to abstractions offers no way forward. Concepts like landscape quality and sustainability can only be endowed with practical meaning if we can investigate them from the secure foothold of experience. Field visits and excursions to demonstration projects are therefore of considerable value. For example, if someone argues that wind turbines are an intrusion in the landscape, it helps if we can visualize an actual situation where the person can describe in concrete terms what qualities are being affected, and what feelings and thoughts this engenders, and what interests are at stake. If conversation partners can put themselves in the position of the other person through such a concrete experience, we can start to appreciate the pluriformity of the real world. This makes it important to ensure the participants in the dialogue are diverse, as their different perspectives on a concrete situation will enable them to explore the substance of the abstract concept of landscape quality. In this way, dialogues reveal shared facts (joint fact finding) and give meaning to value-laden concepts. Postponing judgement and consciously exchanging perspectives creates space for new ways of thinking.

5
De Zeeuw, F. (2018). Zo werkt gebiedsontwikkeling. Handboek voor studie en praktijk. Praktijkleerstoel Gebiedsontwikkeling TU Delft en Stichting Kennis Gebiedsontwikkeling (SKG).

6
This example also demonstrates that spatial concepts are a product of their time.
The interrelated challenges of biodiversity conservation and climate adaptation and mitigation are so urgent that the concept of the Randstad and the Green Heart in its original form is no longer adequate. Numerous alternative concepts and design studies are being put forward in which urban development and other land uses are based on the soil and water systems. Political and social support for a change of direction is mounting. The question is when decisionmakers dare to set course for a fordable place.

7
A quote from the philosopher Immanuel Kant, from *Critique of Pure Reason*.

8
In my approach to dialogue I follow contemporary interpretations of the Greek liberal arts, including dialectics. This interpretation is well known from, among others, the physicist David Bohm (Bohm, D., *On Dialogue*, Ed. Lee Nichol (London, Routledge, 1996) and William Isaacs (Isaacs, W., *Dialogue and the art of thinking together* (Bantam Doubleday Dell Publishing Group Inc., 1999).
In the Netherlands it was introduced in the form of the 'Socratic dialogue' by the philosopher and writer Jos Kessels, who taught me how to use it.

FREE SPACE VERSUS BOUNDED SPACE

A dialogue requires *free space*[9]. This is also referred to as 'soft space', informal places for free exchange of ideas and opinions. Participants engage in a dialogue in an individual capacity, not to represent a certain lobby group. They practise attentive listening, frank questioning and uncovering assumptions, while divesting themselves of their own prejudices as much as possible. Dialogue therefore goes *beyond* polite conversation. In the beginning this is necessary to establish an atmosphere of trust. Thereafter, though, we must have the courage to be honest about conflicting opinions, because it is precisely this recognition that can generate shared insight and understanding about the task at hand and the possibilities for change. This is not the same as reaching a consensus about desired solutions.

Dialogue is not the means for negotiation and decision-making. That process takes place in the *bounded space*, the place where interests and lobbying play a leading role. It is crucial to distinguish between these two concepts and organize them as separate processes. But they are linked none the less. The strategists among the designers, leaders and officials will have a keen sense of when a concept is ready to be moved from the free space to the bounded space. People who can make this connection between the two spaces are indispensable. In the example of *An Energetic Odyssey* the chief designer (Dirk Sijmons) and the curator of the IABR (Maarten Hajer) were able to move from free to bounded space by involving senior officials in the Ministry of Economic Affairs. The whole process requires that all those involved adopt a creative and flexible attitude. This skill should be strengthened in the curriculum of designers, consultants, researchers and policymakers, and absorbed into the culture of their organizations as well as into the wider political and administrative culture.

THE POWER OF LANDSCAPE AS INTEGRATIVE FRAMEWORK

The outcomes of design dialogues are varied in nature. In terms of content, the outcome points the way to 'fordable places' in the form of concepts and unifying narratives. In terms of time, it generates a feeling for the 'right moment', the window of opportunity when such a concept, or parts of it, can be brought into the decision-making arena. As we saw in the example of *An Energetic Odyssey*, the EU summit was used for this purpose. The resulting momentum can lead to innovative agendas and the coalitions that form around them. A unifying narrative is therefore also an investment in cooperation and social capital (capacity building) with a wider impact in institutions and society.

In essence, a design dialogue is a broad platform that provides the *mental* space to create concepts for the *physical* transformation of the landscape. The landscape as it is perceived by people represents an integrative framework for exploring the future together. The process can rapidly gain momentum if a sense of urgency, a powerful unifying concept, political endorsement and public support all come together in a favourable way. The design dialogue is not a ready-made method and there is no fixed recipe, but there are vital ingredients.

9
The Latin word *otium* stands for free time, time without obligations or a business or social nature. This freedom is necessary for new ideas to emerge. Its opposite, *negotium*, is the origin of the 'negotiation', the time when business is conducted, when other rules and conventions apply.

What is the Power of Landscape? An Epilogue

DIRK OUDES, PAOLO PICCHI and SVEN STREMKE

'Well, what did you think?' said the woman casually sitting on the hood of her electric car to me, when I stepped out of mine to charge it. 'Excuse me?' 'Well', said the woman, 'you just passed the largest wind park in the country. Can you imagine it used to be difficult to place even 2 or 3 turbines?'. I could certainly remember that period. We had just started to replace fossil fuels with renewable energy sources and many questioned whether we would achieve a full transition. The woman continued: 'Did you know wind energy is one of the first things people mention when they think about this region? This landscape used to be all about long lines of trees and huge agricultural fields. Personally, I just love the idea that those turbines right there are charging my car. Driving here always makes me feel like coming home'. I thought about what she said and replied: 'Yes, here it makes sense. Where I come from, our landscapes are of a different scale. We like small energy plants that fit right in with the landscape, most communities have their own.' 'No large wind parks over there?', the woman asked. 'We have some', I replied, 'but we are mostly big on energy saving, you know what they say about the Dutch. But we also created a whole patchwork of solar landscapes. Boosting biodiversity, obviously. Our mayor can't stop talking about how proud she is of this 'eco-energy' network. Tourists love it too.' The woman nodded and said: 'Who would have thought we could do it? Clean energy, all around us?'

This excerpt from a future conversation about energy landscapes provides a stark contrast with our current attitude towards energy landscapes. Instead of casual conversations, renewable energy sparks intense debates between politicians, policy-makers, civil servants, engineers, designers and parts of the general public. However, this debate mainly revolves around the *what* and the *who,* and, if you consider the urgency, the *when* of the energy transition. 'What' refers to the choice of technology, balancing the energy system and transportation of energy carriers such as electricity, heat or molecules. The 'who' question relates to the actors involved in developing or financing renewable energy and to the fairness implications of the energy transition. 'When' refers to realizing a timely transition to minimize the negative effects of climate

1

2

change. In this final chapter, we argue that this debate should not be limited to the *what*, *who* and *when*, but also the *where* and *how*. This book has illustrated how these questions come together in 'landscape' and introduced novel narratives to engage with the energy transition. We use the term *narrative* to emphasize that all these questions need to be coherently accounted for. Talking about *landscapes* connects these questions and thus provides an excellent starting point for all kinds of debates about energy transition. The previous chapters have all illustrated this *power of landscape*. In the following, we illustrate that power by discussing common issues and pressing questions that will sound familiar to many readers who care about energy transition.

SMALL AND LARGE SCALE → fig. 1

Dan van der Horst, in his chapter, denotes the trend of scaling up in renewable energy projects: both in the horizontal plane (a larger footprint of projects) and the vertical plane (for example height increase of wind turbines). This increase in scale is driven both by the innate characteristics of technologies (e.g., the minimum size required for a concentrated solar power plant) as well as economic parameters. However, the large spatial expanse of renewable energy technology may be considered inappropriate in one landscape and the pride of a region in another.

The power of landscape is that the spatial expanse of energy technology becomes relative to the scale of the surrounding landscape and how this is experienced. Landscape thus helps to resolve the question, or at least points to directions of which spatial expanse 'fits' a certain location. When the spatial expanse of energy technologies fits a specific landscape, landscape users experience that landscape (including technology) as a *whole*. For example, because of the way the wind turbines of the Irene Vorrink wind park in Lelystad (chapter 2.2) are aligned along the dyke, they *together* become a landmark for landscape users. In this way, defining the scale of energy projects based upon existing landscape characteristics is one of the ways to highlight and celebrate differences between regions.

MONO- AND MULTIFUNCTIONAL → fig. 2

In the current energy transition discourse, a false dichotomy between monofunctional and multifunctional projects is often created. Some criticize (some forms of) multifunctional energy landscapes when additional functions such as ecological restauration or recreational facilities increase the costs or the required space of a project. Others criticize monofunctional energy landscapes for their homogeneous and technological character. To some extent, the type of technology affects the potential multifunctionality. Concentrated solar power plants (for example Gemasolar, chapter 2.2) do not easily match with other functions, while energy landscapes with wind turbines allow for many other functions between and underneath the turbines (for example Zahara de los Atunes, chapter 2.2).

Most importantly, for each single technology there exists a range between mono- and multifunctional. Chapter 2.3 for example, argued that although monofunctional solar fields are still common practice, multifunctional solar landscapes are emerging in more and more places. These provide alternative solutions for those seeking to realize more than mere energy generation in their landscape. That chapter

1 'Solar dam' of the Muttsee reservoir (at 2500m altitude) that is used for the pumped-storage hydropower plant Linthal in the Swiss Alps. This dam is 1000 meters long, yet the scale aligns with the scale of the mountainous landscape (Photo by Dirk Oudes).

2 Agriculture and electricity production combined in Donau-Eschingen, Germany. The bifacial PV panels use solar energy from both sides to generate electricity (Photo by Sven Stremke).

illustrated different solutions, varying in number of functions, scale of functions and energy density.

The power of landscape is that landscape provides the ingredients and directions for *how* multifunctionality should materialize in a specific location. This book has evidenced many opportunities for the energy transition to become a catalyst for multifunctionality, though there may be valid reasons to focus mainly on energy provision in certain landscapes. Moreover, multifunctionality may turn out to be inappropriate for specific landscapes or used in attempts to greenwash technology. We have already witnessed signs of 'catalogue thinking' in solar power plant design, where a bench, some fruit trees and sheep are employed to realize additional 'functions', independent of the existing landscape characteristics and spatial qualities.

In its essence, the number of functions should 'fit' the larger surrounding landscape. Put more poetically, landscape is the *muse* of the energy transition, functioning as source of inspiration and reference. Remote, open agricultural landscapes may be appropriate for a lower number of functions compared to other landscapes with a high number of existing functions and a rich variety of landscape users.

Departing from *landscapes* rather than energy *technologies* creates opportunities to make the transformation of our living environment about more than just energy and to customize solutions for each individual landscape with its users. Multifunctionality may be pursued from the start, as was the case with the solar landscapes presented in chapter 2.3. In other cases, multifunctionality comes afterwards and unannounced, as communities start appropriating their landscape. In Larderello, for example, where the pipelines of the geothermal energy landscape are appreciated by tourists and locals. Or the wind farms in Zahara de los Atunes, where the arrival of the wind turbines enabled a huge proliferation of biodiversity between the maintenance roads (see chapter 2.2).

CENTRAL AND DECENTRAL →fig. 3

Throughout the book, we have seen clear examples of centralized energy projects such as the Hoover Dam, Gemasolar concentrated solar power or Larderello geothermal energy landscape (chapter 2.2). Stakeholders from outside the local landscape take the initiative for an energy landscape or affect how energy landscapes are developed by policy, law and subsidy schemes. Proponents of a centralized energy transition stress the urgency of climate mitigation that requires swiftness and thus top-down development of energy landscapes. At the same time, examples such as Southill Solar, solar park the Kwekerij (chapter 2.3) and the wind energy landscape in Viticuso (chapter 2.2) illustrate a much more decentralized approach. Energy landscapes have been initiated, shaped and even financed by local stakeholders. Proponents of a decentralized energy transition point to improved energy democracy and self-sufficiency if energy projects are organized locally. In the current energy transition discourse, these two perspectives are often presented as if it is either one or the other.

The power of landscape is that the central and decentral perspective meet in physical landscapes experienced by its users. A project initiated on the local level is part of the challenge to achieve renewable energy targets for which regional and national governments are held accountable. In turn, national or regional policy may affect choice of location, material form, the type of technology, the scale and number

3

3 Local stakeholders meet with civil servants, designers and other energy professionals in an agrivoltaic fruit farm in Wadenoijen, the Netherlands (Photo by Sven Stremke).

4

of additional functions. Coordination between the national and local level is however still lacking. The Dutch government, for example, advocates multifunctional land use, yet national subsidy schemes do not yet favour the combination of PV and agriculture (agrivoltaic) over monofunctional solutions.

Departing from *landscape* allows for the inhabitants and other users to become more central in the proposed transformation. These users ought to be supported by national legislation. Only in the absence of progress, national policymakers need to find ways to complement decentral decision-making to safeguard meeting (inter) national energy targets. Sven Stremke and Jolanda de Jong (chapter 1.2) showed that we can learn from previous energy transitions. Large-scale infrastructure for transport of energy was concerted at the national scale, while many decisions about the actual energy 'mining' were taken on the local scale. Pressing questions still need attention, such as *who* these landscape users are precisely and *how* exchange and coordination between national and local stakeholders takes place. Jannemarie de Jonge (chapter 3.3) dedicated her essay to the power of the *design dialogue*, where the use of 'free space' fosters 'unexpected linkages with other challenges' and paves the way for the 'bounded space' where negotiation and decision-making takes place. Design dialogues gain momentum if 'concrete *experiences* and *reflecting on these experiences'* are continuously exchanged. Concrete experiences again point to the significance of physical landscapes where transformations take place or are proposed. Design dialogue *about a landscape* functions as an arena where feedback between the central and decentral perspective takes place. National and regional stakeholders will be confronted with the implications of policy and regulation in specific landscapes, while local stakeholders need to consider the characteristics of the larger landscape or the implications for the functioning of the energy system.

LOCALS AND EXPERTS → fig. 4

Few people working on the energy transition will argue participation of local landscape users is not important. Still, participatory processes remain a struggle in renewable energy projects. At the same time, projects often also include a range of experts: energy system engineers, ecologists, hydrologists, archaeologists, acoustic experts, cultural historians et cetera. Expert and local knowledge both constitute valid ingredients for any project, yet it seems often either one or the other is dominant in the decision-making about energy landscapes.

The power of landscape is that understanding a specific site requires both local and expert knowledge and thus brings both together. Local users know what matters: they know of the recent and detailed changes in their landscape, how their landscape works, how they use, experience and value their landscape and what they expect it to be in the future. Experts draw lines between landscapes on the local, regional and (inter)national scale and across larger timespans. This larger frame of reference is required to assess local aspects. Think for example of the preservation of 'red list' species or cultural heritage—they both require insight in the larger 'population' before local decisions can be made.

The book has illustrated the effectiveness of collaborations between locals and experts. Notably the on-site, participatory visual assessment used in Southill Solar

4 Photograph of the energy landscape on the Danish island of Samsø, designed by experts and locals together. The location, amount and the height of the wind turbines were decided together (Photo by Sven Stremke).

5

6

7

(chapter 2.3) and the co-design approach used by Florian Becker that involved collaborating with local inhabitants and the landowner for a solar landscape (chapter 3.1). Chapter 2.2 stressed that landscape immersion is needed to go beyond understanding the technological parts of energy landscapes. A shared immersion of both experts and locals, for example during fieldtrips, supports exchange and alignment between locals and experts. Or as Jannemarie de Jonge put it in chapter 3.3: 'Concepts like landscape quality and sustainability can only be endowed with practical meaning if we can investigate them from the secure foothold of experience'.

HIDDEN AND VISIBLE → fig. 5

The photographs in this book make clear that renewable energy infrastructure is hard to keep out of sight entirely. While the default option still seems to be (the attempt) to hide energy infrastructure, Kate Sherren showed that 'the strongest predictor of support for renewable energy was noticing any kind of existing energy infrastructure: basically, knowing it has and deserves a footprint' (chapter 2.4). Opting for a *landscape* instead of *technology* perspective brings a lot more nuance to the binary distinction of 'hidden' and 'visible' energy infrastructure.

The power of landscape is that it makes clear how a group of users in a certain place and time respond to the arrival of energy technologies. Lara Voerman (chapter 1.4) described the emergence of four different design approaches through time. These approaches nuance the black-and-white thinking in terms of 'hidden' and 'visible' energy infrastructure. Depending on the place and time, one approach may be more appropriate than the others.

However, our increased understanding of the twenty-first-century major challenges such as food security, biodiversity and climate change, presents us with the responsibility to look beyond mere aesthetic considerations about energy infrastructure. The *enrich* approach that Lara Voerman identified tentatively may prove to be a proper candidate for a new default. This design approach draws from the richness each landscape (in potential) has in store for us, be it visually, socially, economically or environmentally. The solar landscapes presented in chapter 2.3 provide ample inspiration on how to *enrich* landscapes while contributing to energy transition.

Convincing landscape users that hiding energy technologies may not be the best 'fit' is not an easy task. Contemporary societal values may, at least initially, motivate locals to keep energy technology out of sight. And yet we learned that the younger part of the population, who has learned about climate change and renewables at school, is keener to embrace energy landscapes in their living environment. Co-ownership and co-design of energy landscapes that provide local benefits in addition to energy generation may shed a different light on the visibility of energy infrastructure for all landscape users.

8 → 216–217

PRESERVE AND DEVELOP → fig. 8

Which landscapes will we 'save' and which will be 'sacrificed' for the greater good of energy supply? This is an often-heard phrase that perfectly illustrates the default negative connotation of renewable energy infrastructure. These connotations and the subsequent evaluation of landscapes as either worth saving or not is problematic,

5 Hydropower plant Solbergfoss operational since 1924 and designed by architect Bredo Greve (Photo by Dirk Oudes).
6 Here visitors can watch the hydpropower plant in action, they can even sit on the stone bench visible in the bottom right of the picture (Photo by Dirk Oudes).
7 Ornate wooden doors at the entrance of Solbergfoss hydropower plant (Photo by Dirk Oudes).
8 In a previous energy transition, peat extraction has shaped the landscape of Nieuwkoop, located in the so-called 'Green Heart' of the Netherlands (Frans Lemmens / Alamy).

because as a result, the landscapes of some communities may be targeted more than those of others. The chapter by Andrea Cardoso and Emma Banks (1.3) has, on a global scale, made painfully clear how our energy demand affects the 'landscapes of others'. Consequently, Kate Sherren rightfully urged us to train the 'altruism muscle'. Arguably, some landscapes may be considered irreconcilable with certain energy technologies, although low shares of renewable energy in some countries indicate this argument may be used too quickly. The key question is where to preserve or develop and to what degree?

Perhaps paradoxically, the *power of landscape* with respect to this issue lies in the knowledge and understanding of the existing landscape. This understanding is not meant to provide arguments against any change, but rather to put the transformation in a spatial-temporal perspective. The first two chapters of the book have taken us on energy landscape journeys through time and space. Mike Pasqualetti (chapter 1.1) concluded that the current transition provides the opportunity to heal, recycle or even upcycle landscapes that have been negatively affected by, for example, fossil fuel extraction. Sven Stremke and Jolanda de Jong (chapter 1.2) taught us that some of the cultural landscapes we love and preserve today, came into existence during earlier energy transitions. Landscape, in other words, thus provides directions for the pace of transformation: places that have changed (relatively) little require additional caution compared with more dynamic landscapes. When transformation takes place, care and attention for the landscape and its users should at least be *on par* with economic and technological parameters. Robert Ferry and Elizabeth Monoian have astonished us by illustrating how designing beautiful energy landscapes can strengthen local identities, preserve cultural and ecological values and facilitate energy democracy. The designs from the biannual Land Art Generator Initiative (LAGI) competition provide us with a first glimpse of future energy landscapes and, simultaneously, remind all of us of the pressing need to keep learning and advancing practices.

LOOKING AHEAD

By complementing the *what, who* and *when* with the *where* and *how* question, a more encompassing energy transition narrative emerges. The answers to these questions, together, provide the building blocks to decide and define how the energy transition takes place in different places, in different landscapes. We hope that renewables become the new 'default' energy source, replacing fossil fuels in the near future. Renewable energy technologies, effective to mitigate climate change, still leave us with many choices to be made during local implementation. Choices perhaps less related to *quantity* but rather to *quality*. Quality of implementation processes as well as the outcome of those: energy landscapes. Decisions that are made about local implementation will have implications, for example on democracy, fairness, costs, energy system and, ultimately, the pace of energy transition. The resulting energy landscapes and their experience by its users does and will continue to mirror these decisions in most parts of the world.

The introduction to this book argued that the energy transition is not so much about changing *technologies* but about a changing *landscape*. The landscapes where we live, work and recreate.

All chapters, in a complementary manner, provided evidence to sustain this proposition. In the first part, we set out to *learn from the past*. The rich history of humanity's energy provision, transport and consumption can be traced in many landscapes. Moreover, energy demand in the past has shaped and continues to shape how we use and value our landscapes today, from recreational use in recycled energy landscapes to places tainted by pollution and social conflict. In the second part, we *questioned the present*. The abundant energy landscape examples and multitude of interpretations of those landscapes evidence that similar technologies are received very differently in different places and times. Not the technology itself, but the (absence of) environmental, social and cultural bonds between technology and landscape shape our response to energy transition. Such bonds obviously increase the complexity of energy landscape evaluation and hint at a degree of subjectivity: an energy landscape may be perceived by one person as a sublime aesthetic experience while the other focuses on the bare soil and destruction of existing landscape patterns. In the third part, we started to *imagine alternative futures*. Using the power of imagination, not immediately restrained by economic or technological feasibility, revealed that energy transition may give rise to unprecedented landmarks in some places and the cultural landscape of the twenty-first century in others. These futures are built upon dialogues between all kinds of people about specific landscapes. We are more confident than ever that a more encompassing perspective on energy transition involving landscape and landscape users will benefit both the quality of the transformation and its timely realization.

We did not yet arrive at the future outlined at the start of this chapter. But we believe that the *power of landscape* can help us to get there. Despite the groundbreaking work of Sylvia Crowe in the 1950s, we are just starting to understand the true potential of landscape. Landscape, of course, is not a standalone *superpower*, it needs to inform and provide feedback to policy instruments such as renewable energy subsidies and planning regulations to reach its full potential. Luckily, these instruments are developed by *people*. People that we recommend to travel, to explore energy landscapes, to converse with locals and experts, to keep innovating and reflecting.

One thing *we* learned from this book is that working on the topic of landscape provides a joyful antidote to the sometimes depressing aura around energy transition: black-and-white responses, failed project proposals and conflicts that can rip communities apart. Departing from the landscapes that people use and cherish, instead of technological performance and economic growth that has dominated the post-modern era and thus much of the initial phase of today's energy transition, certainly leads to different conversations. Conversations in which memories of the past and images about the future are starting to create novel narratives to engage with the energy transition.

SVEN STREMKE
Sven Stremke is Professor Landscape Architecture at the Amsterdam Academy of Architecture, Associate Professor Landscape Architecture at Wageningen University, Principal Investigator at the Amsterdam Institute for Advanced Metropolitan Solutions and founding director of the NRGlab, a research laboratory on energy transition. Sven has been practicing as a landscape architect in Germany, the United States, Spain and the Netherlands before returning to academia in 2006. His research and teaching focuses on the relations between renewable energy and the living environment. Sven has (co)authored more than 25 scientific papers and many book chapters on planning and design for energy transition. Together with Andy van den Dobbelsteen, he edited the book Sustainable Energy Landscapes: Designing, Planning and Development published by Taylor & Francis in 2013. In 2018, Sven participated in the negotiations of the Dutch National Climate Agreement as an expert for landscapes-related questions. Sven is a member of the scientific advisory committees for the German Academy for Territorial Development in the Leibnitz Association (ARL), the Dutch National Consortium Sun & Landscape (NCZiL), and the pre-IBA Luxembourg. Sven is scientific director of the WUR Solar Research Programme, initiator of the Wageningen Energy Alliance and board member of the Dutch Archiprix foundation.

DIRK OUDES
Dirk Oudes is a landscape architect, researcher and associate of NRGlab, a research laboratory on energy transition. Following a five-year period as a landscape architect with different design and consultancy firms, he worked at the Amsterdam Academy of Architecture as a research fellow, contributed as a teacher and wrote his PhD thesis in affiliation with Wageningen University. His PhD thesis is entitled Landscape-inclusive energy transition: landscape as catalyst in the shift to renewable energy. As part of his PhD thesis, he supervised master's students and undertook extensive fieldwork in 20+ solar fields across Europe. The results of his four research projects have been published in peer-reviewed journals. In addition to his work as a PhD researcher, he collaborated, among others, with leading design offices in the Netherlands and contributed as a spatial expert to the negotiations of the National Climate Agreement in 2018. He is frequently asked as speaker, jury member or expert critic and was advisor for the Creative Industries Fund.

PAOLO PICCHI
Paolo Picchi is an agronomist and landscape architect. In the last decade he conducted both practice and research in landscape architecture and landscape ecology and he participated in several projects as a volunteer of the Italian Chapter of IFLA, International Federation of Landscape Architects. His research focuses on the relationship between communities, landscape quality, art and sustainable energy transition with a specific focus on mapping, participatory and transdisciplinary research methods and ecosystem services. He is a member of the NRGlab—a research laboratory on energy transition based at Wageningen University where he conducted the finalization of his PhD Research. He recently concluded his Postdoc Researcher in Landscape Architecture at the Academy of Architecture—Amsterdam University of the Arts. At the Academy, he has been project coordinator of METRO (Metropolitan Energy Transition and Spatial Dimension), a project in partnership with the Municipality of Amsterdam. The project aimed to enhance design knowledge in the field and train public officers from different backgrounds and teams on the spatial dimension of the energy transition through poetic thinking for the local design implementation of the regional energy strategy. He currently collaborates with ENEA, the Italian National Agency for New Technologies, Energy and Sustainable Economic Development in different projects.

MIKE PASQUALETTI
Dr. Martin J. Pasqualetti is a Professor of Geography in the School of Geographical Sciences and Urban Planning, and a Senior Global Futures Scientist in the Julie Ann Wrigley Global Futures Laboratory, both at Arizona State University. He concentrates on matters of energy and society—especially energy landscapes. For his lifelong contributions to energy studies, he was honoured with the Alexander and Ilse Melamid Gold Medal from the American Geographical Society (2015); Distinguished Alumnus of the Year by the University of California (Riverside) (2018); and Elected Fellow of the American Association of Geographers (2019). He has advised several agencies and NGOs, including the U.S. Department of Energy, the National Renewable Energy Laboratory, the U.S. Office of Technical Assessment, the National Academy of Sciences, the Arizona Office of Energy Policy, the Union of Concerned Scientists, and the Natural Resources Defense Council. His latest books include The Renewable Energy Landscape (Routledge) and The Thread of Energy (Oxford).

JOLANDA DE JONG
Jolanda de Jong graduated cum laude in landscape architecture from Wageningen University in 2016. She then went to work as a junior researcher at the department of Landscape Architecture. Together with Sven Stremke, she wrote a publication on the spatial impact of historical and future energy landscapes in the western part of the Netherlands. For the past few years, she has been working at Urban Synergy as a landscape architect on various assignments. Regional landscape challenges are her favourite. Both energy transition and infrastructure projects are recurring themes in her work. She develops visions, advice, landscape applications and designs at various scale levels.

LARA VOERMAN
Lara Voerman is an architectural historian. With history as a starting point, she advises governments and design offices about the future of a landscape or a building. Her specialization lies in unravelling historically layered, complex landscapes. Lara carries out assignments for the Atelier Rijksbouwmeester, the Cultural Heritage Agency, the Rijksvastgoedbedrijf and the municipalities of Rotterdam and Amsterdam. Lara is the author of Dudok by Iwan Baan (2021) and Wonderlijkheden. Willem Marinus Dudok. Netwerken en inspiratiebronnen (2019) and co-author of, among others, De nieuwe grachtengordel. De realisatie van het Algemeen Uitbreidingsplan van Amsterdam (2017) and De Deltawerken (2017).

EMMA BANKS
Emma Banks is an Assistant Professor of International Relations at Bucknell University. She has worked in the Guajira region of Colombia for nearly a decade with Indigenous and Afro-descendant communities. Her research focuses on displacement, environmental conflicts, and post-extractive futures. She is part of a network of solidarity activists that support Colombian movements for a just post-coal future.

ANDREA CAROLINA CARDOSO
Andrea is a Professor in the Business and Economics Faculty of the University of Magdalena, Santa Marta, Colombia, where she also serves as director of the Energy Transitions students' research group. She holds a European Joint Master's degree in Water and Coastal Management from the University of Plymouth, UK, and Cadiz University, Spain. She received her MSc and PhD in Environmental Studies in the field of Ecological Economics from the Institute of Environmental Science and Technology, Autonomous University of Barcelona. Andrea's research addresses the political ecology of the global coal chain, just transition and climate justice.

DAN VAN DER HORST
Dan van der Horst is a climate migrant and disciplinary nomad, interested in both socio-technical and socio-ecological perspectives on societal change. He seeks to understand how we can transition away from our deeply unsustainable habits, and improve our well-being in the process. His main focus is on climate action at the sub-national level and he likes to write about energy landscapes. Due to age and funding luck, he now has extensive experience in leading and supervising interdisciplinary, citizen-oriented and policy-relevant research on the adoption of low-carbon technologies and lifestyles. Dan has co-authored around 100 research papers and enjoys exploring just energy transitions with Master's students, on the MSc in Energy, Society & Sustainability, which he developed. Dan is based at the School of Geosciences, University of Edinburgh, where he holds a personal Chair in Energy, Environment & Society.

KATE SHERREN
Kate Sherren is a Professor in Dalhousie University's School for Resource and Environmental Studies, in Nova Scotia, Canada. Growing up on a hydroelectricity headpond in neighbouring New Brunswick fuelled an interest in anthropogenic landscapes and how they are read and experienced. She has now worked

in Canada, Australia, the United States, and the Falkland Islands across landscapes including farms, energy infrastructure, cities, wetlands, and coasts. She uses a range of social and visual methods to focus on change in multifunctional landscapes, cultural ecosystem services, climate adaptation, and what it all means for our societal capacity to make significant sustainability transitions.

ELIZABETH MONOIAN
Elizabeth Monoian is the founding co-director of the Land Art Generator Initiative (LAGI). In this role she is developing global partnerships between private and public entities around interdisciplinary projects that address issues of climate and sustainability through the lens of creativity. She works closely with cities, universities, corporations, arts organizations, and community groups to design customized approaches to renewable energy installations. She has published, exhibited, and presented globally on the aesthetics of renewable energy and the role of art in providing solutions to the climate crises. Under her leadership, LAGI has received multiple National Endowment for the Arts grants and has been awarded the J.M.K. Innovation Prize, a programme of the J.M. Kaplan Fund. She holds an MFA from Carnegie Mellon University. Her publications include Land Art of the 21st Century, Regenerative Infrastructures, The Time Is Now: Public Art of the Sustainable City, New Energies, Powering Places, Energy Overlays, Return to the Source, and A Field Guide to Renewable Energy.

ROBERT FERRY
Robert Ferry is the founding co-director of the Land Art Generator Initiative (LAGI) and Studied Impact Design. A graduate of Carnegie Mellon University (1998) and a LEED-accredited licensed architect, his expertise is in the design of buildings and public spaces that surpass net-zero and contribute to the regenerative infrastructure of the surrounding city. Through the Land Art Generator Initiative, he supports the critical role of architecture and urban design as part of a comprehensive solution to climate change. As co-director of LAGI, Robert has received multiple National Endowment for the Arts grants and has been awarded the J.M.K. Innovation Prize, a programme of the J.M. Kaplan Fund. His publications include Land Art of the 21st Century, Regenerative Infrastructures, The Time Is Now: Public Art of the Sustainable City, New Energies, Powering Places, Energy Overlays, Return to the Source, and A Field Guide to Renewable Energy.

JANNEMARIE DE JONGE
Jannemarie de Jonge (1961) studied landscape architecture at Wageningen University. She worked successively for the municipality of Ede, the province of North Brabant and research institute Alterra. During this period, she carried out her PhD research into the significance of a strategic, investigative design approach in the service of complex environmental issues. The study examines the typical nature of design thinking, which is compared to and contrasted with scientific and political thinking (Landscape architecture between Politics and Science: an integrative perspective on landscape planning and design in the network society, Wageningen, 2009). In 2007 she co-founded the consultancy Wing, specialized in sustainable spatial development. Additional positions cover a broad spectrum from juries, scientific or strategic advisory boards, educational activities to more activist initiatives such as the founding committee for the Year of the Environment (2015). In 2020 she was appointed Chief Government Advisor on the Physical Environment for a period of four years. She combines this with her work as a partner at Wing.

AUTHORS
Sven Stremke, Dirk Oudes, Paolo Picchi

WITH CONTRIBUTIONS BY
Andrea Carolina Cardoso and Emma Banks, Robert Ferry and Elizabeth Monian, Dan van der Horst, Jolanda de Jong, Jannemarie de Jonge, Martin J. Pasqualetti, Kate Sherren, Lara Voerman

COPY EDITING
Jean Tee

BOOK DESIGN, MAP EDITING
Studio Joost Grootens / Joost Grootens, Clémence Guillemot, Julie da Silva

PRINTING AND LITHOGRAPHY
ORO

PAPER
Munken Print White

TYPEFACE
Antique Legacy

PUBLISHER
Marcel Witvoet, nai010 publishers

ACKNOWLEDGEMENTS
Sven, Dirk and Paolo would like to thank all contributing authors and the students whose work is featured in the book. And all those that suggested places to visit, opened gates to us and took the time to talk about the landscapes dear to them. From the Amsterdam Academy of Architecture, we would like to thank Madeleine Maaskant, David Keuning, Joseefke Brabander and the members of the HDEL advisory board: Dirk Sijmons, Andy van den Dobbelsteen, Jannemarie de Jonge and Lennert Goemans. Furthermore, we thank the Landscape Architecture Chair Group from Wageningen University, the Solar Research Programme, as well as all members of the Energy Alliance and the NRGlab who continue to show interest and contribute actively to our research. Sven would like to thank Sabrina, Luca, Finn and his dear parents for helping to make this dream come true. Dirk thanks Leanne for all her encouragement, as well as Veerle and Stan. Paolo dedicates this book to Roberto Bernoni, Aurora and Tulia Picchi, Gian Luigi, Franca, Giuliano and Gian Francesco Picchi, Filippo and Stefano.

This publication is published in collaboration with the research group High-Density Energy Landscapes of the Academy of Architecture at the Amsterdam University of the Arts. Sven Stremke was professor of this research group from 2017 to 2022. Research fellows were postdoc researcher Paolo Picchi and PhD researcher Dirk Oudes.

Academy of Architecture
Amsterdam University of the Arts

This publication was made possible by financial support from the Creative Industries Fund NL and the Van Eesteren-Fluck & Van Lohuizen Foundation.

creative industries fund NL

EFL STICHTING

© 2022 authors, nai010 publishers, Rotterdam
All rights reserved. No part of this publication may be reproduced, stored in a retrieval system, or transmitted in any form or by any means, electronic, mechanical, photocopying, recording or otherwise, without the prior written permission of the publisher.

For works of visual artists affiliated with a CISAC-organization the copyrights have been settled with Pictoright in Amsterdam.
© 2022, c/o Pictoright Amsterdam

Although every effort was made to find the copyright holders for the illustrations used, it has not been possible to trace them all. Interested parties are requested to contact nai010 publishers, Korte Hoogstraat 31, 3011 GK Rotterdam, the Netherlands.

nai010 publishers is an internationally orientated publisher specialized in developing, producing and distributing books in the fields of architecture, urbanism, art and design.

www.nai010.com

nai010 books are available internationally at selected bookstores and from the following distribution partners:
North, Central and South America
—Artbook | D.A.P., New York, USA, dap@dapinc.com
Rest of the world
—Idea Books, Amsterdam, the Netherlands, idea@ideabooks.nl

For general questions, please contact nai010 publishers directly at sales@nai010.com or visit our website www.nai010.com for further information.

Printed and bound in the Netherlands.

ISBN 978-94-6208-716-3
NUR 648
BISAC ARC010000, ARC008000
Theme code WMQL
The Power of Landscape is also available as e-book:
ISBN 978-94-6208-718-7 (e-book)

Hoover Dam, Arizona & Nevada, USA → 74–75

Canales, Andalusia, Spain → 82–83

Larderello, Tuscany, Italy → 90–91

Imperial Valley, California, USA → 98–99

Las Gabias, Andalusia, Spain → 104–105

Sevilla, Andalusia, Spain → 112–113

Zahara de los Atunes, Andalusia, Spain → 120–121

Lelystad, Flevoland, the Netherlands → 126–127

Viticuso, Latium, Italy → 134–135

Eggebek, Schleswig-Holstein, Germany → 140–141